The Magic of Normal

DR. MAKY ZANGANEH

The Magic of Normal

Hope, Love, and Beyond

Forbes | Books

Published by Forbes Books, Charleston, South Carolina.
An imprint of Advantage Media Group.

Printed in the United States of America.

10 9 8 7 6 5 4 3 2 1

ISBN: 979-8-88750-515-2 (Hardcover)
ISBN: 979-8-88750-516-9 (eBook)

Library of Congress Control Number: 2024923092

Cover and layout design by Megan Elger.

DEDICATION

When I decided to write this book, I was an intensely busy businesswoman working on a variety of different projects, each one more important than the next, all pushing me in various directions. I have always been extremely ambitious, and it is hard for me to prioritize when it comes to dividing my time.

The truth is, I finally started writing the book because life forced me to slow down. Fate decided to change things and pace my life to the rhythm of my cancer treatments. And strangely enough, at the same time, COVID-19 stepped in and put the world on hold. A space-time dimension occurred where everything was punctuated by COVID-19 … different waves in different countries … on different continents … waves that alternated between hope and despair.

I was fortunate to overcome my ordeal with cancer in the middle of the COVID-19 pandemic. Amazingly, my life got back in order, and I was able to continue my new projects in medical research with more conviction than ever.

So, I dedicate this book, which traces my private and professional journey, to all those whose lives have been interrupted and who dream of returning to *the magic of normal* one day. I dedicate it to every patient going through the uncertainty and torment of cancer. I want you to know you are not alone. You are shielded with science, innovation, and discovery. In front of you lies comradeship, courage, and hope.

A Persian expression states, "In despair hides a great deal of hope, and at the end of the darkness of night is daylight."

CONTENTS

CHAPTER 1

My Father: The Superhero

> **Houston, we have a problem ... but failure is not an option.**
>
> —Apollo 13

J*une 2018*

It was a sweltering day in Houston, where the heat can be unbearably intense. I found myself at MD Anderson Cancer Center, taking a moment in their cafeteria. It resembled a hotel lobby more than a hospital, though the conversations around me quickly reminded me of the reality. After a long day, I needed to recharge. I was observing the people around me—some walking around with chemo drugs on a feed, others in line for drinks, each with their own story of struggle and hope.

Among them was a young couple from the East Coast. The husband had a brain tumor. Initially in remission, he was now back for more treatment. They knew the clock was ticking for him and he would die soon—it looked like only a matter of weeks, not even months. They were holding each other's hands, looking at each other as if they had just met for the first time, loving each other like tomorrow would never really come. I talked with them and tried to understand the conditions they were in. Time was so precious to them. Every minute counted. I never really understood the value of time until I spent so much time at MD Anderson.

I ended up spending more than two months there. It was so hard to understand how things were happening and why. It was hard to make any sense out of life in general. Over two months at MD Anderson, I met many such individuals. One mother, juggling the care of her two cancer-stricken children, deeply inspired me with her faith and resilience. She embodied the spirit of not giving up, keeping her children hopeful through the toughest times. These experiences echoed the sentiments of Steve Jobs's final words about the irreplaceable value of love and relationships.

I met a lot of cancer patients at MD Anderson, and I found that all of them had one thing in common: They all wanted to go back to their "normal lives" ... back to "the magic of normal" ... the true magic we often take for granted.

I was there because my father was battling two aggressive blood cancers: multiple myeloma (MM) and chronic myeloid leukemia, which had recently progressed to acute myeloid leukemia (AML).

A few years earlier, I had met Dr. Michael Wang, who is a professor in the department of lymphoma and myeloma at MD Anderson. I met him when I was working at Pharmacyclics, the biotech company that developed a revolutionary oral therapy drug for blood cancer called Imbruvica (generic name: ibrutinib). Dr. Wang is one of those doctors who really cares very deeply about his patients. He helped the company to develop Imbruvica for patients with mantle cell lymphoma and became a huge advocate for our product. He has also become a great friend to me and my family over the years.

In fact, the last time I spoke with him, he told me, "Friendship and loyalty are precious in life." And the truth is that his friendship and loyalty over all these years have been very precious to me. I could never have overcome the challenges I faced in the past five years without his help.

After talking to him about my dad, he asked me to come to Houston and get a second opinion before starting the heavy chemotherapy treatment that had been recommended for him in France. Once I got to MD Anderson, Dr. Wang introduced me to Dr. Guillermo Garcia Manero, nicknamed Dr. GGM, who is the head of myelodysplastic syndromes/AML at MD Anderson.

After being in the oncology business for more than ten years, I knew that systemic treatment could deteriorate my dad's condition very quickly because of the heavy side effects these drugs can cause. After redoing a complete examination, Dr. GGM informed me that my dad's prognosis was not very good and that he probably had only about four more months to live. Keeping all that in mind, he suggested they start the treatment ASAP.

To increase his chances of survival, they recommended treating both cancers at the same time, which was riskier in case one or both treatments failed. Treating one cancer would accelerate the other cancer, so it was hard to decide which one to treat first. But the decision to treat both at the same time was important. I informed my sisters about the MD Anderson recommendation. They are both medical doctors who spend their lives treating patients.

To be honest, it is never easy to be in a medical family. Everybody has their own opinion. Everybody thinks they know best. But we all had one thing in common: He was our father, and we all had our own special love for him. We all had our own lifelong relationship with him. The problem was that we were all highly educated, and each of us wanted to apply all that education to a decision that might help save his life. Anyway, after days of thinking and discussing, we finally decided to begin the first treatment at MD Anderson, hoping to be able to leave Houston after three weeks of treatment.

As life tends to teach us, things do not always go the way we think they are going to go. My father's journey was grueling. After the first chemo treatment for AML, he was hospitalized due to infection risks, extending our stay in Houston to six weeks. But my dad turned out to be quite a warrior. He became an inspiration to all of us. He fought his cancer all the way until he finally made it into remission. Dr. GGM always called him Superman, and he told us that it was a miracle that he went into remission.

Dr. GGM is an incredible human being, full of courage and determination. I learned so much from him and Dr. Wang during this period. Aim high and go for a cure as long as your body can handle it. In other words, fight till the end and never give up. That is exactly what my dad did. He went through a difficult time, but he went into full remission two years after his treatment, returned home with his family, and was able to enjoy life again.

My dad was a deeply spiritual and non-materialistic man who valued family and ethics above all else. If you had walked into his home and seen a very beautiful, expensive carpet and then told him how much you admired it, he would have rolled it up and told you to take it home. He was not attached to anything except his family. He always seemed to realize what was most important and what really mattered in life. The core philosophy and purpose of his life was to always be ethical and to keep his family together. Nothing else was more important to him. His life philosophy, centered on these principles, always guided us. His faith in God remained unshaken, and his love for his family was unwavering.

CHAPTER 2
Memories of Iran

> **They always say time changes things, but you have to actually change them yourself.**
> —Andy Warhol

I am very close to my middle sister Mahshad, the intellectual powerhouse of our family. From kindergarten to university, she consistently excelled academically, earning straight As and obtaining two high school diplomas—one in France and another in Iran. Like my oldest sister Shaby and me, she attended Jeanne d'Arc School in Tehran, a prestigious bilingual institution run by Catholic sisters, until it was closed following the Islamic Revolution in 1979. Despite the challenges, our family's commitment to education never wavered.

Through correspondence courses with Centre National d'Enseignement à Distance (CNED) in France, Mahshad pursued the French baccalaureate independently and later joined the faculty of medicine in Strasbourg. Her journey in medicine, specializing in OB-GYN with seven subspecialties, has made her an inspiring force in my life. I have always known she would be there for me no matter what. And there have been times in my life that I doubt I could have made it through without her.

Her unwavering support and dedication to her patients exemplify the essence of what a doctor should be. She fits every aspect of the definition of a real doctor when it comes to ethics, loyalty, and caring for and serving her patients. She is a very calm person with a big heart. I believe God gave her one skill that he just forgot to give to me, and that was patience.

I remember us all growing up together in Iran, although Mahshad was much closer to Shaby than me. Shaby has been her hero through all those years, from kindergarten through university and even now. They both went through their schooling together. Same schools, same university. Shaby finished high school and went to medical school in Strasbourg, France. She is the big sister everyone dreams of having.

From a young age, Shaby took the role of big sister to heart, starting with kindergarten. During recess, she would come to the kids' yard to make sure no one was bothering her younger sisters. She continued to protect Mahshad and me later at the university campus and even when we were all working or studying at the same hospital. Shaby is still the one I can count on any time of day or night.

Shaby was my grandfather's favorite grandchild. My grandfather had the most admirable personality I have ever known. It amazes me to think he was born almost one hundred years ago. He was very passionate about mathematics and also taught himself three foreign languages (English, French, and German). As an engineer for an Iranian–Swiss company, he participated in the construction of several monuments in Iran that were inaugurated by the leaders of each period.

He was among the few professors of spatial geometry in Iran. He became so renowned that his lessons were broadcast in black and white on the education channel to every student across the country.

He was always there for his students, and everybody admired him for his amazing creativity in finding solutions to mathematical questions. He taught several generations of students. Several of them ended up holding very important positions in Iran at the state level as adults.

He had a very Cartesian mind, which meant everything could be explained by mathematical laws. My grandfather passed on his incredible passion and talent to Shaby. As the first grandchild, she was the one who had made him a grandfather. She also loved mathematics, and the fact that she was fast and always came up with different ways to find mathematical solutions made her one of the top students in this field. She was always helping me with my algebra. Her methodology was beyond impressive. Even the way she gave advice was very mathematical.

I remember I was very sad and frustrated one day, so she sent me a little note: "Don't think about failure or success. Life is the sum of the two, and the result will always be winning because if we try, we win. So do not stop trying, you will find your way." That beautiful concept has always stuck with me.

Mahshad was pretty much the opposite of Shaby. Even if she was an A student, Mahshad was never considered the first when it came to grandchildren. When she told my grandfather she had chosen a field in high school where there would be slightly less mathematics to allow for more biology, he considered it a shame. The bond between the two of them came later when Mahshad was a medical student. Then they started having exciting discussions.

But still, Mahshad never managed to have the last word because, in medicine, mathematics could not explain everything. I knew he was an amazing man and was our grandfather, but I was always a step behind Shaby and Mahshad. I often felt like I was living in their shadow then.

I was too young, which tended to make me an invisible grandchild to my grandfather. I was present, but with so little to say or prove that would make me stand out to him. To be honest, he was always very serious. He was so disciplined and organized that Mahshad and I were always afraid he would ask us to do something or pose a question we could not answer. So whenever we were near him, we tried to remain invisible.

Unfortunately, because life, distance, and political events made travel more difficult, none of us were able to be at my grandfather's bedside when he fell ill and died at the age of eighty-three. I believe, to this day, that remains the biggest regret all of us have ever experienced.

Shaby chose cardiology as her specialty. She has a photographic memory and has become a well-renowned cardiologist. Like Mahshad, her patients are her life. Mahshad says she has "cardiomegaly of the soul." Cardiomegaly is a condition when your heart becomes enlarged. Like Mahshad, Shaby's life is all about serving and helping others. Her kindness and love for people are unimaginable.

Shaby has always been the one with a fiery temperament and boundless energy. And she has an incredible memory. She amazes us all with her elephant-like memory, but even more with her memory for numbers. She is the only person I know who has been able to soften the toughest and strictest department heads at the hospital and then become one of their favorites, just as she became the darling of my grandfather. It is hard to be her younger sister and expect to be noticed. Nothing is more difficult than trying to walk in her footsteps.

Shaby is loved and appreciated by everyone who knows her. This includes family, friends, patients, coworkers, and all the professors and department heads at any hospital she has ever worked at. But she can be stubborn sometimes, and her life becomes about "her way or the highway." That is why when she is in something, she is all in, and nobody can match her dedication. However, the day that she is not in agreement with you, God help you and the entire universe.

I have very distant memories of my hometown of Tehran. My memories keep receding and have become more and more blurry over time. I was born in 1970 under the monarchy, the last royal dynasty after more than 2,500 years of Persian monarchy. The Shah of Iran was competing with the greatest heads of state of his time and was greeted like a king by JFK, Charles De Gaulle, and Queen Elizabeth II on all his trips around the world. He undertook a far-reaching series of reforms and projects called the White Revolution or the Shah and People Revolution. It included many fields: legal (women's right to vote), agricultural, industrial, educational, military, cultural—and later, technological and nuclear.

The goal was to get Iran to an autonomy of excellence in all areas and to be able to not rely solely on natural resources (oil from the south, gas from the Caspian Sea to the north, copper mines, uranium, and gold). He even invested in European nuclear power and ensured that the program could never be dismissed. I find it so interesting that in his interviews in the early 1970s, he mentioned that he was planning to invest in digital. He said that digital would revolutionize the world of the future. In his book *Answer to History*, published before the 1980s, he even wrote about the idea of telemedicine.

The year 1978 was marked by demonstrations and protest movements led by an Islamic religious leader named Ayatollah Khomeini. He completed his fourteen-year exile in Iraq and then went to Neauphle-le-Château, near Paris. The Shah of Iran had to leave the country in January 1979. Ten days later, the Islamic revolution began with the coming to power of Ayatollah Khomeini, three of his followers, and his spokesperson.

Shortly after the Islamic Revolution, hoping to take advantage of the post-revolutionary political instability in Iran and the fear of contagion from the Shiite Islamic revolution in Iraq, Saddam Hussein attacked without warning. It was September 1980, and Saddam Hussein and his Iraqi army bombed the Iranian bases and the Abadan refinery in Southern Iran, one of the largest refineries in the world. The Iran–Iraq War went on for almost eight years. It did not end until August 1988, and it claimed more than a million lives.

Anyway, my sisters and I lived through the revolution of 1979, and we were all together in Iran when the war began in 1980. That was a time I would never wish anyone to have to experience in their lifetime, but I do believe it shaped our lives and changed our way of thinking. The three of us became survivors in life. We would never be the victims, no matter how many challenges we would have to face in the years ahead.

The events we lived through during the revolution and the Iran–Iraq War changed who we were forever. It changed what we thought, what we felt, and what we would be able to endure in life. We lived through the closure of the schools during the revolution and the new rules of wearing a chador after the schools opened again. Worn mostly by Muslim women, a chador is a piece of cloth that is wrapped around the head and upper body, leaving only the face exposed.

I remember that during the war, we had to stay in school even when there was bombing close by. I also remember the fear that spread not only through our family but also through all the people around us. The fear of parents with sons, who had to send their sons to the front line of the Iran–Iraq War even when they were young teens.

We constantly had to face the fear of bombing during that war. Many of the people at the time would hide in the mountains near Tehran to avoid the Iraqi rockets at night. As if this was not enough, we also had to face the fear of robbers and people who were hungry and needed money. There was a shortage of gas, as well as a shortage of food.

Life completely lost the meaning of normal. Whatever a normal human being could or should experience in their lives was forbidden. Even the simplest things, like going to a party, holding your boyfriend or girlfriend's hand in the park, or wearing normal clothes outside your home, were forbidden.

During this period, and even after many Iranians had gotten out of the country, education remained of top importance. There were many highly educated and brilliant people, like Maryam Mirzakhani, an Iranian mathematician who, in 2014, became the first woman and Iranian to be awarded a Fields Medal. There were also many Iranians who joined NASA or became leaders and entrepreneurs of very successful companies around the world.

I was eight years old when the revolution started. I just remember people going out on the streets, yelling and setting everything on fire. I remember the gunshots and how people were hiding in different houses. I remember the long nights in my grandpa's basement, with all the family. We had no electricity, just the lights from our candles. We all listened to the radio to try to find out information about the bombing.

I remember trying to play board games or just drawing or reading books to pass the time on those long nights. I remember the sound of the red siren announcing an Iraqi bomb approaching its target. I remember the sounds of bombs like thunderstorms. And even after so many years, every time I hear a thunderstorm, I jump for a chair to hide beneath. I still cannot handle those sounds.

I also remember waking up the day after hearing those sounds with all of us trying to find out which family nearby got hit the night before. But I believe the most terrifying moments were when we never knew if the bombs would hit our home or not. Everybody had to safely prepare their homes for whatever might occur. We put tape all along the windows in the shape of a cross so that in the event of a bombing in our neighborhood, the tape would keep the windows that had been broken by the shock waves together. Taping the windows would also help prevent any injuries from the bombing.

We also had to put all our decorative glass and crystal in the closet in hopes that they would not shatter. Our furniture and sofas were always stored against the walls in case our home was destroyed. We did not want there to be any clutter if the time came when we had to immediately flee the house. So many changes, all based on an instinct for survival! It was somewhat like the landscape we faced during COVID-19, where we couldn't imagine everyday life without a mask or hydroalcoholic gel for our hands, or being separated from others by plexiglass panels.

Anyway, to this day, I still find it hard to believe that Iran lost more than a million people in that war and that so many young people became handicapped because of this terrifying event in history. Only God knows why this war started and why all those young people had to die.

As much as the climax of the revolution had united the different parties in opposition to the Shah of Iran, after the revolution, the minority parties were less and less tolerated and were considered enemies of the Islamic Republic.

One night, my parents went to their friends' house and left my sisters and me at home. It was a weekday evening, and we went to bed early because we had school the next day. A little before midnight, we woke up to the sound of machine guns. My sister Shaby went to look out the window and saw a white Mercedes, a few armed men, and a machine gun set on the grounds of our next-door neighbor's house.

Shaby made us all move away from the windows. Then a voice came over a loudspeaker, saying, "We will count to three, and if you don't come out, we'll shoot." The voice counted to three several times, and then we heard the machine-gun fire.

At that time, we didn't know what was going on. We were scared and confused. We did not know who was in the house next door, as the neighbors we knew had left and rented the basement to new tenants. Around midnight, we got a call from my parents, who could not get back to our house because the street was blocked off. The military personnel blocking the street told them that they were arresting people at the last house on the street. We were scared and confused.

The truth of the matter was, our house was the last house on the block! It was at the dead end of the street. So, when my mother heard the news, she totally fell apart. My parents decided to go to a private clinic in our neighborhood, where they were finally able to call us on our home phone. Remember, at this time, nobody had a mobile phone. My parents finally found out that the police had made a mistake and all the violence was not going on at our house but at the house next to ours.

My father tried to reassure us over the phone and told us that, above all, we should not leave the house. We were terrified. It seemed like this horrific event had been going on for so long. Shaby held my ears between her legs so I wouldn't hear the sounds of the loudspeaker or the machine gun. I remember her holding Mahshad and me so tightly in her arms, trying to protect us, that we could hardly breathe. But we held things together as best we could. We immediately knew to shut all the windows even though there was a point when we all became aware of the horridly awful smells that even the windows could not block.

Around 1:00 a.m., silence set in, and my parents were able to come home. It was a difficult scene for anyone to look at, and it was right next to our house. There were shards of glass, blood, and smoke. We never saw anyone come out of the house, so after hearing the loudspeaker and so much machine-gun noise, we assumed there were no survivors.

Looking back, maybe the strangest thing was that the day after this shocking and gruesome night, we got up and headed out to school. All of us knew it was important not to talk about what had happened. And strangely, our neighbor's house had been completely cleaned up. There was no trace of the horrors of the night before. It felt like we had just had a bad collective nightmare.

During this period, it was very hard for us to obtain the visas we needed to get out of the country. There were no US or European embassies open in Iran. However, we were very lucky that a friend of my dad living in Germany was able to help us get German visas. Although Shaby did not get a German visa, she was able to get a French visa because she had been accepted to medical school in France. Getting authorization to leave the country was one thing, but getting our visas was another thing. But the most difficult part was getting a ticket for a flight, as there were very few flights leaving the Tehran airport at that time because of the war.

My dad had left us behind nine months earlier to go to Germany. He took one of the last flights leaving Tehran at that time. He headed to Germany to prepare for our lives there. Me, my mom, my sisters, my aunt Mahnaz, and her two daughters, Niloufar and Maryam, were still in Iran, waiting for the next flight leaving the country.

I really do not remember much about those last three months before we left Iran. The nights in the mountains were particularly long and scary. We had with us a so-called survival suitcase containing our identity cards, passports, cash, and precious jewelry. The fear of bombings and finding our house destroyed on our return from the mountains added to the fear of being attacked by thieves who were interested in stealing our suitcases. They knew that people running from the war would not be carrying shoes or clothes in their suitcases, but that these cases would be packed with the most valuable items they owned.

The Iran–Iraq War continued in Tehran. Everything going on was beyond imagination. But believe it or not, we still had to go to school and take our final exams no matter what was happening around us. Daily bombings became just a part of our lives.

I will always be grateful that my mom knew people at a lot of different travel agencies. She tried to book ten different flights with different airlines for the entire family. That way, we could get on the first flight out of the country as soon as the airports reopened. Then one day, one of the travel agents my mom knew contacted her and told her they could get us tickets from Tehran to Frankfurt via Austria.

She got the tickets, and we were finally able to leave Iran. I will never forget that last night before we left for the airport. I was with my sisters, listening to music in my parents' bedroom. The music was Elvis Presley's "My Way." There we were with our luggage, packing our bags, knowing this would be the last time we would ever be in our home in Iran. Sometimes, we try to look at everything differently and keep all those images in our memory. There we were, trying to figure out how to say goodbye, knowing that in just a few hours, everything would disappear.

The last few weeks in Iran were some of the most emotionally difficult times I can remember. We were so busy that we really did not have a chance to prepare for the life-changing transition we were about to face. We tried to say goodbye to everyone. We tried to memorize the smallest details before leaving. We were putting so many important times and memories behind us. My sisters and I were so young. After all the ups and downs and all the unbearable moments and endless seconds, as a family, we decided that staying in Iran was not an option. It was too late to make up our minds and move in another direction or come up with a different plan. It was time to move on.

We knew that nothing would be like before! Nothing would ever be the same. Decisions had been made. These were one-way tickets without a return. We knew that by leaving Iran, we would probably never be back or live there again. We were on our way to the airport, to a new continent. I remember having a tightness in my chest that last night. It felt like my heart was being squeezed with a lot of doubt, hesitation, and so much that was unknown.

To eternalize those moments, we took a lot of pictures. That way, we would be able to relive every moment. We thought we would be able to own the times and locations. We thought we could hold on to the times and places where we had power, fun, and success. Years later, the pictures are the only traces of something that proves the existence of the events and our life in Iran.

A new page had been turned. There are times when we are ready to pay anything to have something we really want. Pay anything to have the moon. At the end of the day, we try to find the easiest solution to get the things we want, only to find out everything cannot be bought, nor is everything for sale.

Distances, times, forgetfulness ... sometimes, we are so far away from things that we think the past never existed. And when we combine a long time ago with a faraway place, well, it just gets worse. Everything becomes not only far from our eyes but from our hearts as well. It is sad but true.

There seem to be bad times, as well as good times badly placed. Then, of course, there are the good times when everything seems good, except ourselves. We just find ourselves at a time when we are not receptive to happiness. This brings us to the all-time essential question. What is happiness? Ideal happiness? We all had so many questions in our heads back then. And the saddest part was, we did not have any answers.

It could sometimes be better, perhaps, to become a fatalist and just believe that everything is predetermined and inevitable. When there is really nothing we can do about something, we have to let things be. We have to let time take its course and let fate take its course. A page turns, and a new page is revealed. What does the future hold for us? At that point in time, none of us knew.

Reflecting on my memories of Iran brings a mix of nostalgia, pain, and resilience. The profound impact of the revolution and the Iran–Iraq War shaped not only our lives but also our understanding of endurance and survival. Despite the immense challenges and adversities, our family remained united, driven by the values instilled by our parents and grandparents. The intellectual brilliance of my sisters and the inspirational figures in our family have always been a guiding light.

CHAPTER 3

Like a German Girl in High School

> **Home is behind, the world ahead.**
>
> —J. R. R. Tolkien

The journey to Austria was one marked by fear and uncertainty. Arriving at Tehran International airport five hours before our flight, we were greeted by the alarming sounds of red sirens and the knowledge that Iraqi rockets were targeting areas nearby. Our terror was compounded when we learned of an additional five-hour delay. After ten long hours in the airport, our flight finally took off, escorted by military jets, making it one of the most significant and nerve-wracking flights of my life.

Upon landing in Austria, we faced a twenty-four-hour wait in the transit area because of visa issues. The officials meticulously processed our immigration papers for Germany, leaving us in a state of endless waiting. When we finally reached Germany, we headed straight to Oldenburg, near Hamburg, marking the beginning of a new and dramatically different chapter in our lives. This transition meant adjusting to a new culture, language, and lifestyle—a stark contrast to the life we had known in Iran.

Everything suddenly changed completely, and I began my new life in Germany. Mahshad got a French visa and joined Shaby in Strasbourg, France. My parents went back to Iran while I stayed with a friend of theirs for a while, and then later with my uncle Hossein Khoee in Oldenburg. I went to school and began learning German. I started my new life in a country I had never been to before.

The German lifestyle was the opposite of my Iranian lifestyle during the revolution. I could hardly believe it. What impressed me the most about Germany was the abundance of merchandise. The supermarkets were full of food, and the restaurants and cafés were full of people. This was in contrast to Iran, where the stores were closed and the supermarkets were empty during the first year of the revolution and the war.

The funniest part is, thirty years later, I could not believe that I was going through the same thing again, not because of war but because of a virus called COVID-19. There it was again—the shortage of food, shelves empty of groceries, and panic—but this time, panic caused by a pandemic.

Anyway, life was quite different then, not to mention that I was a teenager, which is already one of the toughest times in life. I felt like the world had turned upside down. I was starting school without wearing the Islamic chador. I was going to a coed school with boys and girls all mixed together in one place.

The school was completely different from what I had experienced in Iran. There was freedom of speech, and we could say whatever we wanted to say. In Iran, we did not have this luxury after the revolution. I was very good at math and science. I was much better prepared and further ahead than many of my classmates.

In Germany, high school lasts five years, unlike most of the world, where it's typically a four-year program. During my final two years, I was the only girl who chose to major in physics. There were only eight students in my physics class, and I was the only female among seven boys. The class was small because physics and math were considered particularly challenging subjects in high school.

The funniest part about school in Germany was that we were allowed to use calculators, something that was never permitted in Iran. Back home, we had to do all the calculations mentally. On top of that, some of our physics exams were open book. Despite having the textbook right in front of us, these exams were far more challenging than anything I had ever experienced. It was almost ironic—we thought having the book meant we'd have all the answers, but the questions were so difficult that, even with the book in hand, finding the solutions was still a struggle.

Looking back, the one thing I really enjoyed during my stay in Germany was riding my bicycle to school or a friend's house. That was something I was not able to do in Iran. But in Germany, it did not matter if you were the CEO of a company or a student in high school. If it was raining or snowing, everybody rode their bikes everywhere.

What may have been the hardest thing to believe once I got to Germany was that everything was allowed once you turned sixteen. Young people could drink alcohol, smoke cigarettes, and have a boyfriend or girlfriend. You just could not drive a car, which was the opposite of how it worked in the US, where you could get your driver's license once you were sixteen. Still, it amazed me to see young people going out and acting like adults, and their parents really could not say anything.

At that time, I had so many questions and so few answers. I was shocked, and I felt completely lost in my own universe. I was experiencing so many differences between cultures, countries, and governments. I had just left a country where young people had no freedom and arrived in a country where teenage freedom had no limits. I had been living in a country where everything had to happen inside of the homes, and now I had come to a country where everything was allowed outside of the home.

I remember the first night eating outside, at a restaurant in Oldenburg. A young couple was seated in front of us, holding hands and kissing each other. This was a new discovery for me. Before, I had only seen things like this in movies. I had never seen anything like that happening in the streets outside of homes in Tehran during or after the revolution.

You were not allowed to be somewhere like that with your boyfriend in an Islamic country if you were not married. And for me, the question became, "Why? Why do you have to be married to see somebody? Why should girls get married at the age of nine? Nine-year-old girls are just little kids. They are still young children. And why don't women have the same rights as men?"

Why is it that in some countries, there can be gang rapes and nobody even talks about it . . . as if some women are just worthless and their lives are invisible? I cannot believe there are still countries where women are considered to just be pieces of meat that people can do whatever they want with. And I do not think I will ever understand how there can be so much violence in life.

How is it that some people are born in countries where freedom has no meaning, while others are born in countries where anything is allowed? Who decides who should be born where? I guess some people are just luckier than others. I can say I am one lucky girl. I am grateful for where I was born, how I was raised, and how much I have been able to achieve in my life so far.

I give a lot of credit to my parents for raising us the way they did so that we could become the people we are today. We gained a lot of maturity after facing the challenges of war and revolution. They sacrificed their lives for us, and we always had a deep respect and admiration for them. This respect helped us build our lives in a Western country without getting sidetracked by the daily distractions that often affect today's younger generation. Our conscience, integrity, and maturity helped us to stay focused and strive for success outside our own culture and country.

Like my father, my mother is an architect. All her life, she fought to be recognized as a female architect with the same rights as her male counterparts. But it was hard for her, no matter how good she was at her trade for all those years. When we lived in Iran during the revolution, she told the three of us to choose a profession that would allow us to be both financially and socially independent, no matter where we ended up living.

The two professions that allow such independence anywhere in the world are medicine and dentistry, and that is why she guided us to go into these fields. My two sisters went to medical school in France and continued their professions as a cardiologist and a gynecologist, respectively. I decided to go to dental school even though I could have chosen medical school. At that time, my mother thought it would be better if I did not follow the same path as my sisters.

I stayed in Germany for a while. It was an unbelievable time in my life. I learned a lot, I worked a lot, and I fought a lot for my own identity. It was not easy being a foreigner in Germany at that time, especially one who had just come from Iran. I worked so hard to show that I was no different from anyone there. Once my sisters and I were stable and secure in Germany and France, my parents went back to Iran.

Although there were several people looking after me, it was not easy to live in Germany without my parents. But it did show how much confidence they had in their children despite how difficult it was for them to leave each of us in a new environment. We all knew they made the decision to go back to Iran for many reasons: their work, our home, and my grandparents. We have always been a tightly connected family that looked out for each other, and no matter where everyone was, we were all able to keep in touch with each other.

I remember that before my parents left, they gave me an envelope with money inside just in case I wanted to buy a ticket back to Iran. Some days were harder than others, but the whole time I kept telling myself, "It's easy to give up and go back. It's much harder to move forward." Germany helped build my character. It made me tough. It made me a fighter. It made me work hard and never give up, no matter what.

I will always be grateful to my dad's friends, Uncle Hamid and his wife Anne, who treated me and supported me like their own daughter all those years. I was also lucky that my mom's brother, my Uncle Hossein, was there for me during my high school years. We had a lot of fun together. He worked with me at night and on the weekends to help me get through high school. We also went to German language classes together in the afternoon after school.

Uncle Hossein had spent his adolescence in England. He returned to Iran just before the Islamic Revolution. He worked in Tehran as a mechanical engineer for a few years at the time of the bombardments. He also came with us to Germany. After spending time with us in Germany, he left and moved to Canada.

Living in Germany without my parents was challenging, but it demonstrated their immense trust in us and our abilities. The unwavering support from family friends and my uncle was invaluable during those formative years. Their encouragement helped me overcome the hurdles I faced and cemented my belief in the importance of family.

Finishing high school turned out to be the end of my journey in Germany. I remember being very much like a German girl then. I spoke German, and I behaved like the German people did, but I never forgot my Iranian traditions or the Iranian culture I had grown up in. However, I had learned that by forcing myself to integrate into this German culture, I could become one of them.

In 1989, when my parents came back to Germany from Iran, they decided to send me to France for university even though I had applied to Heidelberg University for medical school. My parents wanted me to be with my sisters. To be honest, at that moment in my life, I did not agree with their decision. I did not want to go to France. Having to learn another language and begin my life again in Strasbourg was not what I would have chosen if the decision had been up to me, but I really had no option.

Family and keeping the family together were the main goals of my parents. Looking back, it was the best decision they could have made for me, even though it was difficult to leave Germany after I had put in a lot of effort to integrate myself into the culture and country. I was too young to understand the value of a strong family and the importance of knowing that we are not alone in this world and have a family who will protect and support us, no matter what may happen.

Contemplating my journey, I am struck by the stark contrasts between the cultures I have lived in and the circumstances I have endured. My time in Germany, marked by the challenges of adapting to a new culture and language, ultimately shaped me into a resilient and determined individual. Despite the harsh realities of being a foreigner in a new land, the experience instilled in me a strength that I carry with me to this day.

Ultimately, despite my initial resistance, my parents' decision to reunite us in France proved to be the right one. It underscored the significance of family unity and the strength that comes from knowing I am not alone. As I moved from Germany to France, I carried with me the lessons of resilience and adaptation. I am forever grateful for the foundation my parents provided.

CHAPTER 4
University in France

> **Education is the most powerful weapon which you can use to change the world.**
> —Nelson Mandela

Leaving Germany for France marked a significant transition in my life. Despite the immense challenge of learning a new language, I successfully earned my German Abitur alongside my peers. My hard work and determination were recognized by my high school dean, who awarded me for my perseverance and excellence as a foreign student. His words of encouragement highlighted my strength and commitment—traits that defined my journey so far.

Here is what he wrote to me:

Where there is a will, there is a way. When you arrived at our school you realized it would be a long and tedious path to graduation. Your strength and determination are what helped you to achieve this goal. With admirable energy and great personal commitment, you have mastered your fate and won the recognition and sympathy of teachers and students alike. I wish you happiness and all the best for the rest of your life.

Over the years, I tried to adapt to my new life and circumstances in Germany. At that point, adaptability, flexibility, drive, and determination were the main characteristics that defined me. I wanted to succeed. I wanted to show that I could achieve anything I wanted if I put my intention and attention to it.

Despite all of this, I knew that moving to Strasbourg would not be easy. I was unsure how I could navigate university while trying to maintain the family's reputation and succeed when my siblings were there—all brilliant, famous, and successful. These thoughts weighed heavily on my mind as I moved from Germany to France. How could I adapt to this new environment where everyone looked at me and expected me to be like my siblings?

It was challenging to maintain my identity, hold onto my dreams, follow my path, and ensure my success amid the pressure to measure up to the rest of the family. The pressure was quite intense. The challenge was immense, but I was determined to face it head-on, driven by the same resilience and adaptability that had carried me through my years in Germany.

My two sisters and my aunt Yeganeh, who is the same age as Mahshad, were all at medical school at the same time. Yeganeh is a very fun person, very dynamic and full of joy. We always considered her one of our sisters. The three of them were students together at Louis Pasteur University in Strasbourg, France. And they were not just any students but some of the best students at the school. Thus, for me, the bar was high, as my family's expectations were high.

I was the fourth member of the same family enrolled at the same medical/dental university. I ended up going to work at the same hospital as my sisters and aunt after finishing university. What I remember most about this time was how high the expectations for me were. I will never forget the amount of pressure on my shoulders that I carried around with me every day. I not only had to be a good student, I also had to be one of them.

In France, going to medical or dental school is difficult. A student goes directly from high school to a medical or dental university, but first, they must be accepted based on an entry exam and their high school grades. This is different from the US, where you can apply to medical or dental school after graduating from four years of college.

In 1989, a thousand students applied to medical and dental universities in Strasbourg, France, and only one hundred and sixty of them were accepted into medical school, and only forty students got into dental school. I was in a group of two hundred students out of one thousand students who had been accepted. At that time, I had the opportunity to choose between dentistry and medicine. I chose dentistry.

My sisters were completely immersed in medical school, spending countless hours at the hospital—day shifts and night shifts, year after year, studying and living their lives at the hospital. Because I was able to watch what they were experiencing, I decided it would be better for me to choose a different path.

Anyway, dental school was amazing. I had fun, especially in my second year, when I joined the Dental School Student Association. The association had ended up with a debt of around 250,000 French francs, and the members were trying to find a way to raise funds to get the association back on track. I decided to help them find a way to raise money. My proposal was to charge each student for entry to parties going forward. I became the party organizer, or what I called the "chief of entertainment."

I loved dancing, I loved having fun, and I loved parties. What I never liked were drinking, smoking, and flirting around. I never drank alcohol, I never smoked, and I was much too romantic for the century

I was living in. One could consider me boring, but in reality, I was a fun girl whom almost everybody loved hanging around.

The first parties were held at our condominium. Slowly, more and more people started showing up—not just dental students but also other students from the medical and pharmacy schools. I needed a bigger space, so I began renting locations for Saturday night parties. I charged five dollars per student, and that was the beginning of my life as a businesswoman. Two years after all that began, we were profitable. The pattern continued for the next four years while I was in dental school. It was not only an amazing business experience, but I also made many friends who became part of my life for years to come.

I had spent the early part of my life in three different countries, but I had always dreamed of coming to the US. The reason was that, before the Iranian Revolution, my father was working with a very famous architecture firm in the US. After a year of working on this project, the US company finally decided on a joint venture with my dad's company. The only problem was that the letter of acceptance came a few days after the revolution began. During that time, and specifically at the start of the revolution, all international activities, particularly those with the US, stopped, and everything was canceled.

The US became an enemy of the Iranian government. No one in Iran could do anything with the US or with US companies. All the embassies closed, and the world stopped collaborating with Iran. My dad lost that opportunity. He was young, and he had worked so hard to achieve his dream. Then at the moment when everything had just come into his hands, everything fell apart. Even many years afterward, he could not overcome the disappointment and deception he was forced to deal with in his life.

However, my parents continued to talk about the US. They were always interested in American life and the opportunities that might be available to each of us in America. My mom did everything she could to encourage us to consider going to the US once we received our degrees in France.

My oldest sister Shaby passed her Educational Commission for Foreign Medical Graduates exam—a certification for international medical graduates ready to enter residency or fellowship programs in the US that are accredited by the Accreditation Council for Graduate Medical Education. She was accepted to Harvard University for dermatology, but she never made it to America. She fell in love with a French boy who later became her husband. He finished his degree in gastroenterology in Strasbourg. They had gone to university together, worked at the same hospital, and then got married. It was one of those perfect happily-ever-after love stories.

They went on to have two children and continued working together after the kids came along. Their children did not follow their parents' path to medical school. Sarah went to law school and became a lawyer, and Arman is currently in business school after finishing his master's in law. Interestingly, my parents could never believe that Shaby gave up the American Dream and Harvard University for a French guy she fell in love with in Strasbourg.

My middle sister Mahshad, who also had the option to begin a life in the US after she passed her exam, decided to stay in France as well. As usual, I was the one who decided on a different path. I contacted my best friend, Afrooz Afghani, who was living in Los Angeles, California. We met each other at the school in Iran we both went to until we were around ten or eleven years old. Afrooz left Iran to go to the US, and I ended up in Germany. We did not see or hear from each other for many years. It is hard to believe that without Facebook, Google, social networking, or today's technologies, I found her again.

After fifteen years apart, we met again in Los Angeles. It was incredible how wonderful it felt for both of us to be together again. When I decided to take my US dental exams, I stayed at her home for short periods whenever I had to go to California. Afrooz was the one person who always reached out to help me any time I was in the US. She is like a sister to me.

We have gone through a lot in life together, including an amazing backpacking adventure in Europe that I will never forget. It seems like a lifetime ago. We were so young and full of energy. Afrooz is a very organized, detailed, dynamic, and outgoing person. It is a pleasure to travel with her. She is the master of planification. She always knows where to go, what to see, and which famous places to visit.

We went from France to Italy to Greece to Spain, sleeping on trains and showering in train stations. I remember sleeping on the deck of a boat from Italy to Corfu. We met so many interesting people along the way. We got a cheap hotel in Corfu and then a four-star hotel in Capri when we were totally exhausted from traveling like students.

We stayed in that four-star hotel for a few days to rest up and enjoy life in Capri. It was unbelievably fun there. We got on our Vespas—those Italian scooters—and explored the island. Afrooz and I had some unforgettable times together. I love the fact that we have been friends since we were nine years old, and she remains my best friend today.

In my last two years of dental school, I was extremely busy and working a lot. I was preparing for my US dental exams while studying at a dental school in France. I was traveling between California and Strasbourg. In my last year of school, after spending two weeks in Los Angeles, I went back to France for my final exams. I was overwhelmed with all the studying and traveling. It was a very stressful time. It turned out that I passed all my final exams except one: pediatric dentistry.

I will never forget that day. I had studied everything I could imagine our professor would ask, but I was tired and ended up bypassing something I never thought would be an exam question. I could not believe it when one of the questions was about the tooth decay a child could get because of baby bottles being consumed during the night and the health consequences. Who would ever choose this as an exam subject? Once I got to the exam room and we were all given the question, I nearly fell out of my chair. There was absolutely no way I could write even one paragraph about this subject.

So, I did not pass my pediatric dentistry exam in June. The professor gave me a score of 5/20. If she had given me 6/20, I could have finished dental school at the same time as all my classmates. But she would not make an exception for me. She told me, "No matter how good you are, you should never bypass any subject matter."

Oh man, was I upset! I could not believe what had happened to me. And to be honest, I really did not like pediatric dentistry at that time. Pediatric dentists often find themselves begging kids to open their mouths while the kids yell at them left and right. Instead of doing ten minutes of work, they spend hours negotiating with children. To make a long story short, all my friends were starting their internships at different dental offices in the summer of 1995. I was the only one who had to come back in September just to take one exam.

As I mentioned before, everything in my life happens for a reason. In the middle of August, I was approached by a different professor, Dr. Maniere, who was the head of the Department of Pediatric Dentistry. She asked me whether I was interested in doing my dental doctoral thesis in pediatric dentistry. At that moment, I was much more interested in aesthetic dentistry and implants. Pediatrics was absolutely not my subject.

She persisted, and I found that I was not able to say no, especially when she was the one who assigned me the subject that I had to do research on for my doctoral thesis. I had to write a one-hundred-page thesis and present it to a four-member jury. I had to do all this work to get my doctorate so that I could be recognized as an actual dentist.

Guess what subject Dr. Maniere chose for me to write about? Iron deficiency anemia in young children with tooth decay resulting from baby bottles being consumed during the night.

Yes, exactly the subject that I hated so much. After many days of thinking about it, I said, "Why not?" All my life, I have been competing with myself. I have always been a fighter who never gives up—never ever. No matter how impossible the situation, failure is never an option in my life. I will always do whatever is necessary to overcome failure. I will push myself to work harder than I have ever imagined to prove that nothing can ever bring me down. So I accepted the challenge.

While I was in the middle of preparing for my final exam to get my degree in dentistry, I also began working on my doctoral thesis. As you can imagine, I was very happy to pass my exam in September, as my plan was to be in California by February 1996.

To meet my deadline for going to the US, I told Dr. Maniere that I wanted to present my doctoral thesis in December 1995. She thought I was crazy. Normally, it takes at least a full year to prepare your doctoral thesis, but I was determined to do it in four months. Dr. Maniere told me that it seemed impossible, but if I worked hard, perhaps I would be able to achieve my goal.

The way it worked was that I had to complete the entire thesis thirty days before my presentation to the jury. That meant I had to choose the jury, choose a date, start writing, and be prepared to give the full thesis to the jury by November 20, 1995. This was no easy task, but I went into my hard work mode, pretty much shutting off the rest of my life. And I did it!

During this period, I saw a lot of children in the hospital—many of them in cancer hospitals. I met young kids who were immune deficient and living for a month in a plastic bubble, waiting for their bone marrow transplant. That was my first experience in the world of oncology. It hit me then that cancer was scary, but it definitely piqued my interest.

So I dove in and did something that I would continue to rely on going forward in my life: research. Yes, at this point, I did a lot of research. After days and nights of continuous work, I typed up my thesis on a very old computer that belonged to my sister. I believe it ran on the first version of Windows 3.0. On November 20, I handed in my doctoral thesis just in time for the jury to look at.

I had done it—and in record time. On December 20, I invited my friends and family to my presentation. Normally, no one comes to the doctoral thesis presentation besides a few friends and family members. It is actually quite boring. My thesis, however, was different. All my friends from my class and all my family members showed up. Even the professor who gave me a 5/20 score for my exam was there. The amphitheater was full of people.

I dedicated my thesis not just to my parents, my jury, and my favorite professor but also to the teacher who did not give me that one point to pass the exam because she thought I did not deserve it. I completed my doctoral thesis accompanied by the music of Frank Sinatra's "My Way," which served as the perfect soundtrack to reflect on my unique journey, challenges overcome, and accomplishments achieved.

It was so funny to think back to that day not that long ago. I could not even write a paragraph about the subject, but six months later, there I was, dedicating one hundred pages on the same subject to my professor, the person who had made me so angry before. What a day that was. All my friends cheered. It turned out that I was the last student to finish five years of dental school, but I was the first to become a real dentist by getting my doctorate.

So I believe this explains who I am: always fighting for everything, doing everything in record time, working hard but still having fun all along the way. But as I mentioned before, God forgot to give me one skill: patience. As a result, I have always been in an accelerated mode in life.

After my thesis, I threw a big party. I do not remember how many people showed up. I just know that we were all dancing until five in the morning. It was something to celebrate. I had finished dental school and was headed to the US. I assure you that it was quite an amazing experience.

In France, I had chosen a different path, opting for dentistry over medicine, which led to unique experiences and unexpected opportunities. My involvement in the Dental School Student Association and organizing successful fundraising events marked the beginning of my entrepreneurial spirit. Despite the pressure and rigorous demands, I found joy and fulfillment in my endeavors.

This chapter of my life, characterized by perseverance and triumph, laid the foundation for future successes and adventures, always with an eye toward the values instilled by my family and the unyielding support of those who believed in me.

CHAPTER 5

My Journey through Pediatric Dentistry

> **When we least expect it, life sets us a challenge to test our courage and willingness to change.**
>
> —Paulo Coelho

My trip to California turned out to be much shorter than I had imagined. I spent three months living in Irvine, Orange County, with my best friend's family. I was looking at a possible position at the University of California, Los Angeles (UCLA) in aesthetics/periodontics. The problem was I did not have a green card or the right visa, so I could not extend my stay.

I had to go back to France and apply for the position at UCLA there and also get a student visa. So, I went back to France. But I really enjoyed those three months near Los Angeles. I became involved with the Iranian community. I was so pleased to see what an unbelievably successful community it was.

Every time I went to Los Angeles, I had the feeling I was back in Iran. They were all there: Iranian food, Iranian books, Iranian parties, and Iranian concerts. What a wonderful surprise to be able to feel like I was back home in Iran when I was actually in California. I often find myself thinking back to those days in Iran, even though I was fairly young. I still find it hard to imagine how one event, like a revolution or a war, can change the lives of so many people. Revolution and war forced so many people out of their comfortable lives, which had taken them years to build. Everything was destroyed, and there was no choice but to start life all over again.

So many people had to leave everything behind—their families, their jobs, and their homes. They had to start all over again in a new country, with a new language, in a new environment. So many people trying to adapt, trying to adjust, trying to succeed, and trying to show who they are and what they can do without being judged by everyone around them. That is why I admire so many of the Iranian people—the immigrants who left everything behind and were still able to succeed in high-end professions in a completely foreign country.

I left California hoping that I could go back there one day, as I knew it really was where I wanted to live. It was 1996, yet I knew what I wanted would be very far into the future and was somewhat of an impossible dream. I went back to Strasbourg and got an offer to work in the pediatric dentistry department at the university hospital with Dr. Maniere. At the end of the day, we can never predict life. As I have said before, I believe everything in life happens for a reason, even if we do not see the reason while it's happening, and it takes years to realize how and why things worked out the way they did.

I learned so much working in this department, and I cannot say enough about Dr. Maniere. She is one of the most dedicated human beings I have ever met. She has a heart of pure gold. She has treated so many abused children, as well as children with autism, cancer, and physical and mental disabilities.

I was exposed to so many different situations just by working with her—situations I never imagined I was able or capable of facing in my life at such a young age. Treating young patients demands a lot of commitment, dedication, and very strong emotional stability. You cannot be weak. You cannot ask philosophical questions about life and living or normality. You have to be strong.

It is hard enough for a "normal" child to be treated by a dentist. And believe me, it is not only hard on the child, but it is also hard on the dentist. There we were, confronting those little human beings with their own challenges and fears every day. You can only imagine how hard it is on kids with autism. We cannot even touch them. There must be space in their universe, which means we could not really hold them or keep them seated on a chair. Often, they ended up yelling at the top of their lungs and hitting their little bodies against the wall. There was absolutely no way to calm them down. So how could we possibly expect them to open their mouths so that we could treat their teeth?

There were also abused children who were psychologically traumatized. They needed more psychological help than anything else. I wanted to just hold them in my arms and make them feel loved instead of making them feel traumatized again by treating their teeth.

Most kids with mental and physical disabilities have no idea why they are so different from everyone else in the world. My biggest challenge was that I really was not sure how I could help those children. Unfortunately, by constantly seeing all those kids and spending so much time with them, I became introverted and lost my joy in life. I just could not understand why some kids had to face all that hardship while others got to be normal kids.

Some kids had privileges that others would never have. I do not think I ever asked God so many questions about fairness as I did at that time in my life. I had so many questions in my head. Why do some children and their parents have to go through so much suffering? Why can they not be like everyone else and enjoy a normal life, like you and me?

Maybe the word *normality* is just a word with different definitions based on different conditions and situations. What does "normal" mean anyway? What is really normal? Perhaps someone considers their life to be normal even though it is nothing like the life I consider to be normal.

The truth is, I had become so attached to all those little individuals that I forgot about my own life. My perspective on life changed so much. My approach to life changed. I became more and more aware that society in general needed so much help. Society needed massive action to turn things around. As for me, I needed a bigger project in my life that would have a bigger impact on the world. That was why I went from the dental world to the medical business world.

As I mentioned before, I realized that I should not have been in dentistry from the beginning. I should have gone to medical school because once I transitioned to the medical industry, I was exposed to every therapeutic area that existed. I learned so much about medicine, drugs, and surgery. I now believe that even if I had finished medical school, I would not be as much of an expert as I am today in many therapeutic areas and surgical procedures.

CHAPTER 6

Robots in the Operating Room

> **Any sufficiently advanced technology is indistinguishable from magic.**
>
> —Arthur C. Clarke

In the busy days of September 1997, while I was immersed in my daily visits to the hospital for dentistry, an unexpected visitor arrived. My sister Mahshad's friend Maryam came to Strasbourg. Maryam had known Mahshad in Iran. They went to school together, and after the revolution, Maryam left Iran and moved to America. In 1997, she was working at Computer Motion, which was at the time a leading medical/surgical robotics company in Santa Barbara, California.

Before I tell you about my journey at Computer Motion, I would like to share with you part of an article I recently found in the *American Journal of Robotic Surgery* about the history of robots in medicine and operating rooms.[1]

A major innovation in the field of surgery was made when a robot was first used in the operating room about twenty-five years ago. The robot was a PUMA 200 (Westinghouse Electric, Pittsburgh, Pennsylvania) that was used for needle placement in a CT-guided brain biopsy. Since then, it has been exciting to see how the field of robotic surgery has grown. Part of the reason for the growth is the benefits afforded by robotics that are simply absent in traditional surgical methods. For example, robots offer stability, precision, accuracy, and integration with modern imaging technology, as well as a greater range of motion. Telesurgery using robotics offers multiple other benefits to individual surgical specialties.

Since the introduction of robotic surgery, many advancements have been made in this field. While robots have been in existence for a long while now, their entrance into the realm of medicine is relatively novel. In the 1980s, the field became popular as a way to do minimally invasive surgery. While laparoscopy—an operation performed in the abdomen or pelvis using small incisions with the aid of a camera—was already seeing widespread use, the actions that could be done were relatively limited compared to the believed potential of robotic surgery at that time.

Also around that time, NASA's Ames Research Center started working on the concept of telepresence in surgery, a technology that enables a person to perform actions in a distant or virtual location as if physically present in that location. The center was joined by Stanford University in the 1990s, which led to the development of a

---

1 Jay Shah, Arpita Vyas, and Dinesh Vyas,"The History of Robotics in Surgical Specialties," *American Journal of Robotic Surgery* 1, no. 1 (2014): 12-20. doi: 10.1166/ajrs.2014.1006. PMID: 26677459; PMCID: PMC4677089.

technologically advanced telemanipulator. This served as the building block for future systems.

In 1994, the Automated Endoscopic System for Optimal Position (AESOP) robotic system, owned by Computer Motion, got Food and Drug Administration (FDA) approval. AESOP was an endoscope holder robot with a foot pedal. Later, the foot pedal was replaced by voice control. At that time, however, its functionality was limited. The major benefit was stability in that it offered a steady view of the operating field and eliminated the problems caused by the fatigue and inexperience of the scope holder. However, the technological advancements made with AESOP were not abandoned, and further progress was made.

The ZEUS robotic system, also owned by Computer Motion, has two separate hubs: the patient side and the surgeon side. The surgeon side is designed to control the patient side. The patient side is the one that performs the procedure. It has two arms that are controlled by the surgeon's manipulation on the surgeon side and one arm that is designed to hold the voice-controlled camera. The two robotic arms are fitted with interchangeable instruments. It was initially designed as a cardiothoracic surgical tool for internal mammary artery takedown, but its feasibility for other uses and surgical subspecialties was quickly recognized.

The ZEUS robotic system received FDA approval for limited uses in 2001. In February 2001, it became possible to have a global collaboration of one surgeon with another via the SOCRATES robotic system from Computer Motion. The SOCRATES system is a telecollaboration system that allows a surgeon in a remote operating station to control the robotic arm, view real-time video input from the site of surgery, and obtain real-time audio communication from the location of the surgery.

Besides the ZEUS robotic system, in 1999, the da Vinci robotic surgical system (Intuitive Surgical, Sunnyvale, California) came to market. This system offers the surgeon seven degrees of freedom by allowing the robotic arm to replicate exactly what the human arm does. The da Vinci system consists of the surgeon's console, the patient's trolley (the robot itself), and the imaging system (3D visualization). In 2003, Computer Motion and Intuitive Surgical merged, and the da Vinci robotic system became one of the most ubiquitous and recognized systems throughout the world in the robotic surgery era. Now, in 2024, the da Vinci system performs over 3,500 procedures per day.

Getting back to my journey in 1997, Computer Motion wanted to start a European subsidiary and chose to come to Strasbourg. I believe that was because of Professor Jacques Marescaux and the Research Institute against Digestive Cancer (IRCAD).

Professor Marescaux is a true legend. Everything this one man has done over the years for his patients, for medicine, and for innovation in the medical and surgical fields is beyond belief and without parallel. He is incredibly unique. I have met very few people with so much power, so much knowledge, and so much charisma, and yet, at the same time, he is so human and humble.

In 1992, surgery faced inevitable changes, shifting from the industrial era to the computer era. Knowing the effect this would have on the future of surgery, Professor Marescaux, chair professor at the Universities of Digestive Surgery, came up with the idea to create an original research and training center in Strasbourg, France. In 1994, he founded IRCAD, a cancer research institute focusing on the digestive tract, and the European Institute of TeleSurgery. IRCAD is a center where more than five thousand surgeons from all over the world come to learn about minimally invasive surgery every year.

The most amazing part is that they are trained by more than eight hundred international experts. IRCAD has gained worldwide renown as a leading research and education institute for minimally invasive surgery. This explains why Computer Motion wanted to team up with IRCAD and Professor Marescaux in Europe. The Computer Motion and IRCAD teams would introduce the surgical robots and educate the physicians coming to IRCAD about the new technology.

Over the past twelve years, other IRCADs around the world have also been established: IRCAD Taiwan (the first IRCAD outside France), IRCAD Brazil, IRCAD Lebanon, and IRCAD Rwanda.

In 1997, Maryam was the European head of Computer Motion, and she came to Strasbourg to meet Professor Marescaux. After multiple visits and discussions, I became so interested in her project that when she asked me whether I would be interested in working for them in their European division, I could not have been more thrilled. In November 1997, I started working at Computer Motion as a coordinator of Europe. Interesting title, right? But I did not care. I had my doctorate, spoke four languages, and knew all the medical and surgical teams in Strasbourg—thanks to my sisters and my aunt.

My dad, however, was disappointed that I accepted this job and my new position. The only way he would approve of my continuing with this position was if I agreed to get my MBA. So, while I was working at Computer Motion, I decided to apply for my MBA. I finished my international MBA after eighteen months. I believe my father was quite pleased when I officially got my business degree. As for me, I have to admit it was fun. The school was an affiliate of a Florida school based in Europe, which meant that all the teachers came from the US. It turned out to be a great experience and helped me not only to practice my English but also to learn about all the business aspects involved in running a company.

CHAPTER 7

My Mother: The Rock

> **Being a mother is learning about strengths you didn't know you had and dealing with fears you never knew existed.**
>
> —Linda Wooten

As I mentioned, my dad was not in favor of me leaving dentistry for the medical business. He always thought that dentistry was a safe career for a woman who wanted to build a family and raise a child. Actually, he was right, but that really did not have a lot to do with my life then. It was my mom who always encouraged me to follow my dreams. Also, she was always there to help me overcome the challenges that seemed to be sitting right in front of me so many times.

My mother is one of the most open-minded people I know. I will never be able to find the right words to describe her dedication and the sacrifices she has made in life, especially for her family. Her tolerance and level of acceptance, no matter the circumstances, have always amazed and inspired me. Her courage, loyalty, and fidelity are also nothing short of remarkable. I know I am making her sound like some sort of Wonder Woman, but believe me, she actually is.

She and my father met when they were at university in Iran together. They became sweethearts. They both studied architecture and got married when she was only eighteen years old. She finished high school at the age of sixteen and started university at the age of seventeen. She is a true genius. While she was busy studying, she also had three children—all before finishing her degree.

She has surprised me at every step of my life with her advice. If you knew her, you would see that she is fearless. She always tells me, "Follow your dreams. Move forward. Do not look back. Life is in front of you, not behind you. Just keep going."

From Iran to Germany to France to the US, she always created an environment that pushed me to achieve more. No matter how difficult it was to move and change my life from one continent to another, from one country to another, she supported me in every way she could.

My mother was the reason why I accepted the job at Computer Motion, moved to California, and pursued my American Dream in 2002. She was the one who supported my decisions. She was always right there, watching over me like a guardian angel. Even later in life, when I was pregnant and my situation was very complicated, she was right there for me. I will forever be grateful that she and my father were willing and able to help raise my son, Shaun, all those years while I was working.

I often think to myself, "How can she take on so much? How is she able to be all the things that she is?" She is a woman, she is a mother, she is a daughter, she is a grandmother, but she is also a professional in her field and an experienced career woman. I suppose this is why she understands me and every aspect of my life.

Many years have gone by since I left home and we left Iran, but still, no matter where I am on the planet, I call my parents every day and talk to my mom for at least two hours. It does not matter what the time difference is; she is always there to listen to me. She is there when I laugh, when I cry, when I have a problem, and when I have a broken heart. She is always there to guide me—never judging me, never judging anyone. I can remember her just listening for hours and hours at a time when I was very sad. I could see in her eyes that she just wanted to take all the pain out of my life and put it on her own shoulders.

Until I had my son, Shaun, I never understood the meaning of motherhood. The truth is, I love being a mom. I will always believe it is one of the most challenging and rewarding jobs ever. Just watching every step of your child's development is incredible—the first laugh, the first tooth, the first step, the first day of daycare, the first day of school, the first win in the basketball or football game, the first loss of that game, the first award, the first girlfriend or boyfriend, the first graduation, the day they start college, and the time they leave home to pursue their own life, their own dreams. What a joy to be a part of their cries, laughter, and challenges, not to mention those sleepless nights with a baby that needs to be fed or the nights they are sick.

And who can forget those sleepless nights when they are out with their friends or have an exam the next day? What I have learned is that being a mom means you are willing to put your kids and your family ahead of yourself and your own life. Talk about sacrifice. My mom was always one of these mothers who dedicated her entire life to us, her family. I believe they call that unconditional love.

CHAPTER 8

Joining the Business World

> **The secret of change is to focus all your energy not on fighting the old but on building the new.**
>
> —Socrates

My life changed once I joined Computer Motion. It was an amazing experience. I became part of building a company in Europe and learning all aspects of running a business in Europe and the Middle East, and it all happened in a very short period. In late 1998, I met Bob Duggan, who was the CEO and chairman of the board of Computer Motion, as well as the lead investor. He came to visit Computer Motion Europe. While he was there, he spoke with several European physicians and traveled to some of our centers and hospitals in Europe to evaluate our progress in that part of the world. We had made a lot of progress as a team in a very short period.

Bob is a serial entrepreneur. He is very charismatic and someone I will always admire. I would call him extraterrestrial. His positive energy is contagious, and his enthusiasm, drive, and sense of humor are unmatchable. His intensity and persistence are the two characteristics that have defined him through all the years that I have known him. I really enjoyed our business partnership over the years and learned a lot about investments and business from him.

When Bob came to Strasbourg, I introduced him to Professor Marescaux, and we took him to see IRCAD. He really enjoyed meeting our European team and being able to see what we had accomplished in Europe. We visited multiple places together and met with many of the hospital physicians and administrators. He spoke with such a passion for robotics. I will never forget the day before he left. We met for coffee at the Hilton Hotel in Strasbourg. He asked me, "What do you want to do?" I told him I enjoyed my work at Computer Motion and would do everything I could to help the company introduce robotics to the surgical world.

When he asked me that question, he was looking directly into my eyes. I believe he wanted to see my level of commitment to the company. I tried not to look up or down. I just waited to hear what he had to say. He asked me if I wanted to run the European and Middle Eastern division of Computer Motion as the president of EMEA. I was completely surprised and did not know what to say. I was young—twenty-eight years old—but I knew that I was hungry to learn the business.

Believe it or not, I enjoyed working day and night, 24/7, without any breaks or vacations. We were nine hours ahead of California time, and the Middle East was open on Saturdays and Sundays while Europe was closed. So there I was, working nonstop, and what I remember most was that it was really fun.

But on that day, my brain was working nonstop, and my mind was all over the place. I had a lot of questions that I did not have answers to yet. Building a company and hiring people across Europe, especially at that particular moment when Europe was not a unified entity, with each country having its own currency, rules, and regulations—how quickly could I learn all those details?

Everything raced through my mind at the speed of light, but on that day, Bob told me something I would remember for the rest of my life. It became something I always refer to. He told me, "Take responsibility, and the capacity and ability will follow."

And that was the beginning of my business life. This concept was life changing. I jumped into an unknown business world and learned extensively what to do and how to do it. I worked hard over the years and became a well-established businesswoman. By accepting responsibility, my desire to learn, to make, to progress, and to improve grew and expanded. I have become more able and capable than I ever thought possible.

I accepted the challenge and began to hire more people. I also began traveling around the world to introduce robotics to physicians for all their surgical procedures, including urology, gastroenterology, and cardiac procedures. I traveled to many different European countries and enjoyed the diversity of cultural thinking. We sold AESOP, our single-arm robot, to many hospitals. Selling ZEUS, another one of our robots, was more challenging because we had a competitor, Intuitive Surgical, that owned the da Vinci system that was similar to ours. The problem was, they were trying to sell their product to the same physicians we were. It became an interesting challenge, with many barriers to overcome.

At that time, both companies were focusing on robot-assisted cardiac surgery. But cardiac surgery is very challenging via robotics for several reasons: the complexity of the procedure, limited field of view in minimally invasive surgery compared to direct vision during open surgery, lack of haptic feedback (which is the sense of touch and force feedback), and, most importantly, the learning curve. Mastering the use of robotic surgical systems requires training and experience.

Surgeons need to become proficient at operating the robotic console and translating their movements into precise actions by the robotic arms. Despite these challenges, robot-assisted cardiac surgery continues to evolve with advancements in technology and training, offering such benefits as smaller incisions, reduced blood loss, and faster recovery times for patients.

I remember one day, one of our clinical specialists, Murielle, called me and asked me to visit Montsouris Hospital in Paris. This hospital had our ZEUS robotic system in place. Murielle and our clinical director, Peter Puke, spent a lot of time with one of the urologists at these hospitals, Dr. Guilloneau, as well as the pediatric cardiac surgeon, Dr. Laborde. Murielle and Peter told me about the new procedure named robot-assisted radical prostatectomy via our robotic system. Years later, this procedure, which coupled the benefits of minimally invasive surgery with the benefits of robotic surgery in urology, became the gold standard of robotics procedures.

The main limitation of the use of traditional laparoscopy is that guiding the instruments into the desired location is a challenging feat, as the depth of the pelvis makes it harder to access. Radical prostatectomy via robotics can lead to significantly decreased blood loss, shorter postoperative catheterization times, quicker return to urinary continence, and faster mean return time of erections. In addition, the complication rate is lower.

After seeing the procedure, I called Bob and asked him to come to France and visit the hospital. A revolutionary procedure in the field of urology had been developed with robotics, and we needed his support. After explaining the procedure and the benefits, he totally understood that we should change our direction from cardiac surgery to urology.

As mentioned, cardiac surgery via robotics requires extensive training and involves complex procedures with limited access, unlike radical prostatectomy performed using robotics. Urologists are accustomed to conducting minimally invasive procedures, making it easier for them to integrate robotics into their daily routine and surgical practices. The incorporation of robotics enables them to perform more precise surgeries and significantly enhance patient outcomes.

That was the beginning of the use of three-armed robots in the operating room. But da Vinci's robotic system was better than our ZEUS robot for these procedures. Their robotic arm had seven degrees of freedom, and their system had 3D visualization, which meant that it had more advanced instrument movement, as well as more advanced visualization. So they got FDA approval for robot-assisted surgery for radical prostatectomy in 2001. And that was the beginning of a new era in robot-assisted surgery.

Over the past twenty years, robotic surgery has revolutionized the field of medicine and made a significant difference in the outcomes of patients' lives. This cutting-edge technology is often described as magical because of its transformative impact on surgical procedures, and it has evolved rapidly, becoming more precise, efficient, and accessible to a wider range of medical specialties.

In the coming years, we can expect to see even more advancements in robotic surgery with AI integration. The integration of AI into robotic surgery holds immense promise for the future of healthcare. AI algorithms can analyze vast amounts of data, assist surgeons in decision-making, and even perform certain tasks autonomously. This collaboration between AI and robotic systems has the potential to further improve surgical outcomes, reduce complications, and enhance patient recovery. This may include personalized treatment plans based on individual patient data, real-time feedback during surgery to optimize outcomes, and the development of autonomous robotic systems that can perform complex procedures with minimal human intervention.

The future of robotic surgery with AI is bright, offering new possibilities for precision medicine and improving patient care.

CHAPTER 9

Welcome to the Middle East

> **Be happy for this moment. This moment is your life.**
> —Omar Khayyam, Persian astronomer,
> mathematician, and poet

Sometime in 2000, I went to Dubai on a business trip. Dubai is a city of contrasts, where tradition meets modernity in a dazzling display of wealth and innovation. Its skyscrapers, luxurious hotels, and man-made islands are testaments to its ambition and vision. Dubai is a global hub for trade and tourism, and its forward-looking leaders and infrastructure investments have turned it into a grand and influential city that captivates people globally.

From the world's tallest building, the Burj Khalifa, to fancy shopping malls and lively cultures, Dubai radiates luxury and charm that set it apart as a truly remarkable destination. I had heard a lot about Dubai and thought it might be the perfect place to establish our company, Computer Motion Middle East.

My mom and my sister Mahshad had visited Dubai in 1998 and had given me a lot of information about the area. When I went there, I was quite surprised. It was a very quiet place with a lot of brand-new luxury hotels. The first eight-star hotel in the world, the Burj Al Arab, is located in Dubai. I found it all unbelievable. What a creation. The designers and architects of this hotel had a lot of imagination. I also visited the beautiful luxury hospitals. The hospitals that I visited looked like four-star hotels. I found everything in this country absolutely amazing, although a bit grandiose.

I give a lot of credit to the ruler of Dubai, Sheik Mohammed. In his roles as the prime minister and vice president, his leadership and vision have made Dubai one of the safest, cleanest, and most innovative places that I have ever visited.

The first time I landed at the Dubai airport, I saw a sign that said, "Welcome to the country with Unlimited Possibilities." This sentence has always remained in my mind.

"Unlimited Possibilities." That was how Sheik Mohammed built this country in a very short time. Even big business leaders had never built companies with such incredible quality and details in such a short period. Building a company in a few years is a difficult task, but building a country like Dubai in record time is unheard of. The more I learned and read about him, the more I liked and admired his philosophy.

While I was in Dubai, I really wanted to meet Sheik Mohammed and talk to him about our surgical robotic system. I knew that if there was someone who would understand the future of surgery and the vision for the future of operating rooms, it would be him. I tried calling several different organizations to get access to him, but it just never happened. After a few days, I left Dubai and went to Jordan.

I had a big meeting that was set up at the military hospital of Jordan. I would be the one presenting our surgical robotic system to the cardiac surgeons as part of an important cardiology event. I believe fifty to eighty people were invited to this meeting to learn about robotics and the role it would play in the future of surgery. That was a day I will never forget. It was a very hot day in Dubai, so I put on a very nice red dress to travel in so that I would not feel so hot. I headed to the airport for my flight from Dubai to Jordan.

I cannot remember which airline I took. I just know that it was not the Emirates airline. What a flight! To be honest, I thought I might die on that flight. It was on an old, smelly aircraft. The seats were moving in all directions and felt like they were only half-connected to the aircraft. On top of that, it was a very shaky flight. The weather was not good, and we had a lot of very bad turbulence. Finally, we landed safely in Jordan. At that point, I was just happy to be alive. I got off the flight as fast as I could and went to pick up my luggage at the baggage claim. One after another, people took their luggage and left the area.

Thirty minutes later, there was no one else there except security guards and baggage claim employees. They were all staring at me. Here I was, a blond, tanned woman in a short red dress. I began to feel very uncomfortable. After waiting for about thirty minutes, I realized that my luggage was lost, and I did not have anything besides that short red dress to wear.

I really do not remember how I got to the hotel. I had just an hour and a half before my meeting. I checked in to the hotel and ran around trying to find a place to buy some type of outfit so that I would look professional at my meeting. I could not find anything. Finally, I found a small boutique in the hotel lobby that had some old-fashioned outfits for sale.

Things were not going well. At that particular time, I was very small, and the only outfit that they had was four sizes too large. It was a dark blue jacket with a dark blue skirt, and guess what? The price was $2,000, which was a lot of money to spend on an outfit that was way too large. But I really did not have a choice. I did not have time to go look for anything else, so I bought it. I went to my room and changed my clothes. All I could think of was I looked like a clown, but it was better than looking like a Vogue magazine model in my short and stylish red dress.

On top of all that, I suddenly realized that my complete video presentation and CD that were in my luggage were also lost. Honestly, it felt like the end of the world. But I had no other option except to show up and act as if nothing had happened and everything was under control. I finally arrived at the meeting room. My heart was beating so fast, and I had the feeling that everybody around me could definitely hear it. My head felt like it was too heavy for my body.

The room was full of *men*. Other than me, there were no women there. I could not believe my eyes. There I was, looking like a clown, my heart beating in my mouth, trying to act like I was in control. I stood up, and they introduced me to the audience.

Suddenly, everything changed. I felt an amazing jolt of electricity surge through my body. It was like a force that was growing inside me and pushing me. I spoke with a clear, confident voice. I spoke about how cardiac procedures using robotics worked and the clinical applications of robotics. I explained the vision of robotics and how it would change the future of surgery. I believe that, as a woman, I surprised them. And truthfully, I even surprised myself. To this day, I still find it hard to believe that was me talking. I still have no idea how I made it all happen. I just know that there is nothing more important in life than having the ability and confidence to make things happen.

The day after I left Jordan, right before I left my hotel room, someone knocked on the door. It was the bellman, who arrived with my lost luggage. Although actually, it was not my luggage. It turned out to be all my clothes in a plastic bag. There was no video presentation or CD inside the bag, just my clothes. Even today, I still do not understand what happened between Dubai and Jordan.

Why did they search my luggage? Who was it that went through all my luggage? Where did my presentation and CD end up? Anyway, I left Jordan. What an experience that turned out to be.

A few months after my trip to Jordan, I was invited to Saudi Arabia, which turned out to be another interesting journey. It is harder than you can imagine to go to Saudi Arabia if you are a woman and not married. First, someone had to invite me before they would even give me a visa. I was invited by one of the physicians I worked with to present the robotic system at Riyadh Hospital. The good news was that I went from Egypt to Saudi Arabia, so I had enough time to buy a chador and Islamic outfit, the traditional clothing for women in that country.

When I landed, the man who invited me picked me up at the airport. The first thing he did was take my passport, which he kept during my entire stay in Saudi. He registered me under his name at the hotel. Suddenly, my journey became a little more adventurous than planned. The truth of the matter was, if something had happened to me then, nobody would have ever known I even existed in that country.

To make a long story short, I got to my room, and I had to prepare for my meeting. I would be presenting the robotic system and the future of surgery to a group of surgeons and administrators of the hospital. I put on my chador, got all the necessary videos and presentations, and headed to the lobby. The man who invited me came with his wife to pick me up. We were all together in his car because apparently, as an unmarried woman, I could not get into a car with just a man.

When we got to the meeting, I saw a large number of eyes staring at me as if someone from Mars had just landed at their meeting. The people in the room were all men, and not one of them could believe that a woman would be presenting. They thought my name, Maky Zanganeh, was a male name and not a female name. They were sure I was going to be a man.

At first, I thought they were kidding when they said they did not want me to present. They asked if someone else from my company could do the presentation. I told them I was the only one there and no one else from my company had come with me. It took at least thirty minutes before they finally allowed me to talk. I found it all so interesting. What difference did they see between women and men? Are men supposed to be more intelligent than women? Are women not considered able human beings?

During this trip, I also learned that I could not shake hands with men while I was in Saudi Arabia, and men always had to walk a few feet ahead of women. After I gave the presentation, I was extremely tired and asked for a coffee. My host suggested going to Starbucks. I cannot tell you how happy that made me. I felt like I was on my way to my mom's house. I could not wait to get to Starbucks. It was such a warm and familiar place. But as soon as I got there, I saw curtains everywhere. There were curtains all over the coffee shop, separating one group from another. This was not the Starbucks I knew, but I must admit that it was really interesting.

A customer can take their coffee, and they cannot see anyone but the person or group of people who came with them. What a culture. What traditions. It was completely different from any other place in the world I had ever visited. Nevertheless, I really enjoyed my time in Saudi Arabia. All the people I met there were nice. I did find it interesting to see all the restrictions and limitations women had to face there. There was so much controversy. The malls were full of beautiful, expensive boutiques. I saw many elegant women beautifully dressed under their chador, which covered them from head to toe on those very hot Saudi days.

I found the Middle East business market extremely challenging. Finding money was never a problem, but finding a surgeon with vision was impossible at this point in time. The mentality of these people and their philosophy in life are so different from how people in Western countries think and act. Time has no meaning in the Middle East, and a signature has no value. Trust, confidence, and relationships set the rules in this part of the world. Their philosophy is, "Give it time because you have eternity in front of you."

Although life there can be extremely difficult, especially for women, I still love the Middle East. I love it because it is mysterious and adventurous.

But the most interesting parts of my journey to the Middle East were my trips to Egypt. In one year, I ended up going to Egypt eleven times. I was first invited by the team at Qasr El Eyni Hospital in Cairo, and I landed in Cairo for the first time in September 2000. I remember it being a hot day. A car picked me up and dropped me off at a very luxurious hotel.

Driving in Cairo is just crazy. It is very much like Iran or India. Every car on the road is trying to get in front of all the others. And every driver is better than any Formula One driver. They can see ahead and behind. They can professionally maneuver their cars to cut corners and never hit any people. They are really fun to watch but not so much fun to ride with.

The day after I arrived in Egypt, I went to the hospital. When I arrived, there were people everywhere. I had a meeting with the general director of Cairo University Hospitals. Qasr El Eyni Hospital is one of the oldest, most prestigious university hospitals in the region. It was built in 1827 in Cairo, Egypt. The hospital is affiliated with the

Qasr El Eyni Faculty of Medicine, Cairo University. This is where I met Professor El Fiky.

I had never met anyone so calm, kind, and polite. This man was an incredible human being with a heart as big as an ocean. He offered to give me a tour of the hospital.

When we got to the pediatric hospital, I could not believe the number of patients. There were rooms where you could see six children sleeping in one room and their parents sitting on the floor. Everything was so different from any hospital I had visited before. From the moment I saw the kids, their parents, the environment, and the condition those children were in, I knew that the hospital needed basic medicine much more than a surgical robotic system.

I believe Professor El Fiky read my mind when I saw him the next day. Before I even got a chance to tell him that it was not a good idea to continue the discussion about the robotic system, he brought me to a different floor of the hospital. I could not believe my eyes. I was looking at the latest in technology, videoconferencing, everything. It was all there. And to be honest, I could not understand what was going on. One floor looked so in need of basic medicine, while another floor had all the latest technology and innovations.

I knew that Egypt had great physicians and surgeons. The medicines used by ancient Egyptians are some of the oldest documented. From the beginning of civilization in the late fourth millennium BCE until the Persian invasion of 525 BCE, Egyptian medical practices remained largely unchanged but were highly advanced for their time, including surgery, dentistry, and pharmacology.

Anyway, after spending time in Cairo and going back and forth so many times, I fell in love with the environment, the culture, the people, and their hospitality. I saw the pyramids and the Egyptian museum. I rode camels in the desert. I had dinner on a boat on the

Nile River. I saw the poor places and the luxury locations. What a contrast! On top of that, the military was always around everywhere. It seemed like no matter where I was, I could see soldiers with guns, protecting the country.

Finally, in September 2001, the hospital bought the first ZEUS robotic system and became the first hospital in the Middle East to do robotic surgery. Professor El Fiky, chief of pediatric surgery at Qasr El Eyni Hospital, performed the first robotic procedure within a week of installing the ZEUS system. He completed more than a dozen procedures within the first month.

Working with Professor El Fiky on this project was an unforgettable experience. His personal dedication to his patients, his students, and his staff was remarkable. His interest in technology and computers made Qasr El Eyni one of the most advanced hospitals in Cairo. We were so proud to be working with him and his team, and we knew that surgeons like him would ultimately develop new and exciting procedures to treat more and more patients less invasively with surgical robotics. Professor El Fiky became the center of reference for us in the Middle East. From that day on, we brought all our surgeons from the surrounding Arab countries to Egypt.

The time I spent in Egypt was unforgettable. Also in that year, Israel heard about our robotic system. They heard that we had sold a robot in Egypt, and they contacted me. I could not go to Israel, however, because I am Iranian, and we are not allowed in the country. The general surgeons from Israel came to France instead to look at our robotic system. Israel became the second country after Egypt to get our robot.

After my initial visits to all these countries, I returned many times with Bob and our European colleagues. We were featured in the news and media of the Middle East. It was exciting to see how quickly robotic innovation had followed our presence.

Overall, my journey to the Middle East, from Dubai to Jordan, Saudi Arabia, and Egypt, was an experience I will never forget. The Middle East is the home of spirituality. Each country is different and beautiful in its own way. When you are there, you hear the sounds of the call to prayer five times a day, and it is magical. There are incredible collections of architecture, from mosques to skyscrapers. The landscape is remarkable, from deserts to oceans. It is all part of the magic of the Middle East.

The culture is one of peace and hospitality. I met so many kind, welcoming people there. Kindness and generosity are the cornerstones of Middle Eastern culture and tradition, and despite the stereotyping and discrimination we so often hear in the mainstream media, Middle Eastern hospitality has become world-famous.

Unfortunately, the first thing that comes to mind about the Middle East for so many people is crisis, turmoil, and fighting, some of which are due to radicalism, as well as inequality, sexism, and repression. There is another side of these countries that people seldom hear about or get to experience. This is very sad not only for Middle Easterners but also for the world at large.

The unique culture of the Middle East may be strange to someone from the West, but they can intuitively grasp its main concepts. Everything is about peace, serenity, and personal growth. In addition, knowledge and learning have always been major goals for Middle Eastern sages throughout history.

I have also discovered that there are things I can find in the Middle East that I will never see anywhere else in the world. Things like ATMs in Abu Dhabi's fanciest hotel, the Emirates Palace Hotel. These are no ordinary machines. Some of them dispense bars of pure gold. The

ATMs in the hotel are gold-plated as well and offer curious customers 320 options that range from gold bars to customized coins. Prices are constantly updated to reflect the value of gold in international markets, making it a pricey souvenir that can also be a good investment.

Anyway, I really enjoyed my journeys to so many magical parts of the Middle East. And I will never forget all the incredible times I was fortunate enough to experience there.

Experiencing Middle Eastern culture has deeply influenced my professional journey and personal philosophy. The values of faith, patience, hospitality, and willingness to help others have shaped my approach to work and life.

Embracing faith has taught me to trust in the process and believe in my abilities even in challenging times. Cultivating patience has allowed me to navigate obstacles with grace, resilience, and an understanding that good things take time to unfold. The culture of hospitality has instilled in me a sense of warmth and openness toward others, fostering strong relationships and collaboration. Lastly, the emphasis on helping those in need has inspired me to seek opportunities to bring innovation and positive change wherever they are required, contributing to a more compassionate and inclusive world.

CHAPTER 10

Operation Lindbergh

> **Success is not measured by what a man accomplishes,**
> **but by the opposition he [has] encountered**
> **and the courage with which he has maintained**
> **the struggle against overwhelming odds.**
>
> —Charles Lindbergh

My major achievement and the highlight of my career during my time at Computer Motion came in September 2001, when Professor Marescaux electrified the surgical world with Operation Lindbergh. He performed the world's first telesurgical operation using robotic technology. This groundbreaking procedure, named in honor of Charles Lindbergh, demonstrated the potential of robotic surgery and telemedicine to enable remote surgical interventions, opening up new possibilities for global collaboration and access to specialized medical care.

Using advanced robotic systems in surgery enables precision, dexterity, and minimally invasive techniques, mirroring Lindbergh's emphasis on innovation. Just as Lindbergh's flight across the Atlantic revolutionized aviation, Operation Lindbergh revolutionized medicine by offering new possibilities for complex procedures, improved patient outcomes, and enhanced surgical techniques.

Professor Marescaux launched the first telesurgery operation between New York City and Strasbourg, France, via the ZEUS robotic system, a Computer Motion robot. Sitting at a robotic console in New York, he removed the gallbladder of a patient in Strasbourg. It was the perfect blend of information, technology, and surgery, proving that distance was no longer an obstacle.

Operation Lindbergh was one of the biggest innovations in the field of surgery. Professor Marescaux showed the world that surgery could be performed from a distance via robotics. We showed everyone that the barriers of space, distance, and time can collapse. The signals had to travel over ten thousand miles, resulting in a delay of over one-tenth of a second after an incision was made before the effects were seen. The data link, capable of carrying ten megabytes of data a second, was the result of two and a half years of work by French Telecom.

Professor Marescaux, who had come up with this brilliant idea, asked me to discuss the idea with our US team at Computer Motion. I immediately went to Bob, who liked the idea. Bob came to Strasbourg to meet up with Professor Marescaux. I will always remember this meeting with Professor Marescaux and Professor Leroy at Chez Yvonne, a wonderful little restaurant in Strasbourg. This was where we all agreed to do this exciting project together.

The project took approximately twenty-four months. The Computer Motion engineers, led by Moji Ghodoussi, successfully built a ZEUS robotic system with telesurgery capability, French Telecom handled the networking infrastructure between the two continents, and Professor Marescaux and his team worked on the surgical procedures.

On September 7, 2001, we performed the gallbladder removal surgery between the two continents. I was in the room, carefully observing everyone. The engineers were nervous and eager to see their invention working in real time. The French Telecom engineers were attentive; it was a matter of milliseconds, and mistakes were not an option. Everyone was focused on Professor Marescaux's hands and the surgery on the monitor. I remained quiet. The weather was superb, and excitement filled the room.

Time flew by, and I vividly recall everyone suddenly standing up, shaking hands, and congratulating each other in that historic moment. It was a moment that I will never forget. I felt immensely proud, knowing that all our hard work had paid off. Bob and I, along with Professor Marescaux, made history again.

The surgical team decided to wait a few days for the patient to recover before announcing this miraculous procedure to the world. We planned to announce it on September 13, 2001. All the journalists and media were invited to hear the news at IRCAD and in New York. Two days before the announcement, on September 11, 2001, Professor Marescaux called me and told me to get to the IRCAD amphitheater as soon as possible.

This was a moment in time I will never forget. We watched in disbelief as the Twin Towers came down during a full-blown terrorist attack on New York. But it did not stop there. Airplanes were commandeered and used as weapons. The Pentagon was bombed. This was a day of tragedy that would go down in history for all Americans. Who could ever believe that one day the Twin Towers would be destroyed by two aircraft? The news of the attack was so significant that our surgical innovation never made the headlines.

The strangest thing of all to me was that my sister Mahshad and I had been together in New York just two months before this horrific incident. The team was there, testing the robot. The days we spent in New York were very long. On the day we were flying back to France, my sister really wanted to go see the Twin Towers. We could see the buildings from our hotel window. I told her I was too tired, and we would definitely go see it next time. After all, those buildings had been there for many years, and it wasn't like they were going anywhere. I was wrong. Two months later, this unbelievable tragedy happened, and we never got the chance to go to the top of the Twin Towers.

Operation Lindbergh symbolizes a new era in surgical innovation, where technology transcends geographical boundaries and allows for precision, efficiency, and expertise to be shared across distances. This pioneering achievement has paved the way for further advancements in robotic surgery and telemedicine, shaping the future of healthcare.

In October 2002, I was promoted to global vice president of training and education and moved to Santa Barbara. It was fun to work at Computer Motion in the US. In June 2003, the company merged with Intuitive Surgical, and I decided not to continue working at Intuitive Surgical. I left Computer Motion a few days before the merger.

In an instant, everything came to an end. The merger and acquisition process is never easy for any employee, and for me, it was particularly challenging to say goodbye. Leaving Computer Motion behind was a bittersweet moment, as it marked the conclusion of my first business venture.

I had poured my heart and soul into building the European office and contributing to the integration of robotics into the operating room. The journey was filled with hard work, dedication, and a deep sense of purpose. Letting go was tough, but I took pride in the impact we had made and the legacy we had created in advancing the field of surgical robotics.

I did not stay until the last days of the company. I heard that Bob gave a very nice speech. Others always mention that it was one of his best speeches ever. But I was so sad that the companies merged that I just did not want to stay and be any part of that last day. So instead, I took off for Hawaii to attend an aesthetic dentistry event. That trip to Hawaii was amazing. I went to Maui and visited Hana and the waterfalls. It ended up being a trip I will never forget. It helped me decide that it was time to find my own serenity and start anew.

CHAPTER 11
The Story of Pharmacyclics

> **There is no better exercise for the heart than reaching down and lifting people up.**
> —John Holmes

After I left Hawaii, I went back to California. In June 2003, after the merger of Intuitive Surgical and Computer Motion, the two leaders in surgical robotics, I decided to take a few months off. I left Santa Barbara and went to live in Los Angeles. I decided to do post-education training in aesthetic dentistry at UCLA. It was an interesting experience, but it was not at all what I wanted to do. Transitioning back to dentistry after my time at Computer Motion was a significant adjustment.

My world suddenly narrowed down to one room, focusing on a very specific environment—the realm of thirty-two teeth. The shift to aesthetic dentistry posed even greater challenges compared to my previous experience in pediatric dentistry. Patients in this field are often seeking immediate results, adding a layer of stress to the environment. Adapting to this new setting was tough, requiring me to recalibrate my skills and mindset to meet the demands of aesthetic dentistry and deliver the desired outcomes efficiently and effectively.

Around September 2003, Bob Duggan called me to see what I was up to. I told him I was enjoying my time at UCLA, but I was not passionate about what I was doing. He asked me whether I would be interested in working with him at Robert Duggan & Associates, his investment company.

Bob was a top-notch serial entrepreneur and investor, so this looked like a great opportunity for me to learn about investing and evaluating companies in different sectors of the industry. I always wanted to learn more about investing and how to become an investor. So I left UCLA and dentistry for the investment business, and I joined Bob's company around September 2003 as vice president of business development. The title was not important to me. I looked at it as another opportunity to learn. My job was to become an expert in assessing companies and finding the right ones to invest in.

The first company I looked at was YPNet, a Yellow Pages company servicing small businesses. This was my first financial investment alongside Bob. I made about three to four times profit from this investment. This was not bad for a four-month investment. From September to November 2003, I looked at a lot of companies, from fashion to healthcare to energy.

Then in November 2003, I was sitting in the Duggan & Associates office in Santa Barbara with Mike, Bob's office manager. A list of fifteen companies came up on the fax machine for us to look at. Some were in energy, some were in healthcare, and Pharmacyclics just happened to be one of them. For some reason, after looking at all of them, Pharmacyclics was the one that caught my eye. The early 2000s posed significant challenges for the biotech and pharmaceutical industry. Rapid advancements in technology and growing competition created a complex landscape for companies operating in this sector.

Developing innovative drugs and therapies required substantial investments in research and development (R&D), with no guarantee of success. The industry faced pressure to deliver breakthrough treatments while navigating stringent approval processes and addressing concerns around drug safety and efficacy. Additionally, market volatility and shifting healthcare policies added another layer of uncertainty, making it a challenging period for companies to thrive and maintain a competitive edge in the ever-evolving biotech and pharmaceutical landscape.

Pharmacyclics, a biotech company, was founded in 1991 and became a public company in 1995. When I first became aware of them, their lead drug candidate was motexafin gadolinium (MGd). The management team at the time was testing this drug in several different oncology clinical trials. The company had two phase 3 trials for the treatment of patients with non-small cell lung cancer (NSCLC) with brain metastases. The data looked good, and it seemed like this might be a promising treatment for patients with NSCLC with brain metastases. At that time, I remember the stock was at seven dollars a share. I tried to gather as much information as possible over the next couple of months so that I could discuss it with Bob.

I went to Europe over Christmas to be with my family. Bob was in Santa Barbara, where he was very busy with some personal projects. I remember calling him over the holidays to speak to him about Pharmacyclics. The stock had gone up to nine dollars a share, but Bob was not interested. By the time I returned to Los Angeles after the holidays, in January 2004, Greg Wade, an analyst at Pacific Growth, had written a report about Pharmacyclics and its pipeline. At that point, the story was more intriguing and finally caught Bob's interest. The stock price had increased to fourteen dollars a share.

In April 2004, Bob and I met with Greg Wade and visited Pharmacyclics in Sunnyvale, California. I remember this day very well. It was the first time I had ever been to Silicon Valley. Interestingly, Pharmacyclics was just two blocks away from the Intuitive Surgical facility. I have always had this competitive spirit concerning Intuitive Surgical. For some reason, at that moment in time, I was truly upset that Computer Motion had merged with Intuitive Surgical.

Computer Motion was the first company I ever worked for, and I became very emotionally attached to it. Intuitive Surgical always seemed like a competitor to me. Loyalty and fidelity have always been at the core of my life. This is why I did not go and work with Intuitive Surgical after the merger.

Retrospectively, I believe that the merger was the best thing that ever happened to Computer Motion. The two companies could not continue their disagreement over some key patents, and together, they could become a stronger, more unified company with one vision and one mission: patient-friendly, robot-assisted surgery in the operating room for all minimally invasive surgical applications.

Bob merged Computer Motion in exchange for 33 percent ownership of Intuitive Surgical. And I must say, it is wonderful to see how much Gary Guthart, the CEO of Intuitive Surgical, and his team have accomplished over the past twenty years. Anyway, so many of these thoughts were going on in my head as we passed Intuitive Surgical on our way to Pharmacyclics.

That day, we met with two top executives at Pharmacyclics. They were both very bullish on the MGd phase 3 trials, and they were quite optimistic they would get FDA approval. We were dealing with what appeared to many to be a highly confident management team at that time.

On our way back from San Francisco, Bob told me, "You invest, I invest." To be honest, I did not expect that. But I understood the message: If I am recommending something, I should believe in it enough that I am willing to put some skin in the game. At that moment in time, it was hard for me to put all my reserves into Pharmacyclics, but retrospectively, that was one of the best things I ever did. I am so grateful for that. I sold my Intuitive Surgical stock and borrowed money from the bank. Finally, both Bob and I invested in Pharmacyclics in April 2004. The stock price then was around fourteen dollars a share.

The story of Pharmacyclics is an unbelievable story of how it is possible to turn a failing company around in just a few years. A lot of people have talked about it, and a lot of people have written about it. But the truth is, I was very close to the events that happened from 2003 to 2015. How did everything start? How did everything end? What were all the events in between? The reality is that the real heroes of this story were the patients willing to take an experimental drug, the physicians willing to try an unapproved drug to help their patients, and the researchers, employees, and consultants working endless hours to develop this drug.

I believe it is a story worth writing about because the best part of the story is the number of patients who have been helped after the launch of Imbruvica for blood cancer. I still cannot believe we were able to turn this company into one of the most successful biotech companies in history and introduce a blockbuster drug that has changed the lives of so many patients. It is hard to describe the feelings I have experienced, knowing the effect this life-changing drug has had on so many patients and their families. I cannot imagine anything more gratifying than playing a role in saving someone's life.

I believe that anyone who has ever wanted to be in the fields of healthcare and business or who wants to start a biotech company in the field of oncology should read/know this story. My hope is that it just might inspire someone to build a similar company that could also help save the lives of the countless patients still out there, waiting for a cure.

For those of you truly interested in the business details, you will find a more complete summary of everything that occurred from 2003 to 2015 later in this book.

While I was following the Pharmacyclics investment in 2005, I went back to France, although I kept my place in California. I got a very nice job offer to be the CEO and general director of a private company called Pole de Competitive. The company was started through a government initiative to bring small businesses into the field of healthcare in Strasbourg, France.

I accepted this opportunity because of Professor Marescaux, the man who led the initiative. He came to Los Angeles and offered me the general director position at Pole de Competitive, Innovation Therapeutics, which I accepted. And so I went back to Strasbourg. But while I was working at this company, I continued to follow Pharmacyclics.

Working at Pole de Competitive allowed me to learn a lot about healthcare companies, their needs, and their challenges. I joined Professor Marescaux for one year to help implement the competitiveness cluster. After finishing my commitment in early 2007, I left Pole de Competitive and decided to continue investing and become personally educated as an investor.

From 2004 to 2008, I continued to follow Pharmacyclics as an investor. Then, in August 2008, I decided to join the company as the vice president of business development, and I moved to Sunnyvale.

When I moved to Sunnyvale, I really did not know how long I was going to stay. Time was short, and the road to success looked long. It was not easy to see any light at the end of the tunnel. If you really want to achieve something, you have to truly care about it. You have to obsess about it. Achievement and success require a lot of time, a lot of sacrifices, and a lot of tough choices. People underestimate how much effort goes into chasing a dream before it becomes a reality. But there was a good reason I went through all that. However, I never totally understood the reason until ten years later when I was at MD Anderson, helping my dad get through his blood cancer treatments.

Being involved for more than thirteen years in Pharmacyclics, an oncology company, as an investor and managing the company as COO allowed me to learn a lot about cancer, especially blood cancer. I learned about different treatment options and was extremely fortunate to be able to meet a great hemato-oncologist. And that was how I had the ability to help my father get the very best treatment possible with the very best hemato-oncologist. We were able to get my dad into remission.

From 2008 to 2015, all of us at Pharmacyclics worked hard with one goal, one purpose, and one vision: At Pharmacyclics, we were fully engaged in creating a patient-friendly, small-molecule drug company whose purpose was to improve the quality and duration of life in the field of oncology and inflammation.

In late 2011, we decided to partner with Johnson & Johnson. That was the best decision that was ever made at the company. This partnership helped us build our company internationally and launch the product worldwide. The truth is, this partnership never would have happened without Dr. Paul Stoffels and the entire executive team at Johnson & Johnson.

Dr. Stoffels is vice chairman of the executive committee and chief scientific officer at Johnson & Johnson. He is a visionary leader who inspires and drives transformational innovation to bring years of life and quality of life to millions of people around the world. He spearheads the Johnson & Johnson research and product pipeline by leading teams across all sectors to expand company-wide innovation. He did his medical studies in Belgium and began his career as a physician in Africa, focusing on HIV and tropical disease research.

Dr. Stoffels was a young student and colleague of Dr. Paul Janssen and made a name for himself in the early 1990s by leading the way with breakthrough research in HIV drug resistance and drug development. His search for more effective ways to treat HIV infection led him into entrepreneurial territory. In 1994, he cofounded two companies. One company, Virco, worked on phenotyping all the viral strains found in patients, and the other, Tibotec, developed new drugs to defeat drug-resistant strains.

In 2002, Dr. Stoffels joined Johnson & Johnson as part of the acquisition of Virco and Tibotec, as he was the CEO of Virco and chairman of Tibotec. He then led the development of several breakthrough products for the treatment of HIV that helped transform this devastating disease from a death sentence to a chronic and treatable condition. Dr. Stoffels later told us that the reason he chose to partner with Johnson & Johnson was that they were prepared to leave them alone as small companies in the group so they could continue the work they were doing and build their companies. And that was the exact reason those of us at Pharmacyclics chose to partner with Johnson & Johnson.

We wanted to keep our small company and build it by collaborating with Johnson & Johnson to develop Imbruvica and commercialize the product worldwide. Dr. Stoffels knew the value of keeping a small company alive by giving it the help and resources it needed to build its business. The first time Bob and I met Dr. Stoffels was in Santana Row at Hotel Valencia in Santa Clara in April 2011. We had dinner with him at a steakhouse there. From the day we met him, we were impressed and inspired by his entrepreneurial mentality, his humanitarian character, his scientific knowledge, and his fight to put the right medication in the hands of the patients who needed it.

We deeply admired Dr. Stoffels's philosophy of making a difference in a patient's life. His dedication to everyone involved in helping patients was spectacular and had a tremendous effect on us and the decisions we made moving forward.

Anyway, five years after Bob and I joined the company as CEO and COO, respectively, we launched Imbruvica in the market for mantle cell lymphoma and chronic lymphocytic leukemia (CLL). This was record time for any oncology drug: five years from the investigational new drug application (NDA) to the launch of the product. We received three breakthrough therapy designations to accelerate our FDA approval. We were awarded Best Partnership of the Year in 2011 for our deal with Johnson & Johnson. We also received awards for Best Research, Best Company, and Best Drug (the Prix Galien award).

In 2012, Bob was nominated as a finalist for Ernst & Young's Entrepreneur of the Year. And in 2013, I was nominated as a finalist for Ernst & Young's Entrepreneur of the Year. I was also honored as one of the Top 10 Women in Biotech in 2013 by Fierce Biotech.

Finally, in 2015, we merged our company with AbbVie for $21 billion. We sold Pharmacyclics in less than four months—in record time again. The time frame of this sale was considered unheard of.

The interesting part is, over the last few decades, it has taken an average of about twenty years for a typical Fortune 500 company to reach a market capitalization of $1 billion. In 1998, Google reached a $1 billion market cap in just eight years, which was considered unheard of. In 2004, Facebook reached the same goal in just five years. In 2009, Uber did it in just three years. I found it interesting to actually learn the amount of time it took these companies to hit the $1 billion market cap.

At Pharmacyclics, we started with a $15 million market cap in 2008, and seven years later, the company was valued at $21 billion. And I believe this was due to the amazing performance of every individual involved in pushing our plan forward.

But let's not overlook the journey to this monumental success—it did not materialize overnight. It took thirteen rigorous years of unwavering commitment and strategic investments. When Bob and I joined Pharmacyclics, the company's valuation hovered below $20 million. Through sheer dedication and a robust partnership with Johnson & Johnson, we catapulted our valuation to an astounding $21 billion when we sold it seven years later. This remarkable financial trajectory, however, is not just a testament to our business acumen. It underscores a deeper, more profound narrative.

If it weren't for the investments of Bob, me, and other investors who saw potential in our endeavors, if our team hadn't executed their roles with exceptional prowess, and if our collaboration with Johnson & Johnson hadn't flourished, the real impact of our work and the life-altering drug we developed would never have reached those who needed it most. This isn't just a story of financial success; it is a testament to how business achievements can translate into significant human impact. Through our efforts, we were able to bring hope and relief to countless patients, illuminating the profound intersection where business success meets human health.

As we reflect on these milestones, it's important to remember that the true value of our work lies in the number of lives we have touched.

The journey from a modest start-up to a multibillion-dollar entity wasn't just about increasing shareholder value; it was fundamentally about developing solutions that could significantly improve patient outcomes. This is the legacy of Pharmacyclics.

Today, I am so proud to have been a part of this unbelievable, unforgettable journey, and I cannot find the words to thank the team who worked so hard over the years to help so many patients in need. We all really have to thank all the patients and physicians who trusted us and joined our clinical trials. Without all those incredible people, it would never have turned out the way it did.

And today, five years later, I am so happy that we merged with AbbVie. I have so much admiration for Rick Gonzales, chairman of the board and CEO of AbbVie. He runs a global biopharmaceutical company that employs approximately forty-seven thousand people worldwide and markets medicines in more than 175 countries. Prior to AbbVie's separation from Abbott in January 2013, Rick was a thirty-year Abbott Laboratories veteran.

Rick is an incredible CEO. His knowledge of all aspects of business is remarkable. His attention to detail and knowledge of everything that is going on in his company is unmatchable. Rick understood the value of a great team and a great product. He saw our team's passion and agreed when we asked him to keep the name and location of the company and most of the existing Pharmacyclics team for several years after the merger. He understood that so many people had put their hearts and souls into this company and wanted to continue to be a part of Pharmacyclics even after the merger.

A lot of analysts and financial markets criticized Rick when he made the decision to pay $21 billion to acquire Pharmacyclics. But years later, people understood why he made the decision. Imbruvica became one of the top ten blockbuster drugs in the industry. The

AbbVie team did an outstanding job in collaboration with the Johnson & Johnson team to continue to put Imbruvica in the hands of many patients in need of it.

CHAPTER 12

A Letter from Professor Marescaux

> **If your actions create a legacy that inspires others to dream more, learn more, do more, and become more, then you are an excellent leader.**
>
> —Dolly Parton

As I closed my chapter at Pharmacyclics and embarked on new adventures, I was grateful to carry with me invaluable lessons learned from some truly remarkable individuals. Though it was difficult to part ways with a place that shaped so much of my professional life, the experience was profoundly enriching. My gratitude extends far beyond these pages—particularly to my parents, who I thank for all my achievements and success in life, as well as individuals like Bob Duggan and Professor Marescaux, whose mentorship was pivotal in my growth. Their wisdom not only propelled my career but also deepened my resolve and expanded my capabilities.

Professor Marescaux and I met when I was still a student in Strasbourg. So much has changed since then, but our relationship remains as strong as ever today. When he learned that I was going to write this book, he sent me a very beautiful letter. I have never felt so honored and grateful as I did to be acknowledged by someone as incredible and powerful as Professor Marescaux.

This letter made me feel very emotional. His acknowledgment was so special to me and meant a lot. It made me feel appreciated and validated, and I was deeply moved by his kind words.

This is what he wrote:

I have been lucky enough to know Maky Zanganeh since she was 20 years old. Everyone at the University of Strasbourg knew these three sisters of Iranian origin, whose charm was combined with intelligence. I then followed the exceptional career of Maky who considered that the practice of dental surgery was just not right for her personal development, which led her to successfully undertake an MBA.

I had the chance to work with her more regularly from 1999 when she was President Director General of Europe, Middle East, and Africa and Worldwide Vice President of Training and Education for Computer Motion, which had developed one of the few surgical robots at the time. At that moment, I could appreciate the tenacity and energy that she put into her role as an ambassador to Bob Duggan, who was CEO at that time. And in September 2001, she made it possible for me to perform "Operation Lindbergh" the first long-distance surgery between New York and Strasbourg. Without her support and determination, this surgical feat would never have been possible.

In 2005 when the government entrusted me with the responsibility of creating the first competitiveness cluster in France, dedicated to the development of "smart medical devices." I remember flying to San Francisco and back on the same day to convince Maky to join us, as General Director in

Strasbourg for a year to help us implement this competitiveness cluster, which she achieved with her own talent and sense of innovation.

In 2007, our IRCAD Research and Training Center in minimally invasive surgery that I created in Strasbourg, looked for an international extension. Again, Maky Zanganeh accepted the position of International Project Manager and negotiated with our first Taiwanese partner, President Min-Ho Huang, so that the IRCAD could benefit from financial support in exchange for its experience. Such a deal would never have been concluded without her know-how. Finally, the episode of her career that impressed me the most, which I gave as an example to all students and interns, was her role in the creation of Pharmacyclics in 2008. Indeed, Maky managed to achieve an outstanding valuation of the company, which made the front page of all American and European newspapers.

Maky Zanganeh embodies the values of work and success, but even more so the values of an entrepreneurial profession at the service of mankind.

One of her characteristics lies in her relationship with time. Indeed, all scientific and pharmaceutical research is always conducted in a situation of emergency, in competition, in the race for results. However, Maky has always understood that precipitation may entail a waste of time, and she has always embodied some sort of quiet strength and calm state of urgency, true qualities for the woman of action that she is. At every stage of her career, she has reminded us that research is at the service of patients, not researchers.

Maky has no age. She is still 20 years old.

- *From her 20 years of age, she has kept the enthusiasm, the taste for new things, for knowledge, and these acquisitions have always been facilitated by her appetite for reading and her ability to read.*

- *From her 20 years of age, she has kept the rare sense of unfailing friendship and loyalty.*
- *From her 20 years of age, she has kept this freshness of soul, almost naive poetry.*
- *From her 20 years of age, she has kept that sense of constant challenge and self-improvement.*
- *From her 20 years of age, she has kept the generosity, this true generosity without any ulterior motive.*

  This is the hidden part of Maky, a treasure at the service of the sick. Thanks to her, thousands of patients have been and will be able to benefit from a state-of-the-art treatment to cure their cancer.

- *From her 20 years of age, Maky has kept this contradiction between her need to be loved, her need to love, and this extreme difficulty in expressing her feelings, the modesty that can make those who don't know her very well believe that her scientific and entrepreneurial spirit has taken precedence over her emotional side, without understanding the teenager living inside her.*

Maky has always sought the shortest path between ideas and their application. When I see how she makes her team work, I think of that machine that tennis players use that spits balls in all directions at hellish speeds. At home, the balls are ideas but it takes at least 3 or 4 rackets around her to turn ideas into operations.

Maky is an example of a fast connection between thought and expression: The integrated circuits in her cortex are so fast that she comes to the conclusion with her communicative enthusiasm while others are still at the beginning.

Throughout her career, the art of making her projects come to life is the secret of an alchemy that combines creation, the ability to share it, and most certainly some ancient virtues that she has acquired through exemplary education: rigor, hard work, courage, tenacity, and honesty.

I had the opportunity to meet her father one day: The discussion was not long, but I understood how much her father's charisma and values were transmitted to her.

Maky has always succeeded because she has the ability to surpass herself, to gather, to train, to be a leader, and not a boss.

- *Her ability to bring people together is due to her ability to listen and her benevolence.*
- *Her ability to train is due to her dynamism, her energy, and her instinct, which means that she has often been able to perceive in others the interest of their project before they even realize its full dimension.*
- *Her leadership ability is certainly due to a natural authority, to which are added rare qualities such as courage and respect for others, two traits that are admired by her collaborators and friends.*

Maky is the most outstanding person I have ever met in my career. The long discussions we have had have always enriched me, and her contagious optimism has made me more determined.

I love Maky because she is courageous, insolent, and elegant … because she has the modesty of those who are above the pack …because her laughter expresses such a communicative "Joie de vivre." This exceptional woman has given so much to life sciences that she deserves everyone's recognition.

CHAPTER 24

Shaun, God's Precious Gift

> **Heroes come and go, but legends are forever.**
>
> —Kobe Bryant

I promised my son that chapter 24 would be dedicated to him, whether my book reached twenty-four chapters or not. So this will be chapter 24, no matter what. You will understand why by the end of the chapter.

Shaun, my son, is the love of my life. I remember the day I felt him in my body. At that moment, I did not know I was pregnant. It was the last day of August 2005. I was in Los Angeles at the Getty Museum with my friends for an open concert. We were picnicking and joyfully listening to the music. I was observing families, their kids, and all the people around me. It was a hot day in Los Angeles, a beautiful one.

I was sitting there, drowning in my own universe, thinking about love, relationships, life, and living. Then suddenly, I felt something strange in my body, as if somebody was just shaking my body to make room for something. I had never had that feeling before, nor would

I ever have it again. A few days later, for some reason, I found myself wondering if I was pregnant.

I went to the CVS Pharmacy and bought a pregnancy test. And there you go! It was Shaun who was making room for himself in my body. Years later, I talked to a friend of mine about this very strange feeling and asked whether she ever felt that during her pregnancy.

She told me, "It's baby spirit." What is a baby spirit? Well, it is the spirit who has chosen a mother or a couple to be their parents. The baby has chosen to give some particular being or beings what is arguably the greatest gift the universe can bestow: a child to raise, love, and nurture.

As soon as I realized I was pregnant, I went back to France for a week to see my middle sister Mahshad, who is a gynecologist. She showed me the ultrasound (echography). Shaun looked like a little bean in the image, but I could hear his heartbeat. Those were the very first things I could see and hear. That was my introduction to my son.

I am always amazed by how the universe is built, and I truly believe that the best innovation ever and the most spectacular creation in life is the human being. How can an egg and sperm come together and build such a complex entity? How can centuries go by and still no one can figure out all the variations that exist in human beings?

After traveling to France, I went to Hawaii and then to Puerto Vallarta in Mexico. As strange as it may sound, I surfed until I was four months pregnant. And you know what? I was actually a pretty good surfer at that very interesting time in my life. I believe it was then that I passed on the abilities to Shaun, who has become a great surfer as well.

Unfortunately, after four months of going back and forth, Shaun's father and I decided that the best thing for both of us was to separate. I felt very lonely during my pregnancy, and the fact that I did not tell anyone I was pregnant made me even lonelier. My decision to keep it all to myself and not tell anyone is something I still regret today. Keeping a secret is never easy, but I found a different way to look at it. I decided I would keep in my heart my most beautiful secret of all time—a secret that I tried to bury deep in my heart to be able to forget, but it is also in the same place that the secret hurts the most. We love most deeply, and finally, we realize that we love our secret from the bottom of our hearts. A heart that only knows how to love, even in secret ... What I can add is that I held on to this love all these years, and the passage of time did not change it ... Forgetfulness is a good remedy if it crosses the blood-brain barrier ... but in practice, it did not pass it.

I borrowed the sentence from Kristin Scott Thomas from my favorite movie, *The English Patient*: "I have always loved you."

I never got to enjoy the time I was pregnant. I never looked pregnant. I never wore any of those cute maternity clothes that show your belly. I never had a baby shower, which would have been a very special occasion for me. My pregnancy was a very challenging time from many different perspectives. It was not just that I had started a new job, but I had also just separated from the person I loved. Believe me, it was not easy.

I hope one day to be able to write about my relationship with the one whom I chose to love for so many years and the complexity of it, but mostly about true love that I will never find the words to describe. I had to experience so many sacrifices. I cried so much during those years that I could fill an ocean with my tears. I think I mentioned before that I don't believe I was born in the right century. I am much too romantic to be living during this lifetime. I cannot understand how people can express their affection for each other through Instagram, Facebook, Snapchat, or text messaging. I would much rather have a beautiful romantic dinner on the ocean instead of spending hours in front of a screen, although I do and will always believe that communication is the key to a successful relationship.

When Shaun was in my belly and I was about seven months pregnant, I could not sleep. So I decided to look for a boy's name. I wanted a name with meaning. I wanted something short, no middle name, something easy to pronounce in all languages and in any country. I went through every name alphabetically, so it took a long time. I fell in love with the meaning of Shaun, which means "God's precious gift." At this moment in time, I knew that was what really described Shaun to me and how I felt about him. He is the most precious gift that God could ever give to me. And I could not be more grateful for anything more than having him in my life.

My pregnancy was a story in itself. The entire time I was working, my pregnancy never really showed. Even when I was in my last month, no one I worked with would have ever imagined that I was pregnant. The truth is, I had only gained eighteen pounds. I worked as hard as I always have, so there was really no reason for anyone to think I would soon be having a baby. I worked all the way through my eight-and-a-half months of pregnancy, traveling a lot, and trying to find ideas and concepts for early stage companies.

At the end of March 2006, I went back to Los Angeles to get ready to have my baby delivered. My due date was May 15. In late April, I found out that I had to attend an important meeting. So I went to my gynecologist to see whether I could have a C-section. I wanted to see if I could have the baby sooner. My doctor told me I was crazy and no way would she collaborate with me on this. I totally understood her viewpoint, but I had no idea what I was going to do.

Serendipity: On April 26, my mom and Mahshad came to visit me in Los Angeles. Mahshad had just had her son two months before she arrived. The minute she saw my belly, she told me there was no way the baby would come soon. Her plan was to stay with me for a few days before she went back to Europe. On the morning of April 27, however, I started having some pain. Mahshad told me to immediately see my gynecologist so that she could do an ultrasound and listen to the baby's heart.

As soon as the doctor listened to the heartbeat and saw the sonogram, she did an emergency C-section. Shaun was born on April 27, 2006. The umbilical cord had been wrapped around Shaun's neck, so he was having trouble breathing. On top of all that, Shaun weighed 8.3 pounds. He was a big baby (considering my size), and he was not positioned right for a natural delivery. I had my C-section on Thursday night and left the hospital on Monday morning.

So yes, I was able to go to my meeting on Tuesday. Believe it or not, no one ever knew I was pregnant or that I had just had a baby a few days before. It was somewhat hilarious! I guess I do not have to tell you I was not the typical mother who spends two weeks recovering after a C-section.

Four weeks after Shaun was born, I went to my parents' home in France and asked my mom to look after the baby for a week. I had to go to Taiwan for the inauguration of IRCAD Asia. That was a day I will never forget, as my mom looked at me and asked, "For one week or for eighteen years?"

To be honest, I really wasn't sure. My work schedule and involvement in so many different things seemed to be totally incompatible with being a new mother. The truth was, I did not know how to balance being a mom and having such a challenging career. I needed to have time to figure it out, and my son needed stability.

Consequently, my beautiful baby boy stayed with my parents and grew up in Europe until he turned five while I traveled back and forth to visit him there. He was definitely a big part of my life. Every two weeks, I would go back and forth between California and France so that I could see him for just a few days. I was thirty-six years old, a single mom, and right in the middle of a very important time in my professional career. I could not see any way that I could manage to take care of this little baby and still keep on working the way I was.

To be honest, it was an exhausting and unbelievably challenging time, both physically and emotionally. Looking back, I have to say there are times I regret not having spent every minute with Shaun when he was so small. I missed so much, but I am also truly happy he got to spend the first five years of his life with my parents. My parents taught him the important and core values of life: family, love, ethics, and provided stability… I could never have provided him with all that considering my busy schedule.

Shaun was growing up fast. His passion has always been for sports and science. He quickly became a cute little active boy who loved basketball. Shaun was actually in love with Kobe Bryant since he was two and a half years old. So of course, he has been a Lakers fan ever since then. I have always had basketball nets at home inside and out so he could shoot the ball. Shaun also developed quite a knack for languages. He started out speaking Farsi, then he learned German and French. Later, when he came to the United States, he also became fluent in English.

When he was three years old, he went to prekindergarten in France. Everybody in my family is multilingual, so I believe learning all these languages just seemed like the natural thing to do for Shaun. French and Farsi are the common languages of all our family members. English and German are also often spoken by the ones who speak these two languages. I am quadrilingual, which means that I could easily follow everybody in the family.

Everything was going quite well until February 2011, when my mom called to tell me that something had happened to Shaun, but the doctors did not know exactly what was wrong. I was in the middle of trying to establish a major partnership collaboration between Pharmacyclics and a Big Pharma company. Apparently, Shaun could not walk very well anymore and was falling all the time. Looking back, I really owe a lot to my oldest sister, Shaby. Shaun was supposed to come to see me in San Francisco, but Shaby decided he shouldn't come until we knew exactly what was happening to him. At first, they thought he had a brain tumor, but after several MRI scans, they eliminated that hypothesis. Every day, Shaun was losing his ability to walk. Eventually, Shaby decided to have him hospitalized, and I decided to go back to France to be with him.

I took the flight from San Francisco to Germany, and I remember it being one of the longest flights I was ever on. By the time I got to the hospital, Shaun was paralyzed from his waist down. He was just five years old, and he looked so weak. As soon as he saw me, he started to cry. He held me so tightly with his weak arms that I thought he would never let go. It was really hard for me not to get emotional. The tears just kept coming. It was so hard to see him like that.

The doctor decided to do a cerebrospinal fluid analysis, which is a painful procedure, especially for a five-year-old. The results came back that Shaun had Guillain–Barré syndrome (GBS). GBS is a condition in which the immune system attacks the nerve cells in the peripheral nervous system. The condition may be triggered by an acute bacterial or viral infection. What happens is that the immune system attacks healthy nerves. The result is paralysis of the lower and upper body that extends with the progression of the disease. This is what Shaun was diagnosed as having. Three to five percent of GBS patients can die from complications, which can include paralysis of the muscles that control breathing, blood infections, lung clots, and cardiac arrest.[2]

To this day, I am so grateful to my sister Shaby for bringing Shaun to the hospital in time. That is what helped him avoid a lot of unpredictable complications. At this point, Shaun could not move anymore, and he ended up in the hospital for more than two months. The only treatment that can help these patients is a special blood treatment that involves plasma exchange and immunoglobulin therapy. At that moment in time, it was hard to know whether Shaun would ever recover or how long it would take him to recover. The first round of immunoglobulin therapy did not work. My parents were devastated. It was very hard to watch them crying every day.

I was exhausted and finding it impossible to believe that something like this could ever happen to someone. Shaun was allergic to the medication, so the poor kid had to take an infusion for hours. It was so hard to keep him in bed and try to entertain him. He was just a little kid having to endure the unusual suffering of this disease and the medications all from a hospital bed. As soon as he fell asleep at night, I would begin to catch up with the day-to-day job that I was now doing during the night. It was an incredibly stressful time.

Finally, after weeks, the medication started to work. Slowly, Shaun started to move his hands and then his legs. But every time he tried to walk, he would still fall. He had to do a lot of rehabilitation to be able to get back to all his normal physical activities. He had to learn how to eat, walk, and write all over again. He had to start everything from scratch. He had to start from the beginning like a little baby, step by step by step.

My dad and Shaun had a very special relationship. I cannot really describe it. Dad adored Shaun and had a certain kind of love for him

---

2 Roger S. Taylor, "Guillain Barre Syndrome," *National Library of Medicine*, n.d.

that he never really had for anyone else in his life. He spoke with Shaun a lot. He always gave him examples of multiple athletes who had worked hard to get their injured legs back again. He was a very spiritual man and a strong believer in God. I was lucky that he spent so much time with Shaun then because I believe he gave Shaun a lot of hope and faith to continue his rehabilitation.

It's so interesting how every time I ask Shaun about this incident, he tells me God gave him his life back. Even though he was so young, he has never forgotten that time in his life. He always talks about it, even years later. We all went through a lot of rehabilitation, but after two years, Shaun finally recovered 100 percent from the disease.

Years after Shaun's GBS experience, he had a community project he was working on at school. The project was all about how to help people. Shaun decided he wanted to help kids with GBS at Stanford Hospital, so he bought some gifts and books for the kids. He also drew a picture and wrote a very beautiful letter that I will share with you. We went to the hospital together, and he gave it to ten kids who were suffering from the same disease he had suffered from when he was younger.

He wrote:

Dear Friend,

My name is Shaun and I am 11 years old. I love sports and science. My favorite sports are basketball, flag football, and surfing. In science, I build robots. I love to demonstrate physics and solve math problems. I live in California, but I love traveling and going to different places. My favorite place is Dubai. I am in 6th grade and we recently read a book that showed that each of us can make a big difference for people in the community or world. My teacher gave us a project where we had to try to make a difference, and I chose to help kids like you with Guillain-Barre Syndrome.

I chose this topic because when I was 5 years old, I had GBS and it was very scary. What made me feel better was that my friends and some other people wrote me letters and they were very helpful. I know how you feel. The worst things were MRIs, staying at the hospital, taking bad-tasting medication, and getting shots. I missed playing sports, my toys, and my family.

Since I know how you feel, I got you some items to cheer you up and things you can enjoy in the hospital. I got you a crazy straw because they are the coolest thing there is and you can drink while lying down. I bought you a stuffed animal to bring you comfort and company while you are in the hospital bed.

The book is so you can read if you are bored. I hope you enjoy these items during this difficult time you are in. You should know that recovery is difficult, but you can do it! I had to learn to walk, to use a fork, and how to hold a pencil. It took about 6 months to recover but now I play basketball and I block people in football, I make touchdowns…

Good luck!

From your new friend,

Shauny

I was always amazed and intrigued by the things Shaun would write at such a young age when it came to his school essays. There was always such honesty and optimism in his words that I would wonder whether he would grow up to be a writer. There was another beautiful essay that he wrote when he was in seventh grade about the same subject as the last one. It touched me so much when I read the last paragraph:

> *When I think of the hospital my heart pounds like a thousand miles. I breathe like I would not be able to again. I cannot believe I won the battle against these germs... When I was very sick, I was very scared and nervous. My family helped me, gave me advice and confidence. Then I learned that having positivity may help my life. Being positive is what I learned. When I look back, that is not all I learned. I learned trust, confidence, the importance of family, positivity, and faith. I know that I have people who love me and know me very well that will help me no matter what.*

In September 2011, Shaun came to live with me full-time in Palo Alto. He needed to spend time with me. He needed us to bond. The truth was, he needed his mom. And so I was about to go through another huge change in my very busy life. This was already one of the busiest times in my professional career, as I was right in the middle of working on a partnership agreement between Johnson & Johnson and Pharmacyclics. From then on, I was challenged with handling both my professional life and my private life at the same time. And believe me, it was not easy, but it was definitely worth it.

When I look back at my life then, what I think about is that I was working a lot and did not get to spend enough time with my son. My mom came to help me as much as she could, but there were times she just could not come all the way from France. So I got a nanny to help me. But there were days when things just did not work out.

I remember a day when we had an earnings call at five in the morning at Pharmacyclics, followed by a board of directors meeting. I was alone with Shaun, and I could not find a babysitter. So I woke Shaun up at 4:00 a.m. and tried to put him in a nice suit with a tie. Now, Shaun was only six years old at the time. It was hard to wake him up at four in the morning. But he was so excited to join my board of directors meeting at the office that once he woke up, it was easy to get him going.

It was fun to have him near me in my meetings. His level of interest in science and business was always impressive, and he always had something to comment on during my meetings, whether it was how to manufacture a drug container or a very simple marketing idea. Another day, I had to bring him with me to a top executive meeting at Johnson & Johnson in New Jersey. This was a one-day trip, back and forth to New York for a few hours of meetings with me, Bob, Dr. Stoffels, and Alex Gorsky (CEO of Johnson & Johnson).

Once again, I did not have anyone at home to take care of Shaun, so I went to those meetings and took Shaun along with me. I remember bringing snacks, computers, and an iPad. I downloaded cartoons and games. I put him in a nice professional suit with a red tie. When we got into the building, Bob read him the credo of Johnson & Johnson that was hanging on the wall in front of the reception area. It was an impressive credo. The culture of Johnson & Johnson is all about patients.

I will never forget when we went into the elevator. I could not remember which floor we were going to. I just knew that as soon as I got out of the elevator, my heart started beating very fast. We were in an amazing place with beautiful furniture. I went to Dr. Stoffels's secretary, and I explained that I had Shaun with me. I asked her if she could find a small room for him for an hour while I was in my meeting. She was so nice, and she welcomed Shaun very warmly.

She brought us to a meeting room, and oh my God, it was huge. There was a big, beautiful board table, and she told me that Shaun could stay in the boardroom while Bob and I went to Dr. Stoffels's office. I set up the computer, snacks, and iPad. I told Shaun to stay calm until I came back to the room. I also asked him to be as polite as possible and to make sure to keep everything as clean as he could. Then I went to the meeting.

The meeting lasted more than two hours. I did not know what Shaun was doing all that time. I just prayed that he was watching some movies and would not get bored and start walking around the room or trying to find me. I will never forget that day because I realized it did not matter that I was a mother; as a businesswoman, I was expected to act professionally.

I realized that I was a mother first, and I did what I could to manage my child, as well as my work. The day after we got home from New York, Shaun was excited but very tired. I believe that a twenty-four-hour trip was just too much for him. I came to the realization that no matter how tired I was, my priority was to take care of Shaun and help him recover from his first business trip to New York.

The funniest thing I remember about Shaun and my busy schedule was when another unexpected meeting came up, and like always, a last-minute meeting meant no babysitter. I did not know what to do, so I called Mani, who had a limo service called Venture Limo. I met Mani and his brother in 2008 when the market collapsed. At that time, he had just one limo and serviced the clients of Hotel Valencia in San Jose. He brought all of us anywhere we needed to go.

As Pharmacyclics matured and we hired more people, Mani provided limo service for us when needed. In 2015, when I left Pharmacyclics, he ended up with more than ten limos and four or five drivers. His business had grown, just like our company. Mani is a great friend, and years later, even after I left Pharmacyclics, he still picks me or Shaun up whenever we need to go somewhere.

Anyway, I called Mani and asked if he could pick up Shaun because of my meeting. Shaun was seven years old. I gave them money and asked Mani to bring Shaun to Toys "R" Us and spend two hours there with him. I told him to let Shaun play with any of the toys that he liked at Toys "R" Us and even let him buy whatever he wanted. So Shaun got to play like the little rich boys going to Toys "R" Us in a limo to enjoy the afternoon. He had a lot of fun. What we would do for our kids! And of course, for our jobs. Even after so many years, Shaun has never forgotten that day.

I was always unbelievably busy during my time at Pharmacyclics. I was in meetings from early morning until late evening. And I was usually reading my emails all night. I did not have enough time to see Shaun. I tried my best to attend his basketball games and parent–teacher meetings. One day, I came home around 8:00 p.m., and Shaun was standing in front of the window, waiting for me. I was so tired. As usual, the nanny left as soon as I arrived.

That was when I really saw Shaun's face. He came to me and held me in his arms. He said, "Mom, I am leaving." I thought he was just telling me something out of the blue, but he was serious. He went to his room and packed some clothes, some books, and some toys. Then he just kissed me and opened the door to leave. I was sitting on the stairs, watching him.

What was he going to do now on such a dark night outside, with nowhere to go? He looked back for a second and told me, "Don't worry, you took a lot of pictures of me. When you miss me, just look at the pictures. I love you, Mom, but I am going to find a family who wants to spend time with me."

My eyes filled with tears. At that moment, I realized there were so many times he was just trying to tell me that he existed and wanted to be with me and spend time with me. But I seemed to never have enough time for him. I had time for others, meeting after meeting, but never time for him. I did not know what to say. What could I say? "I'm sorry"?

It was too late. He was leaving home. It was dark, and he was only seven and a half years old. He looked left. He looked right. The night was silent. It was dark and cold. Shaun looked back. His eyes were full of tears. He did not know where to go. He was scared, but he was proud. Finally, he came back, and he told me, "This time, I will accept your apology. I need you, Mom. I don't want to be with our nanny all the time." I took him in my arms, and we cried for a few minutes together.

It was then that I realized there are times in life when we do not see what we should see, and we take important things for granted. I was not seeing the thing that was actually the most important thing in my life. I suddenly realized I could be losing the most precious thing in my life, and I had to act. From that moment on, I knew I had to slow down and spend more time with Shaun.

So many women today are afraid to take an executive position because they cannot handle the stress of both work and family. Many women in the business world even avoid having a child. And I do not blame them because it is not easy. Between long meetings during the day, too many sleepless nights, constantly reading emails, bringing kids to school, finding nannies, and doing homework, it is practically impossible to get through the week. And the weekends are not any easier. It is still hard work participating in all the weekend activities, like basketball or football. They also have to manage sick days and handle household activities. Seriously, it is crazy when they step back and try to figure out how to do it all.

But as I have always said, God will never give you more than you can handle. I really believe, after years of being in high-level executive positions and juggling my work, my child, and everything around us, I can truthfully say it is worth it. If I had the choice to do it all again, I would do it. The joy of having a child is incredible. Children give us a whole different perspective on life. We are no longer the center of the universe. Our child becomes the center of the universe. And we get to see the world again through their eyes. We just have to tell ourselves, "Keep going."

Shaun's eighth-grade graduation was on June 8, 2020. I cannot believe how fast the time went. There it was: eighth-grade graduation. I remember when he came from Europe and started at the French-American school. He was just five years old. When he reached fourth grade, I switched him to a public school in Menlo Park called La Entrada. I will always be grateful to La Entrada school and especially to Leanne Cummins, Shaun's fourth-grade teacher, who helped me all those years to get Shaun where he is today academically. Without her help and support, I could never have gotten Shaun ready for high school.

Here is what she wrote about Shaun:

Shaun and Maky came into my life in August 2015. I met them at a Meet the Teacher event at our school. Shaun was entering the fourth grade and a new school, which meant he was a bit more nervous than most. He greeted me with his bright brown eyes as he held his mom's hand. He was a bit trepidatious. He introduced himself and told me he was excited about his new school and loved to travel.

Throughout this first year together, I learned about Shaun's character. He persevered as he navigated through his first English-speaking school. You see, he was a fluent speaker in Farsi, French and English, but this was the first time he would be asked to read and write in English. He practiced his reading each day and moved through the levels to catch up with his native English-speaking peers. Shaun had a passion for science, math, history and the stock market.

Although he excelled at all of these, his greatest gift was his ability to connect with people and make friends easily. To this day, you will see he greets all with eye contact, is incredibly polite, invests in relationships by asking questions, and loves to learn about the commonalities he has with others. He loves a spirited debate and has excellent negotiation skills!

Shaun is a deep thinker beyond his years. He is creative and is eager to find ways to solve everyday problems with new inventions. He is constantly building, fiddling, and researching ways to make an impact on the world. He also has a love for the stock market. He can explain investment terminology in everyday terms to someone with no previous knowledge or experience. All of this probably comes from regularly attending his mom's board meetings starting at the age of five dressed in a suit and tie! Despite all of this, his true love is for his family. He has a deep connection with his grandparents in France and speaks with them every day. He holds his grandfather in the highest regard.

Maky and Shaun have a deep bond. As Shaun has grown through the years and Maky battled cancer, their roles have shifted. At 13, Shaun is now Maky's protector and the man of the house. He offers her physical and emotional protection. He is an old soul. He offers her words of wisdom and asks her hard questions about the challenges of life and the intentions of people. When Maky was fighting her cancer battle, Shaun took his role of protector very seriously. It was her job to fight for her life, while it was his job to protect her heart.

Maky chose the perfect name when Shaun was born, not knowing what a beautiful child he would grow up to be. Shaun means "God's Precious Gift" and that is Shaun.

Shaun grew up in an environment where the entire conversation has always been about how to build a company. Where to invest? Why to invest? Innovation. The stock markets. As early as he could, Shaun started buying stocks in different companies and then following those companies. The funniest part is he only invests money in companies where he himself is a customer. His investment philosophy is to invest where he knows the product very well and then become a long-term investor. His biggest success is Microsoft.

Shaun's passion for invention and business is nothing short of remarkable. He reminds me of Albert Einstein. Every day, he seems to come up with a new idea, and believe it or not, he wants to patent these ideas. He wants to become an inventor. He cannot wait to create a time machine and other inventions that he believes will help everyone on the planet live a better life.

I truly admire his determination and knowledge, and I believe we really are a great match. I can talk to him all day about different businesses and listen to his analyses and sense of reasoning for hours. He is like a redwood tree; nobody can move him. He has an amazing amount of pride and self-esteem.

One day, we were talking about life and the importance of working hard. He looked at me and said, "Difficulty and hard work haven't stopped anybody. Why should that stop me?" Sometimes, I have trouble remembering that he was only a fourteen-year-old kid when he said that.

I have always told Shaun that getting him from birth to age ten was a very challenging time for me, and getting from ten to twenty will be a very challenging time for him. I want him to know that he has a family who loves him very much and will always be there for him, no matter what. I always talk about love to Shaun. Maybe a hundred times a day—and I am not exaggerating—we tell each other, "I love you." I want him to learn to love with abandon. Like all of us, he will get his heart broken, but I tell him, "You should always love with your whole heart, and you should never stop loving."

A long time ago, I was reading a very nice article about life and following our dreams. This piece stuck with me for a long time. And I always talk with Shaun about things I am reading. In summary, this piece talked about life, telling us that life is not always easy. The rough times will come, but they will not stay. They will pass.

We are going to endure a lot of disappointment, a lot of failure, and a lot of pain. There will be moments when we are going to doubt ourselves. And we will say to God, "Why is this happening to me?"

But as time goes by, we will learn that we should not give up on our dreams. We should overcome our fears, especially our fear of failure. We should take risks and stop living other people's lives. We should look at ourselves and try to understand and know who we are. We should define our values and start considering what we really want and what we really deserve.

We should align ourselves with the right people, the ones who are unstoppable and refuse to live life as it is. We must be able to love without expectations. We must look for and find the happiness inside us because it is there. The truth is, as long as we believe in ourselves, we can make it through anything. And always remember, it's not over until it's over, so never ever give up.

> **The moment you give up is the moment you let someone else win.**
>
> —Kobe Bryant

Shaun's hero will always be Kobe Bryant. He was my hero too. I really loved watching him play basketball. I also really loved his philosophy and mindset. But what I loved most about him was his exemplary discipline.

Ever since Shaun started to play basketball and football, his jersey had to have the number 24 on it. Kobe Bryant died in a helicopter crash at the age of forty-one. He left us too soon, but he left a legacy that will be remembered forever.

> **It's the one thing you can control. You are responsible for how people remember you—or don't. So, don't take it lightly.**
> —Kobe Bryant

This is why I call this chapter, chapter 24. It is Shaun's favorite number!

CHAPTER 13

Cancer and COVID-19

> **It's only after we've lost everything that we're free to do anything.**
>
> —Chuck Palahniuk

After all those years being part of an oncology biotech company and trying to help so many patients, I believe God realized the game was not over for me. Being a caregiver is one thing, being a businesswoman in the field of oncology was another thing, but most importantly, I was now able to truly understand what it felt like, both emotionally and physically, to get cancer. I learned what it felt like to be a patient by becoming one.

I was diagnosed with breast cancer in December 2019. Every part of it was scary and had its own challenges: getting the announcement, going through the surgery, chemo, and radiation. I still do not know which is better: having a lot of knowledge about cancer or having no knowledge about it at all. And as if that was not enough, on top of it all was the coronavirus pandemic of 2020.

When I found out I was in an early stage of cancer, I realized having hope is one thing, but being in a late stage of cancer with no hope is another thing. Thank God, in my case, I was in the first category. Hope is the key to happiness. It makes us stronger and gives us the courage to overcome challenges. Hope is what I believed would get me through those unreal times going on all around me.

Everything in life happens for a reason, and God will never give us more than we can endure. That has always been my life philosophy, and having faith has always been a key aspect of my life. Despite everything, I still believe I was born under a lucky star.

In December 2019, I went to France for Christmas. I had not planned to visit Europe that year. Instead, I was considering going to Singapore or staying home because my son had his private school entry exam coming up. However, in mid-October 2019, we found out that my dad had lung cancer after being in remission from two blood cancers.

We spent a lot of time discussing the next steps with his medical team. We had two options: surgery or radiotherapy. We were looking at a palliative treatment—radiotherapy—versus a lobectomy, which meant high-risk surgery along with high-risk general anesthesia. Once again, we went through many weeks of discussions before we decided to take the high-risk path, which was surgery. We all agreed we did not want to wait until after Christmas for him to have the operation. The physician gave us an appointment on December 20, 2019. So I decided to go to France with my son Shaun, to be with my dad before his surgery.

Four days after the surgery and after spending the entire day in the hospital with my dad, my sister Mahshad and I came home from the hospital. I took a shower and went to bed. On that night, I had some tachycardia, which is an increased heart rhythm often caused by stress. I was trying to find my heartbeat. Sometimes, I think that by touching my heart, I can calm it down, but to my surprise, I felt a little bump on my left breast. It was very surprising and, at the same time, very scary. In life, I believe we have the right to be fearful, but we have no right to panic.

On December 23, the day after I felt the lump, Mahshad called a radiologist, and they were able to do a mammogram. Yes, it was the day before Christmas Eve. Mahshad is an obstetrician-gynecologist with a huge network in Strasbourg. Being the sister of two top doctors in France, I had access to the best healthcare physicians available. All of this was happening right in the middle of the holiday season, which can be a very challenging time of year for anyone, especially when it comes to medical treatment.

The mammogram confirmed the small tumor, but they needed to do a biopsy to confirm the diagnosis and type of tumor. Everything happened very quickly. When the radiologist informed Mahshad that there was a good chance it was a malignant tumor, Mahshad actually collapsed. She could not feel her feet anymore. This incident speaks volumes about our relationship and just how close we are. As far as I was concerned, I still believed I was living under that lucky star.

When I went for my mammogram, I was able to see a highly renowned medical doctor named Dr. Haehnel. He is a retired medical doctor and pioneer and founded the breast cancer screening facility in Alsace, France, in 1989—the ADEMAS program. Dr. Haehnel has known my sister for a while. They worked together for many years, not to mention Dr. Haehnel's sister was Mahshad's neighbor. The world is so small sometimes.

Dr. Haehnel was at the clinic on Christmas Day to wish his former staff a merry Christmas. As soon as he saw Mahshad, he proposed to do the biopsy immediately. He did the biopsy on Christmas afternoon, and he mobilized the entire pathology department in order to get the results ASAP. Obviously, he did not care whether it was Christmas or not. His kindness and compassion had a profound effect on me.

Three days later, the results came in. I had stage 2 breast cancer with high grade 3 cell cancer, which meant I was facing a lumpectomy, four months of chemotherapy, and one month of radiation, followed by several years of hormone therapy. I was basically in shock. I could not believe all this was happening to me.

To be honest, I could not have been happier that 2019 was coming to an end. I was under so much stress that I was looking forward to starting 2020 and a new decade with a completely different perspective. At that time, I was also very excited to announce that I would be opening my new office, Maky Zanganeh & Associates, in March 2020. My new office would be on Sandhill Road, a famous street in Silicon Valley. The street is in a very expensive area, notable for its concentration of venture capital companies. I was very much looking forward to starting my new business and was definitely not ready for all this other turbulence in my life. In reality, are we ever ready for someone to look us in the eye and tell us, "You have cancer"?

Christmas 2019 immediately became a completely different holiday for all of us. My dad and I were both fighting cancer in the same hospital in France. One of Mahshad's friends is a famous breast cancer surgeon and reconstructive breast physician. His name is Dr. Jean Marc Piat. Mahshad and my oldest sister Shaby worked with Dr. Piat as medical students when he was a young new resident at the breast surgery department of the university hospital in Strasbourg. I felt extremely lucky to be a patient of Dr. Piat.

At that time, I had so many questions running around in my head. First, how could the cancer have made its entry into my body? But the more important question was how could I get the cancer out? How were they going to kill all those cancer cells? I just wanted to get rid of the cancer. I was rejecting my body. I was ready for a double mastectomy or even having my ovaries taken out. But apparently, taking all those organs out was not really a solution. I was devastated at that moment in time. I could not ask *why*; it became more important to just try to figure out *how*.

Mahshad called Dr. Piat, and they decided to do the lumpectomy as soon as possible. He said that a small lumpectomy would be enough and that I would need to go through all the systemic treatment. He also told me that a year from now, I would be totally happy that I had not had a full mastectomy. To be honest, I really did not understand what he was talking about then. At that moment in time, it was all just too much to digest.

In the true spirit of the holidays, I decided to have the lumpectomy on New Year's Eve. I thought that was probably the best way to finish 2019. Get this thing out of my body before the end of the year. I wrote in my diary, "Finally, 2019 is over, and I hope 2020 will be a different year, a better year." At that moment in time, I did not know what was waiting for me and the whole world in 2020.

Who knew it would become the year of coronavirus, the year of the lockdown, the year of school closures, the year millions of people would be infected by this raging virus? And whoever thought this would be the year of over a million deaths from it? Who could ever imagine this would happen in our lifetime? Yet there we were, facing a financial crisis, a stock market crash, a surge in unemployment, and the crumbling of so many small businesses.

But what was even harder to face was all of us locked away in our homes, waiting and waiting and waiting. Nothing in life is worse than waiting. Nothing is worse than not knowing what will happen and how everything will end. Everyone everywhere was beginning to realize that life was super fragile; everything could change in a second. We were all forced to expect the unexpected. They told us we were all in this together, yet we were not allowed to go anywhere near each other. Depending on which TV station we watched, we heard a multitude of different opinions and different sorts of blame. Some stations blamed China and the bats from the outdoor market, which supposedly started the whole thing. There was also a theory that the virus escaped from a lab in Wuhan.

In the US, many newspapers blamed then-president Donald Trump for not taking this virus seriously right from the beginning. Trump blamed the World Health Organization (WHO), which he said should have known better, or did know better and was not sharing what it knew with the rest of the world. But it was the actual numbers that became so devastating when we turned on the TV or radio. The number of tests, the number of people infected, and finally the number of deaths—city by city, state by state, country by country—left all of us wondering when it would peak.

When would the curve flatten? When would it all be over so that things could get back to normal? We just wanted to go back. But there really was no going back. We could only go forward. We quickly found out that there would probably be a new normal because normal as we knew it was pretty much gone forever.

During this crazy period when the world was on pause, my life was on pause too. Everything felt like it was in slow motion, and I was not prepared for this unusual and unpredictable lifestyle. Suddenly, everything around us stopped, and we became unbelievably unproductive, not to mention the side effects of the drugs I was taking and the toxicity going on in my body. This was all beyond my imagination.

Thank God I have always been a strong person. I really do not know how people overcome all these challenges. I was in pain every day. I was so sick. Some days, I could not even get out of bed. I never expected that. I had never experienced it, but it became my new reality. I had to accept that dark side of life during that time.

I started my chemo on Valentine's Day, February 14, 2020, at 7:00 p.m. at MD Anderson in Houston. Dr. Wang and Dr. GGM introduced me to Dr. Valero, a breast cancer oncologist. I had always trusted both these incredible doctors and knew they would make sure I received the best possible care.

The first day, when they put the port catheter in my chest for the chemo infusions, turned out to be very traumatic. I was so thankful to have Mahshad with me the whole day. My mom, Shaun, and Bob also came to Houston for my first chemo treatment. But things did not go well. Twenty-four hours after my treatment, my body could not handle the chemo drugs I had been given. I had so much toxicity in my body that I could not feel anything. I could not even open my eyes. I could not control my legs or arms. And my heart was beating very fast.

We were all at the Four Seasons Hotel in Houston. At 2:00 a.m., we called an Uber and went to the emergency room. By then, I was completely gone. Finally, after giving me intravenous physiological saline solution and calcium, I was able to return to my hotel room around 7:00 a.m. The only thing I really remember about the first four days of my chemo treatment was that I was in bed all day and I could not move.

The fact that I was not home in California did not make things any easier. The MD Anderson team was right by my side and highly skilled. Dr. Valero is a great physician. He is calm, friendly, and extremely knowledgeable. But after the first treatment, I just wanted to be home.

My friend Dr. Michelle Longmire, a dermatologist at Stanford, arranged to get me back home for the rest of my treatment. I owe her a lot because, looking back, there was no way I could keep going back and forth to Houston for my treatment. There was also no way I could stay at the Four Seasons Hotel in Houston for six months during the COVID-19 crisis.

Finally, we left Houston and came back home. I continued my treatment with Dr. Sledge's team at Stanford. How would I describe Dr. Sledge? First and foremost, he is very funny. Overall, he is such an incredibly interesting individual—very academic and very patient but always full of humor. He always had a way of making everybody laugh, especially his patients.

Dr. Sledge told me that my body's reaction to the drugs was not normal and not many people experience the reaction I had to the medication I was taking. Believe it or not, I was the exception. They even decided to stop the last round of my chemotherapy treatment with Adriamycin and Cytoxan because of the high toxicity it was causing in my body. The decision was made to start a new round of chemo with a drug called Taxol.

I must say the scariest part of all this was going to the hospital for treatment in the middle of the coronavirus pandemic. There were signs on the front door of the hospital I was going to that said, "If you are sick, do not come in."

The world turned upside down. We were being told not to go to the hospital if we were sick. We were told to stay at home if we were sick. We were told that if we had any signs of fever or a cough, we should go to a drive-in test center to get tested for COVID-19, but only after having a conversation via FaceTime with a physician who would evaluate whether we were even eligible for a test. This was all happening because the country was unable to test everyone because of a shortage of tests. All I could think of then was that life during COVID-19 was unimaginable.

Like so many people, during this time, I was watching a lot of TV. This was not an easy thing to do because the news just kept getting worse. Every day, people were dying. An administrator for Trump announced that the months of April and May 2020 would be the darkest time in US history because of the number of deaths from the coronavirus. This was beyond discouraging because, guess what, my last four chemo treatments would all be during those two months. The timing could not have been worse.

No matter how I looked at the situation, I could not find answers to my questions. I could not make any sense of things. I could not figure out why all of it was happening then: coronavirus, my cancer, and the market crash. It was like something out of a science fiction movie. A bad science fiction movie. I could only hope there would be a good ending.

The hospitals were overloaded with patients. More than three million people were infected, and over two hundred thousand people died. And that was just three months after the pandemic had been announced. Nurses, doctors, and healthcare workers were suffering from exhaustion. Also, I knew from my own experience and everything I saw around me that even doctors have their limits. They are human beings, like you and me. They were doing everything they could for their patients. In many cases, that included sacrificing their own lives for the good of their patients.

God knows just how many healthcare workers around the world died while helping others. Doctors everywhere were trying all sorts of drugs in the hope that they might work. The ICUs and the majority of hospitals did not have the capacity that was needed for this kind of pandemic. Shortages of ventilators, diagnostic tests, masks, and gloves. It was beyond what anyone could have imagined. Researchers from labs around the world and almost every pharmaceutical company were trying to find a vaccine or some miracle therapeutic drug.

But what the rest of the world failed to understand was that we could not produce a miracle overnight. It takes years of R&D to bring a drug to the market, from synthesizing a molecule to launching a product, even if everything goes right. It is absolutely a tour de force, and something like this usually takes years to launch.

There they were, taking a generic drug that is used for lupus and malaria, named hydroxychloroquine, and giving it to COVID-19 patients. Apparently, by administering this drug at an early stage of the disease, or as soon as there are any symptoms, the chance of surviving or getting a lighter case of the disease is higher. But again, we did not have a randomized trial to prove any of these things. It was just a case-by-case approach. Later, they announced that another drug that was usually used for autoimmune diseases, named remdesivir, could help patients with more advanced cases.

But no matter how the world tried to find a solution to avoid the spread of the disease, there seemed to be no light at the end of the tunnel. The only real solution that made sense was to wait eighteen to twenty-four months, best-case scenario, to get a vaccine. In the meantime, 60 to 70 percent of people would have to get infected in order to get the immunity that was so essential to survival. That meant a lot of deaths, especially among older people and high-risk patients, like those with cancer or diabetes.

There were many different forces out there, all trying their best to save lives, find a cure, or discover the right drug. There were so many doctors out there trying to make the right diagnosis and searching for firm answers to all the questions that so many people had for them. The truth was, no one knew everything. The saddest part of the

COVID-19 situation was the patient's fear of going to the hospital for urgent conditions like heart disease, a heart attack, or a stroke.

All planned surgery was stopped. All preventive cancer detection was stopped. All the clinical trials for developing new drugs for other diseases were stopped or slowed down. The medical and surgical world was put on hold so that everyone could just concentrate on COVID-19, as if other life-threatening diseases did not matter anymore. I was still optimistic about the power of science and medicine when it came to finding answers and cures. And I deeply hoped that would happen sooner rather than later so that we could avoid losing so many lives.

We were dealing with a disease that involved and overshadowed all other diseases. We were satisfied with the minimum of monitoring and examining chronic pathologies. We prayed not to have another surgical medical emergency for fear of landing in an emergency room with COVID-19 patients. Provisional recommendations were created, specialty by specialty. Once again, we were evaluating the risk–benefit ratio, risk of the treatment, or the absence of treatment, and the only factor that tipped the scales on one side or the other was COVID-19. There it was again.

We were all facing a mysterious worldwide disease that seemed to change week by week. The knowledge and understanding of scientists, the revelations and decisions of politicians, and the strategies of the WHO changed every week as well. At no time in the history of medicine were the recommendations and treatments so controversial. Everything, from the opinions of medical experts to the decisions of state and local politicians, kept changing from one week to the next. Opinions and decisions kept changing week by week, from one medical team to another, from one country to another. It was never harder to watch the news, but after watching, it was even harder to try to understand it.

I believe there was a moment when we all realized there was just one single word that could define the emotions of human beings, scientific or political. And that word was *humility*.

The psychological pressure on doctors was at its peak. Do not make a mistake in your priorities. Do not run the risk of bringing the patient out of their home for a medical examination. Do not enter your own home without immediately putting everything you wore that day in the washing machine.

There was also an immense amount of pressure on the hospitals, especially at the beginning of the pandemic, when everyone was surprised by the explosion of the pandemic and the shortage of medical supplies—even the shortage of basic needs. Then there were the overwhelming capacity problems in ICUs, the shortage of ventilators, the decision to resuscitate or not to resuscitate, to treat or not to treat, to take the risk of one's own death from COVID-19, or the risk of complications from drugs never evaluated before for this bold new disease.

During a time of sickness, we recognize people and distinguish between friends and enemies, but some judgments can be wrong. The first time I was treated with Neulasta, I really hated it. It was like the bombing of Hiroshima in a body weakened by chemo. Neulasta stimulates the growth of white blood cells. It is used to decrease the incidence of infection by treating neutropenia, a lack of certain white blood cells caused by chemotherapy.

Every time I was treated with Neulasta, I would get sick for at least five days. I cannot describe the pain that I went through. My white blood cell count increased to forty thousand every time, when the normal range should be between four thousand and ten thousand. When so many white blood cells are going around the body searching for all the bad cells and cannot find them, they do not know what to do besides kill the good cells. That is when the body gets upset and starts to fight back. This is a war that starts inside your body, and the only thing you can do is wait until the war is over.

I asked my doctors whether they could change this treatment and find an alternative therapy because I really could not tolerate it. But in this field of cancer, the treatments are very standardized. There is very little personalized treatment. There is absolutely no room and especially no space for medicine a la carte, which is basically customized medicine. I thought Neulasta was my worst enemy because I could hardly withstand the side effects.

By the end of my chemo, I realized Neulasta was my ally, the one that had protected me from the illness that appeared to be spreading throughout the world. The persistent cough, fever, and unexplained shortness of breath—all those symptoms turned out to be COVID-19 symptoms a few weeks later! My bone pain was beyond imagination. It was as if someone had put me under a pressing machine and pressed down on each one of my bones.

I remember a quote that had a powerful effect on me:

> **Pain doesn't tell you when you ought to stop. Pain is a little voice in your head that tries to hold you back because it knows if you continue you will change.**
>
> —Kobe Bryant

And that quote kept me going through my pain.

I definitely lived through some historical events during my cancer treatment. I remember looking forward to the day when I would have the port-a-cath removed. It was June 4, 2020. And strangely enough, the port came out during the two days the curfew took effect in our region and across the US.

As if the COVID-19 lockdown and the cancer were not enough, the death of George Floyd provoked a mass movement across the entire US, with confrontations, looting, gunfire, tear gas, and accidental deaths, causing almost unimaginable collateral damage.

All the symbols of wealth and the American Dream were targeted: the White House, Beverly Hills, and even the residential district of Palo Alto. All those triggering factors and the huge injustices and atrocities were just drops that made the cup overflow. The people, already weakened morally and economically by the COVID-19 pandemic, were ready to explode. And every one of us was witnessing this social explosion indirectly.

It was very much like my body with chemotherapy: intending to save my life but causing collateral damage to my body, my mind, my relationships, and the way I looked at my life, others, and the world. Nothing had ever happened like this before. It was a completely new experience, unprecedented, in my personal life.

During those very unusual times, I came to realize the similarities between COVID-19 and cancer: not only do the two begin with the letter *C*, but they also both come at us in life like a tsunami. Both come at a time when they are least expected. Both get us to pray that we will get through the crisis as well as possible with the least amount of damage. During either crisis, we approach life differently afterward. Even when it seems like the crisis is over, the uncertainty persists.

We are left wondering, "Is it really over? Has the wave changed direction? Should we fear a second wave? When will the second wave be? Will it hit harder than the first wave, or will it lose its strength? And as time goes by, will weariness win?"

Then there is the anxiety at each annual medical visit when we are faced with the fear that the doctors will find something again and the disease will start all over. During all this, we are also faced with the fear of not having the necessary resources in case of recurrence or complications.

Finally, we did not know whether it was actually the disease, anxiety, or uncertainty that created symptoms like those that COVID-19 exhibited. Retrospectively, some COVID-19 patients have seen that the illness changed their bodies even after recovery. For example, they may still experience extreme fatigue, difficulty breathing, and memory loss. This has become known as *long COVID*. One day, the patient feels good—the next day, exhausted. They try to walk, they try to work, but the body does not follow. They are tired and have trouble concentrating.

The COVID-19 pandemic completely changed the world. There was a world before and a world after. Nothing in this current life resembles how we lived before. It is neither exactly the same nor different. Around us and in us, everything has changed, even constancy. I no longer know what to believe. It is much like the scientific community right now. They did not know what to do—actually, nobody knew what to do. We were constantly faced with the choice of using a mask or no mask, lockdown or no lockdown, curfew or no curfew. This was how life went on during that time.

We could not even imagine going out without a mask or disinfectant. We were forced to try to keep our distance, avoid crowds, avoid meetings, avoid hugging people, and even avoid shaking hands.

In this new world, I felt I was losing all of my landmarks and losing my taste for life. It became hard to actually feel the joy of living. COVID-19, cancer, isolation, social distancing—it all became part of the same fight.

By mid-June 2020, more than ten million people around the world had been diagnosed with COVID-19,[3] and more than half a million people had died from this unpredictable virus.[4] Uncertainty and fear spread throughout the world, and the worst part was that nobody knew what was really happening.

At the end of June, I started my radiation treatment. Everybody told me that radiation would be easier than chemo. I believe they are correct, but easy or not easy all depends on a person's mindset. During chemo and radiation, the one thing we really need is calmness. We need words of encouragement and hope, nothing more. The mind is full of so many thoughts and questions, so anything negative adds to the condition and seems to stimulate the body to reject the treatment it's getting.

I believe that is how my story went. My stress during my treatment was inevitable. I had all of the worst side effects of chemo and radiation during those unfortunate and uncertain times. Who could ever believe that an athletic, healthy woman like me would have to go through all those unexpected events?

After two treatments of radiation, I developed an inflammation of the cartilage in my sternum, which caused pain in my bones again. The stress of my daily treatment and trying to work gave me tachycardia. Every time I had radiation treatment, I would get so emotional. I do not know why, but the tears just kept running down my face even though it was just a three-minute treatment.

---

3 John Elflein, "Number of Cumulative Cases of Coronavirus (COVID-19) Worldwide from January 22, 2020 to June 13, 2023, by Day," Statista, May 22, 2024, https://www.statista.com/statistics/1103040/cumulative-coronavirus-covid19-cases-number-worldwide-by-day/.

4 KFF, "This Week in Coronavirus: June 18 to June 25," June 26, 2020, https://www.kff.org/policy-watch/this-week-in-coronavirus-june-18-to-june-25/.

To be honest, I always seemed to get a strange feeling after radiation that I really cannot describe. I felt like I had lost the integrity of my body and my body had been reduced to just the area of radiation. As much as the chemotherapy targeted the whole body and the effects were more visible on the hair and face, radiation felt like the symbol of femininity and motherhood was being targeted. I suffered from burns and discomfort so severe that I could not stand contact with my clothes. There were times I could not even move my arm, and I experienced a great deal of pain in my sternum. I just could not handle all the changes that were occurring in my body.

After one month of radiation therapy, I finally felt free—free like a bird and hopefully free for the rest of my life. I would not wish anyone to have to go through what I went through. Although I can assure you that it was an experience that opened my eyes to my own life, putting the value of life itself and the importance of time into perspective.

I never had the same type of confidence in my physical appearance before that I gained during that period of my life. Before, when I would look at myself, I would always find something wrong. But when I went out with my bald head and people looked at me as if I were ten feet away from death, it now makes me laugh.

So I guess you can tell why the quote below is one of my favorites.

> **A bird sitting on the tree is never afraid of the branch breaking, because its trust is not on the branch but on its wings. Always believe in yourself.**
>
> —Charlie Wardle

CHAPTER 14
Recovery

> **Though nobody can go back and make a new beginning, anyone can start over and make a new ending.**
>
> —Anonymous

It was July 2020, and I was happy to report that I had finally finished all my radiation treatments. But it was not easy. My entire body had become completely and unbelievably tired. I could not recognize my body or myself. My physicians told me that I had to start exercising. I had to move and walk. But it was not easy. My sister Mahshad tried to help me walk around my swimming pool. She put multiple chairs around the swimming pool so I could sit and rest after walking a few steps.

Standing by the pool, I felt an overwhelming mix of loneliness and determination, as if each step forward was both a small victory and a reminder of how far I still had to go. It was hard to believe I was still so sick.

By the end of June, my family had to leave for France because their US visas would expire by June 30. I decided to send Shaun to France with them because he was tired of the life he was being forced to live. He had been home since March 2020. He had not gone to school because of COVID-19. He had not seen his friends because of my condition. He was in a roughly five-month lockdown at home because of my immune system and sickness. Even though he did not want to leave me alone, I convinced him to go to France and told him I would join him once I finished my radiation treatments. So they all left.

While I was having my radiation treatments, I called my friend Landan Laurusaitis, who is a professional private trainer and coach in the Bay Area. I met Landan in 2015 at his studio, The Performist, in Palo Alto. I worked out with him once in a while at his studio. He is an amazing coach who is very disciplined and very talented.

Landan is also a very inspiring individual, so I thought perhaps he could help me get through a time when I really needed to move and exercise. I knew I could not do it by myself. I did not have the energy, motivation, or courage. I was so tired, physically and emotionally, that I could not see any light at all at the end of the tunnel I had been living in for way too long.

Here is how Landan described our time together:

I met Maky in 2015. I can't remember meeting a more high-energy person than Maky. She was always very busy. She called me after many months of not hearing from her. She contacted me when she was going through her radiation treatment. She had experienced a lot of pain and problems during her treatment, and I think she had a lot of courage to ask for help.

We always had good communication, but I think she reached out to me like I was a life preserver. I started going to her house, but it was not all about training or exercise. It was about encouragement, helping her to overcome her daily challenges, helping her to gain her energy back.

My role was to help her heal. Our goal was to get her strong enough to live the next chapter in her life. I get very close to the people I work with. I'd see her about five days a week. She was not the typical client, and I am certainly not the typical coach. I come from an entertainment family and do things with an individual flair. Coaching is boring. I say, "Let us perform."

Maky was all in. She is a competitor, but not someone who is trying to be the best or look the best among others. She wants to be her best self. Maky owns her own position and has a mindset and drive I am able to hack into. This woman just wants to feel alive. She is very agile and has incredible stamina. She has the grease fire and spirit to keep things going when the resistance sets in.

While I was working with Maky, I also got to know and work with her son, Shaun. I saw many of Maky's unique qualities in her fourteen-year-old son. She's a good mom and very protective of him. Their relationship is not the normal mother-son relationship. They go back and forth on things like they are best friends. He is a very talkative and funny guy.

Sometimes they had let each other have it, but I always saw the best parts of her in him. They have a genuine friendship, different from anything I have ever seen. He gets his confidence from her.

At fourteen, he has already developed a strong work ethic. I felt very privileged to be around them both. Shaun has already found his place in the world, and I am convinced he's going to be great at whatever he does. I was excited to be his friend, his mentor, his coach, whatever made sense on any given day. I am a "giver," and I just wanted to help make Shaun and Maky happy and healthy. And like I said, it was a privilege for me to work with both of them.

Landan worked with me every day after I came back from the hospital. He pushed me to exercise, and step by step, he got me going. By the end of the treatments, I began to gain more energy, so I could actually go up and down the stairs without any shortness of breath. Landan really had to work hard to strengthen my body. He was very patient with me, and I cannot thank him enough for helping me get back to a normal life.

As strange as it may sound, the day after my last treatment, I took off for France to have all my tests done there. The interesting thing was that all my physicians—my oncologist at Stanford, Dr. Sledge, and my physicians in France, Dr. Bagot and Dr. Achille—told me they had never seen a patient like me, who had actually experienced all the side effects of chemo.

My heart had been impacted by the time I received my third Adriamycin treatment. This is a chemo treatment that can be very toxic to the heart. My ejection fraction (EJ—a measurement of the percentage of blood leaving the heart each time it contracts) dropped very low. My cardiologist in Palo Alto, Dr. Ramtin Agah, and my internist in France, Dr. Bagot, recommended stopping Adriamycin to my oncologist. Otherwise, it would be very hard for me to recover.

The good news was that all that exercising I did after my radiation therapy paid off. When I was in France and had my cardiac scintigraphy (a diagnostic imaging technique used to assess the function and blood flow of the heart), my French cardiologist, Dr. Raphael Hebras, told me that I had fully recovered and the EJ was back to a normal range—which today is 62 percent.

I would like to take this opportunity to thank all the staff of MD Anderson (Dr. Vincent Valero) and Stanford (Dr. Sledge and Kathie Smith [RN]), the French medical team (Dr. Jean Emmanuel Kurtz, Dr. Achille, Dr. Bagot, and Dr. Hebras), and Dr. Agah, as well as all my friends around the world, for helping me get through this very difficult time in my life.

I must also admit that I never could have gotten through all the treatments and procedures going on in my life without Mahshad. She made it her responsibility to not only keep track of my health but also help me get through all my pain.

She was there for me from day one. Moreover, she was the one who made an appointment for me and accompanied me to my mammogram on Christmas Day, contacted the surgeon, and scheduled the operation. She also dropped me off at the nail shop to remove my nail polish two hours before going to the hospital for surgery, because it was forbidden to have nail polish on when undergoing general anesthesia. She was also the one who took the surgical biopsy (breast tissue and lymph node) from the operating room to the pathology center for analysis on New Year's Eve.

Later on, Mahshad took care of collecting the histology slides to send to California because my oncologists in the US did not want to start chemotherapy without reviewing the slides themselves (the rules of each hospital). She was also the one who came to Houston for my cardiology checkup, my catheter placement, and of course, my first chemotherapy on the evening of Valentine's Day.

She was the one who changed the ice cubes on my head, hands, and toes. She was the one who watched me at the hotel, managed the complementary treatments, monitored the Neulasta, and took me to MD Anderson's emergency room in the middle of the night for my breathing difficulties. After my first chemo treatment, it took me twelve days to recover before starting the second round of chemotherapy.

Mahshad was supposed to leave after my first chemo treatment, but because of all the side effects and my condition, she extended her stay to attend my second chemo treatment at Stanford. The pandemic had started by then, and for the second treatment, we went to the infusion center covered from head to toe. Mahshad took her box of Clorox so she could disinfect everything we touched. Everything had already been disinfected by the hospital staff, but it was not enough for her. She herself had to make sure everything was clean.

My second chemo treatment was worse than the first, and my condition was deteriorating every day, so Mahshad decided to stay as long as necessary to be with me. The COVID-19 lockdown was already established in Europe and the US. So Mahshad managed her medical practice remotely by teleconsultation, and with the help of her colleagues, she was able to attend to her patients for those five months.

But that was not all. Mashhad left her three kids—Sasha, sixteen years old; Dorian, fourteen years old; and Inès, thirteen years old—alone with their father, Thierry, in France for five months during the lockdown and pandemic. And she did it just to be with me.

She took care of her children via Zoom. She actually helped them do their homework and prepare for their tests at school. She did everything she could to keep me safe and help me get through this unthinkable phase of my life. I think that tells you a lot about our relationship and the kind of person my sister is.

I also had a lot of help from my mom and dad, who gave me all the love and confidence they could to get me through everything I was enduring. It was not an easy time for them. They had never watched me have to face anything like that. I could feel they were broken, like there was a vase inside them that had shattered into a million pieces. But they didn't want me to see how they were feeling, and they stayed strong. They came to live with me and acted like coaches and cheerleaders, helping me start every morning with hope and faith for a fast recovery.

My closest family and many of my friends around the world were always behind me, either sending messages or calling me every day to see how I was doing. There were always people who would bring me food or gifts and just leave things outside my door. Remember, this was all happening during COVID-19, and I really couldn't let anyone come inside.

But I cannot tell you how much I appreciated all the love and support that was left on my doorstep. I would like to take this opportunity to thank my friends, Dr. Behnaz Bakhshi, Leanne Cummins, Mary Anne, and Oscar. I would like to thank Thierry for his presence during difficult times, his moral support, his calmness, and his discreet and efficient help. He always helped us when we needed help during my treatment and my father's hospitalization.

I also want to thank Darian, the son of my friend Ana Sani, who wanted to express his solidarity. At ten years old, he decided to cut off all his long hair when he found out I had cancer and had lost all my hair. Darian had never let anyone cut his hair before. I was very touched when he also decided to donate all his hair to cancer patients.

But the most important person who helped me get through everything was my son, Shaun. There was no way I could ever have gotten through the most devastating time in my life without his positive energy and acceptance of my condition. Shaun never showed any fear or signs of being scared of what I was going through. He was my light at the end of the tunnel that I lived in for so many months.

> **Don't let the past steal your present.**
>
> —Confucius

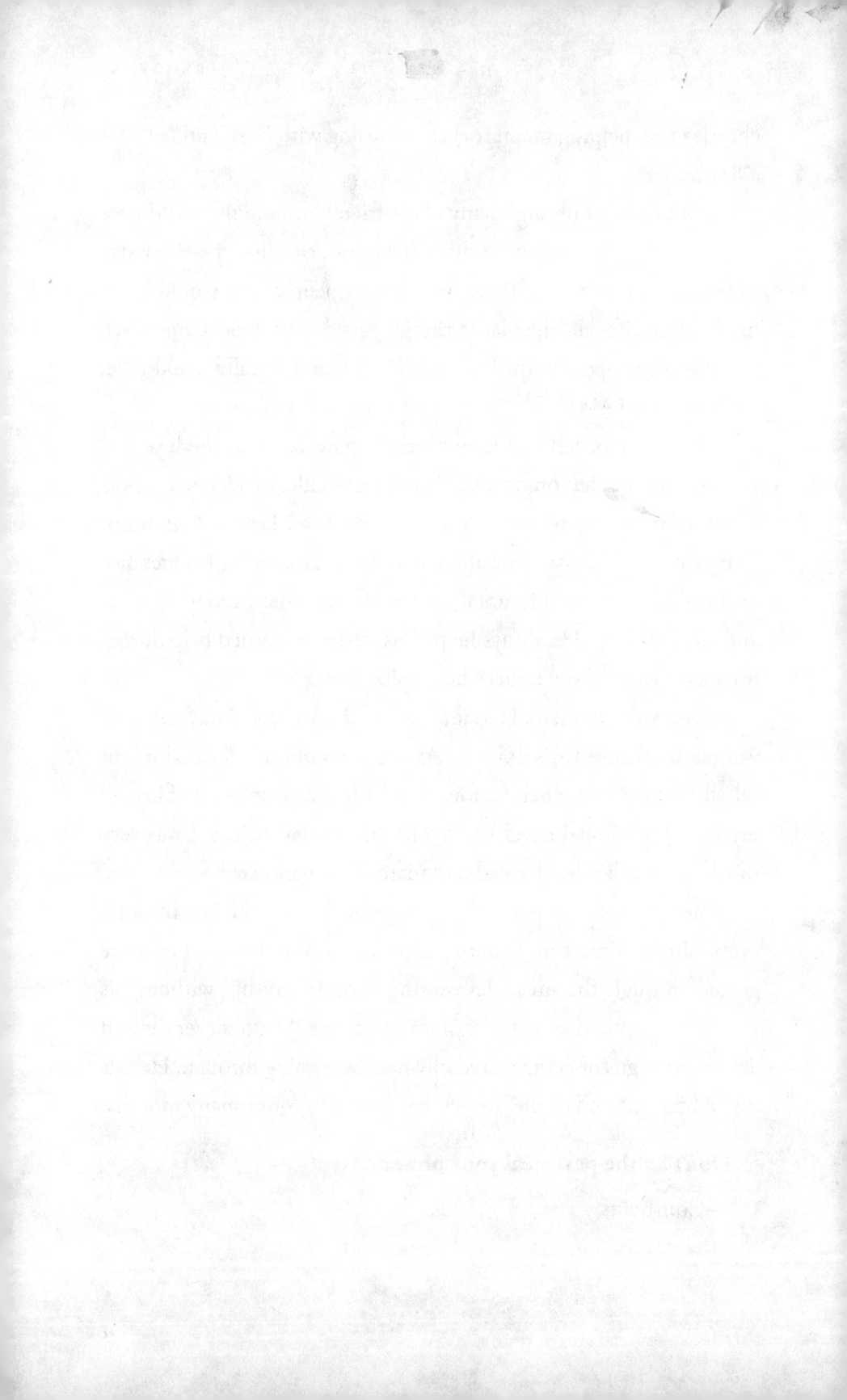

CHAPTER 15

"My Way"

> **You never know how strong you are until being strong is the only choice you have.**
>
> —Bob Marley

There is a correlation between a broken heart and cancer. I did not know about it until I read a scientific article about the stress of people who lost a loved one and the emotional effects of cancer and heart disease. The year 2019 was quite a stressful one for me in many aspects. It was a year when I began to experience a lot of doubt. I could not quite put my finger on it, but there were a lot of little signs in front of me that I did not want to accept. My intuition told me something was just not right.

But there are times in our lives when we just do not want to face reality, so we push back and try to ignore what is going on. My heart was broken into multiple pieces, but I was the only one who could feel it. Just me, nobody else. I ignored my heart. I did not listen to the inner voice telling me I was doing the wrong thing. The pressure on my heart and mind was so much that my body started to fight itself, and suddenly, it manifested in my left breast and became a little tumor.

Like anything in life, if we push too hard on something, it breaks. That is when cancer shows up, knocking on the door. We tend to ignore the stress factor. We always believe that cancer or any catastrophic event only happens to others, until one day, out of nowhere, the world collapses in front of us. If the cancer is at an early stage and curable, it will pass like everything in life, just leaving a big scar to remind us that our time is precious, and we need to love and respect ourselves first and foremost. Also, we need to believe in ourselves and our ability to fight.

Now that I have been through all my treatments, I feel blessed that this world gave me a second chance to look at everything more carefully and grab the opportunity to live the life I want to live. I have come to realize that a lot of cancer patients do not get this second chance. It was not easy going through those treatments.

There were times when death seemed like it would be a lot easier. Every time I had chemotherapy, I was so miserable that I just wanted to throw in the towel. I was so tired and so weak emotionally that I could not see any light at the end of the tunnel.

But as I said before, I believe hope is the main key in life, and when I looked at Shaun and into the eyes of the people in my family, that was what gave me the energy to continue. That was the only thing that allowed me to move forward and helped get me through all the pain. I got through it so I could be there for them. Time is the healer, but the scar never goes away. It is there to remind us to savor every moment in life—and to live it without fear, hesitation, or doubt.

Remembering that I will be dead soon is the most important tool I've ever encountered to help me make the big choices in life. Because almost everything—all external expectations, all pride, all fear of embarrassment or failure—these things just fall away in the face of death, leaving only what is truly important.

Remembering that you are going to die is the best way I know to avoid the trap of thinking you have something to lose.

You are already naked. There is no reason not to follow your heart. Your time is limited, so do not waste it living someone else's life. Do not be trapped by dogma—which is living with the results of other people's thinking. Do not let the noise of others' opinions drown out your own inner voice.

And most important, have the courage to follow your heart and intuition. They somehow already know what you truly want to become. Everything else is secondary.

—Steve Jobs[5]

In life, I have learned to let come what may come and to let go of what has to go. If, despite all the efforts we make in life to get what we want, it still does not happen, then it probably should not happen. I have learned to submit myself to the force of nature, to accept it, to even accept the unacceptable. And to adapt to the unacceptable.

During a biological crisis spanning millions of years on Earth, the species that have survived are those that have been able to adapt or even mutate. The environment changes the brain, and the best thing is, we also can change our minds. We can choose acceptance over

5 "Steve Jobs Quotes," Goodreads, September 23, 2024, https://www.goodreads.com/quotes/427317-remembering-that-i-ll-be-dead-soon-is-the-most-important

resilience. A lion always stays a lion, even in a cage. The difficult times in life should not make us doubt ourselves or lose our self-confidence. This is what I have learned over time. Time is a teacher who makes us take exams before even giving us a lesson.

I have learned to live in the present, to enter fully into the moment. I have learned not to remain locked in my past or to let myself be overwhelmed by projections of the future. And lately, I've learned to thank life every morning for being present in me and around me. I've learned to honor life whenever possible and respect it on all occasions. I've learned to energize life with my resources and my limits. More than ever, I've realized that time accelerates as I get older and that it is important not to add years to life but life to years.

During a period of seven months, I went down. I hit the bottom of the ocean, physically and emotionally. But I came back up fast, and I can tell you that after seven months of treatment, I was back to the magic of normal, back to my normal life. The only thing that was not normal was the world we were living in. COVID-19 was still present around the world.

Sure, kids started going back to school, but many of them Zoomed from home for a long time. Terms like *Zoom* and *Google Doc* took a new place in the dictionary. Children became isolated. They could not see their friends. The teachers and staff made heroic efforts to keep the kids engaged. Unemployment went through the roof. People were suffering from a lack of money, from depression and uncertainty, and at the end of the day, nobody knew where things were headed. The economy was shaky, and nobody could predict the future. People hoped for a vaccine for any future pandemic, but nobody will know for a long time what effects any new vaccines will have on people. The world is still searching for a therapeutic drug that can be relied upon.

It is a shame that it took an invisible virus to open people's eyes to appreciate life. Life before COVID-19 was pretty much out of control. People never saw their families. They took everything for granted. They never saw the value of *life*, *love*, and *living*. I really want to go back to a normal life before COVID-19, but with my new perspective, which is this: "When the world is falling apart in front of you, remember nothing—*nothing*—has more value than your family, the people you love, and the simplicity of life."

I have recently realized there are four things in life that we cannot buy, no matter how much money we have: *health*, *love*, *time*, and *happiness*. COVID-19 did not care who was a millionaire or who was homeless, who was wealthy or who was poor. COVID-19 did not care about skin color. COVID-19 just cared about one thing: children. COVID-19 rarely touched the children. COVID-19 knew they were the innocent human beings that would eventually change the world and perhaps create a *new normal* with more *love* and *respect*.

The phoenix is a mythical bird that symbolizes rebirth and immortality in Greek mythology. Burned by fire, the bird comes back to life in its ashes. Today, rising from the ashes means knowing how to bounce back from failure, from the difficulties of life, from any challenge or obstacle. I am now in the best shape of my life. I have more energy than ever. I have accepted new challenges in my professional career. I recently joined Summit Therapeutics, again a failed company that Bob and I decided to take over and build into a successful company or perhaps even more.

I am determined that our new venture, Summit Therapeutics, like Pharmacyclics, will make an impact on the medical world and once again help save lives. There are so many things that inspire me to jump in again. As Steve Jobs said, "Push the human race forward."

I was so touched recently by the February 21 mission to Mars. The Perseverance rover, a Franco-American collaboration, and Hope, a space probe from the United Arab Emirates led by a woman of Iranian origin, Sarah El-Amiri, were both out at the same time to conquer Mars. These two words, *perseverance* and *hope*, truly summarize my life's journey and, above all, what defines me for my new project, Summit.

> **You have seen my descent; now watch my rising.**
>
> —Rumi

Today, I feel like a phoenix. After all the ups and downs in my life, after all the difficulties, I am back to living my normal life ... I am back to the magic of normal.

As I look back on the moments of my life, the music of Frank Sinatra's "My Way" has been the perfect soundtrack to reflect on my unique journey. From being the last song I listened to when leaving Iran, to my last day in dental school, and the final song played at my father's passing, this music has resonated deeply with me. It symbolizes the challenges I have overcome and the accomplishments I have achieved.

Each note marks a milestone in my life, representing years of hard work, dedication, and unwavering determination. In these moments, I feel a sense of pride and fulfillment, knowing that I have indeed lived life on my own terms: "I did it my way."

Two Years Later

CHAPTER 16

My Father: The Super Angel

> **Once you choose hope, anything is possible.**
>
> —Christopher Reeve

January 2022

It was a cold day in Strasbourg. On January 30 at 5:36 a.m., my dad closed his eyes in room 635 of the Institut de cancérologie Strasbourg. He lost his last battle, but he won the war of his life. Despite all his suffering in the last three months, not once did he ask, "Why?" The only thing he asked was, "My God, help me to endure it."

We were all working on different treatment plans, and letting my dad leave his body was not an option. We were not prepared to arrange my dad's memorial service/the celebration of his life. How to prepare such a ceremony in such a short period of time? We were still in the middle of another wave of COVID-19 (Omicron) … time was lacking … to prepare for eternity. How could I present my dad, whom I have always known? How to summarize eighty-one years of his tumultuous life, spread over three continents and four countries?

To my "Baba," "Dad," "Babairadj," and finally "Dady." It is this last nickname that I will keep since he became a grandfather: adored Dady.

If there was a word that defined him, it was *love*—love above all, love beyond love, unconditional love. All the people who knew him felt it. They felt that extreme, respectful affection from him even when linguistic communication was a barrier, because he spoke just Farsi, his mother language.

The second word that defined him was *courage*—the courage to endure ninety days lying in a hospital bed, unable to eat, drink, or move but conscious all the time. Trying to talk to each member of the family to give them his last advice about life and living.

It was so strange, the last ninety days of his life. Dad could see beyond the wall. He could read my mind, everything that was going on in my head. My sister Mahshad and my mom had the same experience. He was like an angel. He was a spiritual being with a mission. As if he came from another place in his own painful body. That is why I called him a super angel. Who could endure his physical condition? All the pain and suffering and still being conscious and fully aware.

The "Dady's girl" that I was and that I remained until his last breath, until his last heartbeat, with his once-strong hand in mine, until he flew to the sky to join his parents whom he cherished so much …

He was born in 1940 in Abadan, an oil city in southern Iran, on the edge of the Persian Gulf, in a traditional and affectionate family, where the simplest values of life were honesty, loyalty, sincerity, politeness, and respect. "Politeness first, health next, and then education"—these are the pillars that he transmitted to his children and grandchildren.

At eighteen, he moved to Tehran, the capital of Iran, to study in the inaugural class of the Faculty of Architecture at Meli University. While teaching at the university, he founded Iradj Zanganeh and Associates. His work earned him multiple awards and recognition at the architectural research center in Iran. He created an architecture school, M&I—Mahin and Iradj School, with my mom, an architect herself. He was the representative of Iranian architects for a few years and carried their voice.

After many years of hard work and building his own brand and his creation, my dad decided to expand his company internationally, so he went to the US to do a joint venture with the largest American architecture firm, named HOK, for architectural project exchanges between Iran, the US, and the Persian Gulf countries.

The Iranian Revolution of 1979 and the collapse of the entire Iranian society changed the path of life of my father. He had to cancel his joint venture agreement that he had received a few days after the Iranian Revolution because of political reasons in Iran. All his dreams fell apart as if nothing ever existed.

Later on, he decided to create a new architecture company with his engineer and architect friends. He built the medical school in Urmia, the municipal library in Shiraz, and the first thirty-three-story skyscraper in Tehran. He participated in the construction of the international airport in Tehran in collaboration with ADP Paris.

My dad met my mom very young at university. They got married very quickly and they had the first baby in the family and also at the university! Shaby, who became the darling of all their friends. Together, they led and stood side by side in student life, family life, and professional life. He was a father fully involved in the education of his children and the education of other children or students in difficulty. He was passionate about education, loved books, paper, reading, and writing. Back-to-school and back-to-school shopping were very special moments for him … remained special until the end of his life. He only missed them the year when he was in the hospital because he was in pain and could no longer walk. Anyway, he was my father, my advisor, my coach, my mentor, and my hero.

My dad wanted matriarchal dominance for his family and helped my mother equip herself and take on this role. In fact, this was his last request, he reiterated a few weeks before his death. He asked her to stay strong and continue the role for which he had prepared her for so many years … to stay strong when the time of that eternal absence came and dominated the eternal silence … to stay strong when his breathing stopped forever.

It's not easy to live without him. How can I continue to not hear him, to not see him, to not hold his hand, to not massage his painful legs? I will miss all those times when I showed him how to work his iPhone, which he brilliantly used to record a thousand poems that he had written in the past few years, adding musical backgrounds while recording those poems. What a beautiful gift he prepared for us, his children and grandchildren, all those years.

He wanted to help us envision that time when he would no longer be here with us. He wanted to help us understand the core of life, which is integrity, and the value of life, which is family and love, in anticipation of the day when he would no longer be here. Each poem is a message that comes from beyond; he consoles us, even about his own death, with his own voice.

That voice that was missed so much in his last week of life when he lost the ability to talk. He was trying to speak only with his eyes, limited by a dry mouth, facial features that made expression difficult, and the weakness of muscles to even show something. He spoke to me with his eyes and let me guess, and I tried my best to guess what my father was trying to tell me in this non-verbal language. But we managed to communicate with our eyes and our hearts. That reminded me of when my son was born: I learned to guess what he wanted with this wordless language, and I anticipated the day when he could speak and express himself, which comes naturally most of the time to all human babies.

But this time for my father, the lost voice would never come back. He was not even angry anymore for not being able to speak. He let me guess with all his kindness. Ultimately, my role as his official translator will remain for eternity, and when words are absent, it is this deep look that will speak.

Twenty-four hours before he passed away, Mahshad and I told my son Shaun and our mother to go and say goodbye to him. My dad would not let go until he heard from them and made sure that they were OK if he left this world. I wish I could have recorded their talk with my dad. Shaun's last words were so touching. How could he say goodbye to someone who raised him all those years? And how could my mom let go of her soulmate of fifty-eight years?

The turning point of the last hours was when my mom decided to play one of my dad's poems for him. He always loved to listen to his poems. As he heard his own voice reciting the piece recorded on the iPhone, his face became so peaceful—a little smile on his face, a little body movement even though he was almost in a coma. We could feel that he could hear and feel what was happening around him.

It was from the introduction of his own book, the one that his grandchildren, Sarah and Arman, hurried to have printed for him a few weeks earlier. He dedicated this book to his children and grandchildren and thanked my mother for fifty-eight years of shared life. He reassured himself that the message had been conveyed and he could finally rest in peace—and in his way, convince himself to end the long illness, the extreme pain and suffering of his tired body.

That is the introduction of his book, recorded by him and played from his iPhone when Shaun and my mom said goodbye:

I dedicate this book to my dear and loving wife, my faithful companion for 50 years of life together. A life where you had to be patient, tolerant, and very solid, and a thousand adjectives of this kind that you had ... and I was amazed by it. I thank her for all her kindness and all her efforts. The efforts for me, for our children, and for our grandchildren. I will pray for her, for her health, and that her wishes come true.

May God accompany her every moment.

Love you,

Iradj Zanganeh

I dedicate this book to my grandchildren so that they each know how much I love them. In the future, even the nature of reading will change. We must write short passages to be read. The subjects of the scriptures will also be different. The thoughts and wills of human beings will change too. So much so that reading an entire page might be difficult. This collection of short poems I leave for you as a memory from Dady.

Maybe that's not a bad thing, since the subjects I write about are love and human beings. Because as long as the universe continues, it will always be about love and humanity. But maybe it will change form and combinations. We cannot subtract love and human beings from this infinite universe even if it is probable that there are other living beings on other planets.

Even though it is more than probable and even certain. But the relationship between human beings with other living beings and finally between the planets is a relationship of love, balance, and humanity—or in any case, the current meaning of humanity. "Humanity," which will perhaps change its name, and also "love."

Without humanity and love, or the equivalent of these two words, in the future, there will no longer be a world worthy of the name to live in.

Love you,

Dady

My dad always talked about the power of the brain, that we can control our minds and overcome anything in life just by using our mind power. He had shown at times that this power even surpassed the limits of medicine. He was considered the Superman of MD Anderson.

But even medicine does not have absolute truth, and it is far from being all-powerful. There is also the power of nature and the overpowering force of time. Life on Earth is a battle … but my dad succeeded in his eternal life.

January 2024 – Two Years after His Death

The distance between two points in eternity is an instant. Life and death disturb all the laws of physics and mathematics. Distance, space, and time blend together and become one. Is eternity measured in distance or time?

What I know is that eternity is in every second, every minute, every hour, and every day since my dad's death … an eternity of sorrow, an eternity of sadness, an eternity of impatience, an eternity of waiting, not even knowing the reason for the wait… waiting to wake me up and tell me his last three months, his suffering, and his death were just a horrible nightmare.

He always told me that he would like to change space and time. We froze time on these rare moments of happiness in the summer of 2021 when we had given ourselves a break between illnesses and the pandemic. Unfortunately, my dad could not see the world after

COVID-19; the period of his hospitalization and death was during the COVID-19 peak in France. With five hundred thousand new cases per day, thirty-five thousand hospitalizations, and saturated intensive care units ... with all the restrictions and constraints we had to undergo ... wearing the mask in the ambulance, for exams, and in the hospital, even during the transfusion sessions when he lacked oxygen ... In February 2023, everything related to COVID-19 disappeared ... that pinched my heart, since he was no longer there to see it ...

I wish he could be here when the political wave in Iran started in September 2022. I so wanted to know his reaction to this wave of protest in Iran for a year, and finally recognition and praise of the Shah of Iran after forty-three years of revolution.

I so wanted him to be here to comment on the geopolitical events in the Middle East, his vision of the war between Palestine and Israel, to tell me his prediction of the future map of the world ... I so wanted him to be there to share with me the chapters of *Forty Rules of Love*, a book written by Elif Shafak, and absorb the forty rules of love and spirituality. I know that we would have been equal in being attached to the family and detached from the world ...

Since his departure, the world has changed, and my world too. I have more questions than answers, I have more uncertainties than certainties. He has never stopped being present. A presence that goes beyond space and time. This is perhaps the definition of infinity and eternity. I attach myself to the idea that we are energy, and depending on the frequencies, we are visible or not, and that he has moved to the side of the invisible.

He saw me birthed; I saw him die. He lived life before me, then with me. I have always known life with him, and now it's about two years since I discovered life without him. As Shaun says, "without your physical presence in this world," I am enjoying the moments when he comes into my dreams.

Here is how the grandchildren reacted after his death: Shaun wears his scarf and wants to chat with him for hours and hours ... he is missing talking with my dad about the rules of business, world events, and their involvement in the world of finance, his desire to lead, think, and go in the opposite direction of where everybody watches the news and follows other people's opinions.

I wish that my father could be there to listen to him patiently and give him his opinion. Dorian still asks for his help, Sasha bursts into tears, Sarah isolates herself, Arman feels his absence more and more, Inès reminds us that he forbade us to be sad for more than one day, Mahshad is constantly working to better understand life after death or life after life, and Mom goes back and forth to his grave.

Since he passed away, there is not one day that I am not thinking about him. He left too soon, and I blame myself for not having tried all the research protocols at the time (the product of Johnson & Johnson and their innovative CAR T drug). His platelets were too low, his body was too weak, but he asked me multiple times to keep him alive for six more months so he could finish his talk with Shaun and his other grandchildren, and so he could give them his last wisdom and advice about life.

With Mahshad's support, I tried to convince the physician to give him Daratumumab, the multiple myeloma drug, but it was a few weeks too late. I wish I could have brought him to MD Anderson, where the physicians would try everything possible to help the patient stay alive. But we were in the COVID-19 period and travel was problematic. I still blame myself for not having been able to make the impossible possible.

The unthinkable happened on January 30, 2022. The unbelievable became the reality of our daily lives—he followed the light, he became celestial. He always listened to me and came to my aid every time I asked him for help over the last two years. For me, it is the most beautiful proof to say that death does not exist—but absence, yes.

His love is still the only thing that maintains the pillar of the family. It is the root. It is the trunk of the family tree of life. His love is unifying, surrounding, and endearing. This is our meeting point, our point of intersection. It is this point that connects us. And it is this point that contains eternity. Thank you, Dady, for this infinite love that knows neither beginning nor end … nor time … nor space.

I had the honor to be his daughter. I had the chance to be by his side until the last second in room 635 on January 30, 2022, and to feel his last heartbeat at 5:36 a.m. I left my heart in that room. It has been two years now. He said that death is only an instant; I add life too. I promised myself to let him go and not keep him between two worlds. I will do my best. Death lasts an instant; absence lasts an eternity.

"Dady, I love you to infinity and for eternity..."

Two weeks after my father passed away, I was invited to speak at the United Nations. I had the honor of being a speaker at the United Nations' seventh International Day of Women and Girls in Science assembly conference in February 2022, during the esteemed closing ceremony.

The event aimed to celebrate the incredible women and girls in science, and my talk focused on the importance of education. I shared my own life story to inspire young girls and women, emphasizing that education is the foundation for success. I encouraged them to take chances, learn from mistakes, and never give up on their dreams.

Education, I emphasized, is the key to unlocking opportunities and breaking through the perceived barriers of gender, language, culture, and borders. My message to all girls and women worldwide was to pursue their dreams and keep moving forward—with life ahead of them, not behind. I wished my father could have been there to hear my speech, as I am certain he would have been proud of me.

At the conclusion of my talk, Her Excellency Amal Mudallali, ambassador and permanent representative of Lebanon to the United Nations, offered her condolences for my father's passing, a gesture that touched me deeply as she acknowledged my father before closing the ceremony.

After my dad passed away, it was incredibly challenging for my mom to remain focused and motivated. My dad was her everything. They were an inseparable and unstoppable couple. From their university days to raising us kids, building a family, and navigating life's challenges, they did everything together. It was daunting for my mom to carry on when all their decisions had always been made jointly. She always turned to my dad for guidance, and somehow, a glimmer of hope and solutions emerged when they hit a wall.

I am amazed by her strength as she honors my dad's last wish to keep the family united. It is an arduous task to calm down all of us and all our teenagers—the kids who suddenly lost our family's pillar. I have immense respect and unconditional love for my mom. I see her fighting as a woman and a mother, pouring her heart and soul into the family, going above and beyond in every way. I wish I could be like her as a mother.

In the past two years, Shaun's life has undergone a profound transformation. He faced numerous challenges, starting from his eighth-grade online graduation during the pandemic and my cancer treatment. His high school journey began amid the COVID-19 pandemic, forcing him to adapt to virtual learning and isolation from his friends. Despite the setbacks, Shaun remained resilient and supportive, especially during my cancer treatment, choosing to stay by my side.

As he entered his sophomore year in September 2021 and returned to in-person schooling, another wave of challenges emerged. October 2021 was when my father fell ill, prompting Shaun to travel to France to be with him. Witnessing his grandfather's deteriorating health, Shaun made the decision to stay in Europe, supporting him through his hospitalization and cancer treatment until his final moments. Throughout this period, Shaun continued his studies online, demonstrating remarkable strength and maturity. The loss of my father marked a profound and difficult chapter in Shaun's life.

My dad always told me that Shaun was an unusual kid and that I had to be very patient with him. He was right. I have witnessed Shaun's growth into an independent thinker and leader during these past years.

On April 27, 2024, Shaun celebrated his eighteenth birthday, marking a significant milestone in his life. Time seemed to have flown by, and I marveled at his journey toward independence. Shaun's unwavering determination, self-confidence, and courage have always been sources of inspiration for me. It feels like just yesterday that he entered this world, forever altering my life. As a son, he has been the greatest blessing I could have ever hoped for, bringing immense joy and purpose into my life from the moment he was born.

Watching him grow and evolve over the years has been a journey filled with love, laughter, and cherished memories. From his birth to this day, we have faced numerous challenges together, each one strengthening our bond as a family. I am incredibly proud of the person he has become. His unique path, though not without its obstacles, has always been guided by his authenticity and integrity, a source of immense pride for me. I have learned invaluable lessons from him, and I am grateful for the wisdom he has imparted.

He is my angel, my protector, a precious gift from God. And he is my life, as my father always told him—"Nafase Mani," meaning "he is my very breath."

It has been two years since my father passed away, but his presence continues to guide us. The love he bestowed upon his family remains a unifying force, transcending the boundaries of time and space. His teachings on the power of the mind, integrity, and the importance of family and love are legacies that we carry forward. Though death claimed him in an instant, his absence is felt eternally, a testament to the profound impact he had on our lives.

CHAPTER 17

Women, Life, Freedom

> **When the whole world is silent, even one voice becomes powerful.**
> —Malala Yousafzai

Years have passed since I left Iran, and the world around me has transformed in ways I could never have imagined. I journeyed from my life as a young girl in Iran to becoming a successful businesswoman in the US. It was a very challenging road, full of surprises, unpredictability, and uncertainty. When I left Iran, I had no clear destination, only a steadfast faith that everything would be alright.

Despite being separated from my family and friends for years, I always believed in a brighter future. Becoming who I am today and living the life I live now would not have been possible if I had not come to a country where I could be free to grow and pursue my dreams—a freedom especially vital for women. Sometimes women do not have this privilege to do what they want to do, especially in those countries where women have no choice but to follow the rules imposed by others, overshadowing the desires of the heart.

In ancient Persia, the role of women was not only highly respected but often considered equal to men. Women could own land, conduct business, receive equal pay, travel freely, and, in the case of royal women, even hold their own council meetings on politics. The titles of respect given to Persian royal women seem to originate from the earlier Elamite culture and most likely from the Median Empire, the immediate precursor to the Achaemenid Persian Empire (c. 550–330 BCE) founded by Cyrus the Great (r. c. 550–530 BCE). Cyrus established the Persian paradigm of religious and expressive freedom within his empire, and also upheld the dignity and autonomy of women of all classes.

This model was maintained by the Parthian Empire (227 BCE–224 CE), although because of the loss of documents and artworks after the fall of Parthia to the Sassanian Empire (224–651 CE), the details of women's lives during this period are not as well known. The Sassanian period, however, is well documented, and women's rights were maintained at the same level, if not higher, than under the Achaemenid Empire. Persian women continued to enjoy this high status in ancient Persian culture until the fall of the Sassanian Empire to the Arab Muslim invasion in 651 CE. Since then, women have continuously fought for their freedom and the ability to shape their own destinies.

The recent events of September 2022 highlight the power and resilience of Iranian women and the fearless spirit of women globally in the fight for freedom and women's rights. In September 2022, a twenty-two-year-old woman, Mahsa Amini, died in detention for violating discriminatory dress codes for women.

This tragic incident sparked widespread pro-women's rights and pro-democracy protests across all of Iran's thirty-one provinces. During the protests, security forces violently cracked down, resulting in mass arrests, documented beatings, internet and telecommunications shutdowns, and the use of live ammunition against protesters. Hundreds of protesters, including women and children, were killed, and many more were injured.

In October 2022, I remember following on Facebook and Instagram a horrific night of massacre and arrests during the student revolt, particularly at Sharif University, known for its elite student body (many scientists in Silicon Valley and NASA in the US came from this university in Tehran). Many students were arrested and placed in Evin Prison, alongside activists, lawyers, journalists, and brilliant Science Olympiad students.

One comment on social media—whose author is not revealed here for the sake of safety—was a deeply moving remark proclaiming:

> *Whether you are ready or not, whether you want it or not, the people of Iran are going to win. The students of Iran are driven by great ambitions for their country. They don't just want freedom; they seek justice, cultural integrity, and environmental protection. They have shown that they are more than ready to decide for themselves.*
>
> *These students who have been fighting for a year now who have been beaten up, arrested, poisoned, raped and killed yet despite death hanging over their heads they keep coming to the streets every day.*
>
> *Many prepare testimonies in case they don't come back, but they all share the same resolve: "If I die, don't worry, celebrate. The others will continue. It is time for us to show once again to the world we made history. We are making it right before your eyes and we make it forever … whether you are ready or not, whether you want it or not, we are going to win."*

It has been estimated by various sources—which must remain confidential for obvious reasons—that during the protests, over fifteen thousand people were arrested, more than one thousand were injured, seven hundred lost their eyesight from shotgun shells known as birdshot (small metal pellets that are less likely to kill from a distance but can blind people in a crowd), and over six hundred died, including sixty children under the age of twelve, such as Kian Pirfalak, who aspired to work with Elon Musk at Tesla.

Facial recognition technology was used to identify protesters in middle schools, high schools, universities, and on the streets, leading to further arrests and the prevention of students and professors from continuing their studies or professions.

Executions were frequent. Among others, Mohsen S. was executed after eighteen days of arrest because he had kicked a trash can and knocked it over on the sidelines of a demonstration against the regime. Relatives and families of the executed and those who died in the demonstrations were also arrested.

As I reflect on these events, I often find myself overwhelmed with empathy for the parents who lost their children. I cannot imagine the pain of seeing their loved ones tortured, raped, beaten, or executed. They spent years raising, protecting, and helping them, yet it only takes a minute for them to be killed. Years of nurturing and protecting by families can be undone in an instant.

The Iranian song "Baraye" by singer-songwriter Shervin Hajipour became a protest anthem, garnering over forty million views in less than two days.[6] Hajipour was arrested, but the song continued to resonate globally for its powerful message of the Women, Life,

6 GRAMMYS, "Shervin Hajipour Receives Best Song for Social Change Award for 'Baraye' | 2023 GRAMMYs," GRAMMY.com, February 6, 2023, https://www.grammy.com/news/shervin-hajipour-baraye-winner-best-song-for-social-change-watch-2023-grammys-65th-grammy-awards-acceptance

Freedom movement. In 2023, Hajipour received the Best Song for Social Change award at the GRAMMYs for "Baraye."[7]

Since the Women, Life, Freedom movement began in Iran, repression and cruelty have escalated worldwide. This global inaction raises questions about the role of the international community in defending human rights.

For example, there were the events of October 7, 2023. The world was turned upside down, but not for everyone. The world witnessed a tragedy as 1,400 innocent young people from Israel were killed and 250 people were taken hostage by Hamas at the Gaza Strip border.[8] This led to further horrors, including unilateral bombings by the Israeli government on innocent people in the Gaza Strip while the Hamas leaders met in their palace in Qatar.

All this resulted in over 35,000 deaths in Gaza, including 14,500 children, 80,000 injuries, and the displacement of over 1.5 million people who had to leave their homes and walk toward unknown places. They became refugees, facing famine and a lack of water, fuel, medicine, and painkillers.[9]

Despite the images and testimonies from surviving journalists in Gaza, the rest of the world continues to lead a normal life. It feels like

---

7 Recording Academy, "Shervin Hajipour Wins Inaugural Best Song For Social Change Special Merit Award For 'Baraye' | 2023 GRAMMYs," GRAMMY.com, February 5, 2023, https://www.grammy.com/news/shervin-hajipour-baraye-winner-best-song-for-social-change-watch-2023-grammys-65th-grammy-awards-acceptance-speech.

8 Jaclyn Diaz, "Hamas Attacked Israel 1 Month Ago. Here's Where Things Stand Now," NPR, November 5, 2023, https://www.npr.org/2023/11/05/1210641727/israel-war-hamas-latest-updates.

9 Michelle Nichols and Emma Farge, "UN says Gaza death toll still over 35,000 but not all bodies identified," Reuters, May 13, 2024, https://www.reuters.com/world/middle-east/un-says-gaza-death-toll-still-over-35000-not-all-bodies-identified-2024-05-13.

we are shouting into the void, living a never-ending nightmare, with many turning a blind eye to the atrocities.

How much more brutality and horror must we witness before the world takes action? Where is the United Nations? Where are the human rights ambassadors? How can we accept this as normal? What is normal? Where are the individuals who speak eloquently but fail to act? Where has humanity gone? Has brutality and cruelty become the new normal?

During the COVID-19 pandemic, we wondered whether one day we would see the world without a mask. We thought we were united against an invisible but common enemy. Rich countries sent vaccines to poor countries to try to eradicate or at least limit the damage throughout the world in terms of human loss and the slowdown of economies. We finally understood that the destiny of human beings was to be united to each other, and our collective vulnerability was put to the test.

But apparently, it was just an illusion. God tried to show the world that life is fragile, but apparently, human beings have short memories.

My beliefs are shaken, and I feel ashamed for humanity. While we are investing billions in healthcare and medical advancements, striving to develop innovative products to fight against cancer just to give cancer patients a few more months to see their loved ones, a single bomb in a war zone can tragically claim thousands of lives in an instant. Confronted with the harsh realities of death, disfigurement, hunger, and infection, survival constantly hangs by a thread for many.

It doesn't matter where you live on this planet Earth. Some are lucky to be born in a peaceful, free country, while others are just unlucky and have to endure war, injustice, pain, and suffering. Around the world, the cycle of brutality and cruelty persists despite our technological advancements, access to knowledge, and infinite data. We still continue to prioritize weapons, building nuclear arms, and allocating huge amounts of money to destroying the world instead of investing in education and the well-being of future generations.

I hope that one day we will stop fighting and start building, creating, and educating the new generation. Teaching them to create and not to destroy, to love and not to hate. Reflecting on the struggles and resilience of women worldwide, we must continue to advocate for freedom and equality.

Let us remember Malala Yousafzai's words: "One child, one teacher, one pen, and one book can change the world."[10] Together, we can build a future where every voice is heard and every life is valued.

Despite ongoing challenges, the achievements of Iranian women in recent years have been impressive. Notably, two Iranian-born astronauts are women: Anousheh Ansari, the first space tourist in 2006, and Jasmin Moghbeli, the SpaceX commander who conducted the mission aboard the International Space Station from September 2023 to March 2024.

Moreover, two Nobel Peace Prize winners of Iranian origin are women: Narges Mohammadi in 2023 (still in detention) and Shirin Ebadi in 2003. Additionally, Maryam Mirzakhani, an Iranian woman, was recognized as the best mathematician in the world and was the first female recipient of the most prestigious award in mathematics, the Fields Medal, in 2014. She progressed from Sharif University to earning a PhD at Harvard, lecturing at Princeton, and becoming a professor of mathematics at Stanford University.

Unfortunately, Maryam died of breast cancer at the age of forty in 2017. These accomplishments highlight the resilience and deter-

---

10 ThatOneRule, "Malala Quotes," December 9, 2023, https://thatonerule.com/rule/malala-quotes/.

mination of Iranian women, continuing the legacy of their ancient predecessors in striving for equality and recognition.

As we look back on our journey, from the tumultuous times in Iran to our new lives abroad, it becomes clear that the past, with all its hardships and triumphs, has irrevocably shaped our present and will continue to influence our future. Our memories of Iran are a mosaic of beauty, suffering, love, and hope, reminding us of the strength of the human spirit and the perpetual quest for a better tomorrow.

CHAPTER 18

The Final Chapter

> **You can't wait until life isn't hard anymore before you decide to be happy.**
>
> —Jane Marczewski (Nightbirde)

Within the pages of this book lies the narrative of my life, each chapter a stepping stone on a path that has led me to this moment: a journey of resilience toward progress and hope.

Hope acts as our compass, urging us toward growth and offering light in times of darkness. It kindles a flame within us, illuminating the path through life's complexities, which often yields clarity with the passage of time. In life's journey, we navigate depths, confront challenges, and scale summits symbolic of overcoming the improbable and arriving on the edge of new eras. I have faced the impossible, battled the improbable, and contemplated the unimaginable to reach this point.

Throughout my career, marked by risks and discoveries, I have gleaned profound insights into the spirits of cancer patients. I have learned that in the fight against cancer, we must aim high and strive for a cure as long as the body permits. A 2 percent chance is not a 0 percent chance.

However, my personal encounter with cancer, coupled with caring for my father in his final battle with the disease, underscored the importance of addressing fundamental needs first. While advancements in anti-cancer drugs are crucial, it is imperative to consider the holistic prognosis, encompassing access to diagnostic imaging, safe and patient-friendly surgical care, and the management of cancer-related complications, such as infections. Infections pose immediate risks and severe consequences, highlighting the need for comprehensive care beyond treatment.

Bob started to invest in Summit Therapeutics in 2019, and he became chairman and CEO. I joined the company in November 2020 after recovering from my own cancer. The company was an anti-infective company and had an antibiotic drug candidate for the treatment of *Clostridium difficile*, a bacterium that causes an infection of the colon, often after using antibiotics.

After many months of intense observation that shed light on the important yet under-acknowledged role the microbiome plays in sustained recovery from infections treated with antibiotics, we decided to pivot Summit's attention to patient- and physician-friendly oncology therapy.

Standing atop the metaphorical summit of our company in Sand Hill, Atherton, California, felt akin to reaching the pinnacle of Everest: our "Summit." The groundbreaking achievements of Summit Therapeutics, particularly the preliminary results of our cancer drug in clinical trials of lung cancer announced on the evening of the American Society of Clinical Oncology (ASCO) annual meeting in 2024, filled me with professional pride.

At our annual congress, ASCO 2024, we announced our Chinese phase 3 clinical trial results (conducted in China, sponsored by our partner Akeso, Inc., with data generated and analyzed by Akeso). It was with immense pride that we announced in front of this assembly of researchers, doctors, and families that our efforts had borne fruit.

We continue to develop a treatment that promises to change the game and restore hope of betterment to so many cancer patients around the world. Through our determination, perseverance, and hard work, we aim to turn hope into reality. Our goal is to be able to provide families with access to more patient-friendly treatment for their loved ones affected by cancer.

This milestone, not driven by financial gains but by the acknowledgment of our contributions to medical science, felt like a triumph over time itself. As a cancer survivor, this moment represented defiance against the constraints of mortality, offering hope to millions grappling with pulmonary metastases and striving to extend their time with their loved ones while enhancing their quality of life.

Innovation comes at a cost, and the pursuit of safer and more effective treatments than just chemotherapy is paramount for cancer patients seeking longevity and improved quality of life. Every month holds significance for those battling cancer, propelling our mission forward. Bob (chairman and co-CEO) and I (president and co-CEO) have invested in Summit Therapeutics to provide optimal therapy for our patients. While the cost of treatment may decrease over time, it is imperative to invest in reshaping the current treatment landscape for improved outcomes and, ultimately, the quest for a cure.

From 2022 to 2024, I achieved significant milestones in my career. I was appointed as the president and CEO of Summit Therapeutics and received numerous awards and honors. In 2022, I was featured in the article "CEO Appointments: 21 Women Who Became

CEOs in 2022," published in *Business Chief Leadership and Strategy* in August 2022.[11] The article highlighted the fact that women make up only 15 percent of chief executives in Fortune 500 companies, and globally, only 5 percent of CEOs are female.[12]

In the month of this writing, October 2024, I am happy to be able to live in the magic of normal again, and to be fully engaged and professionally involved in the fight against cancer that has profoundly disrupted so many lives.

Wherever Dady is, he must be proud of us. He must be smiling at all that we have accomplished. It is him I think of in this moment of triumph. His wisdom, courage, and love have always been a source of inspiration for me. I feel his presence and his unwavering support.

Looking up to the sky one last time, I whisper a silent "thank you." We will keep moving forward, innovating, and fighting for a better world. Dady, thanks to you, you have taught us by example to never give up, to believe in our dreams, and to work tirelessly to make them come true.

I could not conclude this moment without expressing my deep gratitude to those who have been by my side throughout this journey. Mom and Dad, your love and support have been unwavering pillars. My son Shaun, your patience, understanding, and inspiration have given me the strength to carry on, even in the toughest times. My sister Mahshad, for your unconditional support. Your faith in me and determination have been a guiding light in the darkest nights.

Bob, we were like two halves of a whole in our business endeavors. We formed a magical team, a branded entity known as "Maky & Bob."

11 Kate Birch, "CEO appointments - 21 women who made CEO in 2022," Business-Chief, August 15, 2022, https://businesschief.com/leadership-and-strategy/ceo-appointments-21-women-who-made-ceo-in-july-2022.

12 Ibid.

Whenever we joined forces, people witnessed something extraordinary, and they often remarked that magic unfolded in our presence.

And to all those who did not abandon ship during all the storms, who fought in their own way, whether near or far, but always by my side, I thank you with all of my heart and soul. Your commitment, dedication, and professionalism have been essential to our success.

This victory is also dedicated to all those who have fought, and continue to fight, against cancer. Your courage and resilience are an inspiration to us all. This victory is as much yours as it is ours.

I look toward the future with a heart filled with gratitude and determination. We have shown the world that with faith, perseverance, and teamwork, anything is possible. And this is just the beginning of our journey.

The words of Victor Hugo and Stephen Hawking have always resonated with me:

> **The tragedy of life lies not in death but in failing to truly live.**
> —Victor Hugo

> **Nothing is eternal.**
> —Stephen Hawking

Yet within our finite existence lies the potential for infinite impact—a testament to the enduring power of Life and Love.

CHAPTER 19

A Letter from Bob Duggan

> **If you look at the lives of the world's greatest geniuses—like Edison, Socrates, Da Vinci, Shakespeare, Einstein—you discover they all had 24 personality characteristics in common. These are traits that anyone can develop. It makes no difference how old you are, how much education you have, or what you have accomplished to date. Adopting these personality characteristics enables you to operate on a genius level.**
>
> —Dr. Alfred Barrios

It makes me smile when I look at my own story. I have been to so many different places and met so many different people. There were those who taught me well, stood with me, and helped me advance to where I am today. I can never thank these people enough. Bob Duggan is one of these incredible people who inspires me every day to spread my wings even further to reach new heights in this marvelous game we call life.

Bob has an innate knack for envisioning and developing a better future. He has been my business partner in many unprecedented successes. We continue to work together to this day, searching for ways to enhance what Bob refers to as "the betterment of mankind."

Bob is quite a writer, and he recently wrote a letter for me that I know I will keep forever. Here is what he wrote:

Twenty years ago, Maky made (she would say I took) a decision. She was leaving aesthetic dentistry and pediatric dentistry and joining Computer Motion, the world's first surgical robotics company. We had a small office in Strasbourg, France. That day in November of 1997, and that decision was heaven sent. It was one of those rare miraculous right places, right time, right person … right everything … moments.

Well, by the time you are reading what Bob Duggan thinks about Maky as an executive you are well into her life's story and the "busyness" of business is but one chapter, albeit an important chapter in Maky's amazing biography.

It is true that people who quickly rise up in the ranks of business executives see the road ahead, know what role they want to play, and attain that role by assuming responsibility for achieving the desired objectives that future job requires, day in and day out.

The word executive is derived from the word "executor" which means "an individual who gets intended things done or produced." Business organizations seek affluence and prosperity for all involved. Their ultimate success depends utterly upon getting things done! That is what executives do, it is why they are necessary.

Not only did Maky assume responsibility for her assigned task, and those to follow, but soon she was supporting and assisting her teammates near and far, ensuring that others were producing what they were supposed to produce on time, with quality and on budget.

Over a short period of time, Maky earned the leadership position across all of Europe. Emphasis on "earned." Quickly the local team and fast thereafter the entire Euro team could see she was leading the way in getting the job done. Team morale rose to greater and greater heights as objectives and key results were achieved. She loved her team and her team loved her. Let's say Maky duplicated Computer Motions vision, organized her troops and did whatever it took to get the job done.

Now moving on to Maky's second business venture. Pharmacyclics was all Maky!

She picked the company, she evaluated the company, she studied the road ahead, she called out what was needed, and she pursued its success relentlessly. Maky is not a one-woman band. But she does strive to outwork and out-produce everyone else. She would never advertise this nor is it her objective to prove it, but it is her nature, and others follow her lead because they admire her style, appreciate her inclusiveness, and like Maky others enjoy the sweetness and happiness of success. Maky is both quick to validate and fast to get teams back on track if focus is missing or results sputter.

Leading by example and always ready to be of service to others, Maky's teams become willing to join her in doing what it takes to achieve big picture success. Maky is purpose-driven. Making a significant difference for the betterment of life is foremost in her mind's eye. All great leaders share an urge to be of service to others and make a lasting difference for the betterment of life. Maky's willingness to serve others and her absolute confidence in the fact that "take responsibility and the ability will follow" amplifies her innate, inborn, inherent genius power. The essence of Maky's leadership success is caring about what goes on.

In summary when Maky assumes responsibility for accomplishing a purpose she brings intensity and clarity which is unmistakable. She does not lack courage. The courage needed to get things started, to get things done.

The respect Maky has earned exists far and wide. It exists in recognition of her inspiration, purpose, and competence.

Finding or coming upon a better business associate, a better and more loyal friend in life, a better soulmate, would be impossible to do.

—Bob

Bob is an American decabillionaire and currently the world's wealthiest biotech executive, entrepreneur, philanthropist, educator, and human rights activist. He has received numerous awards and acknowledgments for his work in the fields of technology, entrepreneurship, philanthropy, and activism.

His numerous awards and acknowledgments include

- Congressional Medal of Merit from US Senator Ron Paul,
- Knight of the Legion of Honor in France by President Jacques Chirac,
- Key to the City of Shanghai, China,
- 2016 Venky Narayanamurti Entrepreneurial Leadership Award from the University of California, Santa Barbara (UCSB), College of Engineering, and
- 2024 Santa Barbara Medal of Honor—the highest award given at the UCSB.

Bob's entrepreneurial journey began with Sunset Designs, a company that supplied Jiffy Stitchery kits. It achieved significant success before being sold to the Reckitt & Colman group. Bob later ventured into the food industry with Paradise Bakery & Café, known for its "Chocolate Chip Chipper" recipe. Paradise Bakery distributed cookies to major corporations, such as McDonald's, Kentucky Fried Chicken, and Disney World. The bakery was acquired by Chart House in 1987 and is now owned by Panera Bread.

Bob went on to found Communication Machinery Corp. (CMC) and Government Technology Services, Inc. (GTSI), both pioneering companies in their respective fields. CMC was the third company in the world to create and sell Ethernet node processors, a computer networking technology utilized for establishing local area networks and providing a gateway to the internet. The corporation was sold to Rockwell International.

In the 1980s, Bob founded GTSI and sold new computer technologies and services, primarily to government agencies. GTSI was an early pioneer in the new field that would become e-commerce. In 1996, GTSI was the largest reseller of microcomputer software and Unix hardware to the US government. It was ultimately acquired by UNICOM Global.

In the mid-1990s, Bob co-founded Metropolis Media with his son Demian. It was an organization with the purpose of helping former communist countries transition to free-market societies and enable consumer advertising. Metropolis Media is now owned by French advertising giant JCDecaux Group.

Bob was a founding shareholder of Computer Motion, a leader in patient- and physician-friendly surgical robotics, in 1990. He served as the company's chairman and CEO from 1997 to 2003. In 2003, the company was acquired by Intuitive Surgical, Inc. in exchange for 33 percent interest in Intuitive Surgical. In 2004, Bob invested in Pharmacyclics, Inc. to focus on patient-friendly oncology therapy. He assumed the roles of CEO and chairman of the board from 2008 to 2015. Pharmacyclics was acquired by AbbVie for $21 billion in 2015.

For the past fifteen years, Bob has dedicated his life to spreading the insights from Dr. Alfred Barrios's 1980 article in the *National Enquirer* magazine about the twenty-four characteristics geniuses have in common.[13]

Bob firmly believes, as Dr. Barrios asserted, that these traits are inborn and innate in every individual and that everyone has the potential to unlock their true genius. His mission is to expand the understanding and application of these characteristics worldwide.

After years of research to understand the etymology of the word *genius* and the common traits shared by geniuses, Bob founded his company Genius, Inc. This company is his legacy, aimed at helping people to become aware of, understand, and apply their innate, inborn abilities to become geniuses.

In one of his notes on the subject, Bob questions the meaning of genius and emphasizes that everyone is born with the seed of genius potential within them.

> *What is genius? What exactly does it mean to be a genius? Frankly, I have never encountered a single individual who has not heard of the word genius. Better yet, no one is allergic to the word, and even further, very few people realize their full genius potential.*
>
> *So, what is genius? Is it a beautiful voice only gifted to a few, while the rest of us struggle to even hum a song? Is it the brush-stroke of Van Gogh or da Vinci, while the rest of us fumble to even draw a stick figure? Is genius really restricted to a very few people who, through some quirk of genetic programming or*

13 "The 24 Characteristics that Geniuses Have in Common," Delphine Ryan, September 23, 2024, https://www.delphineryan.co.uk/the-24-characteristics-of-a-genius.

> *twist of DNA, come up with incredibly clever ideas or develop brilliant theories and bring them into existence? Or is genius a gift from God, untaught and unexplained, as it is to most of us?*

Bob explains that the word *genius* comprises the prefix *gen-*, meaning "to bring into existence, to create effects, or to make happen," and the suffix *-ius*, which means "that which contains."

> *As we are all born with the potential capability of being a genius, then why do so few of us manifest this quality in daily living? Good question! Consider a comparison: we are all born with a set of functioning muscles, and yet not all of us, or even most of us, in fact, very few of us become great athletes, champion boxers, amazing dancers, or singers. Being unaware of our potential is a factor. The rigor of training is another factor, omitted understanding of the basic traits and characteristics that really hold us back from operating on a genius level. We simply don't believe it.*

> *Trained muscles develop invariably well; untrained muscles tend to waste away over time. It is the same with genius. These are traits that anyone can develop. It makes no difference how old you are, how much education you have, or what you have accomplished. Adopting these personality characteristics enables you to operate on a genius level. You do not have to take the word of Dr. Barrios or anyone else. Simply with interest and intention to uncover what is true for you, read over the twenty-four characteristics, select one you like, learn, and decide for yourself if there is truth in this.*

Bob encourages individuals to explore these characteristics, learn from them, and decide for themselves whether they hold the key to unlocking their true genius.

In his commencement speech at UCSB for the graduating math and science class of 2024, he explained these twenty-four characteristics and how the graduates could use them in their daily lives. This message is for anyone who wants to succeed, achieve their goals, follow their passion and purpose in life, and strive to be a genius.

> *It's an honor and privilege to be standing before this extraordinary class. I would like to begin by saying that it's also been an honor and a privilege to know Chancellor Yang for the last 30 years. He has been a mentor, a leader and inspirer throughout the entire UC system. The UC system has never had, nor ever will have, a better Chancellor than Henry with his great wife Dilling to lead this group and treat you as family and have you become a member of the Gaucho family of UC Santa Barbara; Henry we thank you.*
>
> *UCSB, to me not only means University of California, Santa Barbara, it also means "You Can Survive Better."*
>
> *Now, each of you standing on the threshold of a new era … commencement is not only a celebration of what you've accomplished, but the beginning of a new era. It's a bi-specific word.*
>
> *All of us in attendance urge you to embrace your dynamic power of curiosity, your willingness to take chances and to use your elastic energy which has no boundaries to propel you forward in life, a successful life it will be. You have drawn upon your inherent courage in the face of formidable challenges, and your ability to learn from your mistakes has set each of you apart. Always keep in mind, that is your innate drive, your inborn courage, your inherent imagination that will shape and create the effects you desire to bring into existence.*

As you navigate the uncertainty of the future, do so with a sense of adventure and spirit of exploration. Know that what you do counts. Life needs your help, your cooperation, and your love. Take risks. Push the boundaries and dare to dream big in support of the betterment of the human species. Strive to improve the conditions of life whenever and wherever possible. Learn from your experiences as well as the experience of others and let them guide you towards a future filled with endless constructive possibilities.

As you embark on this new chapter, always keep in the forefront of your mind that you possess the potential power to create your own destiny as well as contributing to the positive survival of humankind. Let your curiosity and love for your fellow humans inspire you. Allow your imagination and idealism to drive you towards greatness in ways both small and large. Life needs your help and participation. What you do counts; it counts a lot.

To you the extraordinary, extra-ordinary class of 2024, the world awaits your unique talents, your bold ideas and unwavering determination to live life; life up into a superior condition.

Go forward, conquer all obstacles. The future is yours to bring about; to bring into existence. Always be a proud Gaucho.

Bob continued to mention that these are the twenty-four characteristics that Dr. Barrios listed that, if observed, studied, and practiced, will enable anyone to come up with, develop, and effectively operate new and fruitful ideas.[14]

---

14 "The 24 Characteristics that Geniuses Have in Common," Delphine Ryan, https://www.delphineryan.co.uk/the-24-characteristics-of-a-genius.

The Twenty-Four Characteristics Geniuses Have in Common

> **If you look at the lives of the world's greatest geniuses, you discover they all had 24 personality traits in common. These are traits that anyone can develop. It makes no difference how old you are, how much education you have, or what you have accomplished to date. Adopting these personality characteristics enables you to operate on a genius level.**
>
> —Dr. Alfred Barrios

1 - DRIVE

Geniuses have a strong desire to work hard and long. They're willing to give all they've got to a project. Develop your drive by focusing on your future success and keep going.

2 - COURAGE

It takes courage to do things others consider impossible. Stop worrying what people will think if you are different.

3 - DEVOTION TO GOALS

Geniuses know what they want and go after it. Get control of your life and schedule. Have something specific to accomplish each day.

4 - KNOWLEDGE

Geniuses continually accumulate information. Never go to sleep at night without having learned at least one new thing that day. Read. And question people who know.

5 - HONESTY

Geniuses are frank, forthright, and honest. Take the responsibility for things that go wrong. Be willing to admit, "I goofed," and learn from your mistakes.

6 - OPTIMISM

Geniuses never doubt they will succeed. Deliberately focus your mind on something good coming up.

7 - ABILITY TO JUDGE

Try to understand the facts of a situation before you judge. Evaluate things on an open-minded, unprejudiced basis and be willing to change your mind.

8 - ENTHUSIASM

Geniuses are so excited about what they are doing, it encourages others to cooperate with them. Really believe that things will turn out well. Don't hold back.

9 - WILLINGNESS TO TAKE CHANCES

Overcome your fear of failure. You won't be afraid to take chances once you realize you can learn from your mistakes.

10 – DYNAMIC ENERGY

Don't sit on your butt waiting for something good to happen. Be determined to make it happen.

11 – ENTERPRISE

Geniuses are opportunity seekers. Be willing to take on jobs others won't touch. Never be afraid to try the unknown.

12 – PERSUASION

Geniuses know how to motivate people to help them get ahead. You'll find it easy to be persuasive if you believe in what you're doing.

13 – OUTGOINGNESS

I've found geniuses able to make friends easily and be easy on their friends. Be a "booster," not someone who puts others down. That attitude will win you many valuable friends.

14 – ABILITY TO COMMUNICATE

Geniuses are able to effectively get their ideas across to others. Take every opportunity to explain your ideas to others.

15 – PATIENCE

Be patient with others most of the time, but always be impatient with yourself. Expect far more of yourself than of others.

16 – PERCEPTION

Geniuses have their mental radar working full time. Think more of others' needs and wants than you do of your own.

17 - PERFECTIONISM

Geniuses cannot tolerate mediocrity, particularly in themselves. Never be easily satisfied with yourself. Always strive to do better.

18 - SENSE OF HUMOR

Be willing to laugh at your own expense. Don't take offense when the joke is on you.

19 - VERSATILITY

The more things you learn to accomplish, the more confidence you will develop. Don't shy away from new endeavors.

20 - ADAPTABILITY

Being flexible enables you to adapt to changing circumstances readily. Resist doing things the same old way. Be willing to consider new options.

21 - CURIOSITY

An inquisitive, curious mind will help you seek out new information. Don't be afraid to admit you don't know it all. Always ask questions about things you don't understand.

22 - INDIVIDUALISM

Do things the way you think they should be done, without fearing somebody's disapproval.

23 - IDEALISM

Keep your feet on the ground—but have your head in the clouds. Strive to achieve great things, not just for yourself, but for the betterment of mankind.

24 - IMAGINATION

Geniuses know how to think in new combinations, see things from a different perspective than anyone else. Unclutter your mental environment to develop this type of imagination. Give yourself time each day to daydream, to fantasize, to drift into a dreamy inner life the way you did as a child.

Reflecting on my journey, I realize how fortunate I have been to encounter mentors and partners like Bob, who have inspired me to push beyond my unwitting, self-imposed limits. My experiences have taught me that success is not just about personal achievements but about how we align with others in pursuit of high purpose, benefiting all of mankind. The values of responsibility, perseverance, and a relentless pursuit of excellence have been my guiding principles, enabling me to navigate through diverse challenges and triumphs.

As I continue to strive for the betterment of life and the advancement of humanity, I am reminded that the true measure of success lies in the positive impact we leave behind and the legacy of inspiration and dedication we create for future generations.

CHAPTER 20

A Deeper Dive into Pharmacyclics

> **For as long as we are on this Earth, there will always be new adventures to take, new mountains to climb, and new experiences to learn from. The goals we set and the success we achieve are all means by which we do. What matters along the way is that we pause every now and then to take stock of what we have accomplished and who we are before we set off on our next exciting journey … a journey of a thousand miles must begin with a single step.**
>
> —Lao Tzu

I have written this chapter for those of you who are interested in diving deeper into the story of Pharmacyclics. I will share more of the facts, figures, and business details that will help you understand more about how we went from a failing start-up to a historical success. And I will not only take you through it step by step, but I will also share what I have learned along the way. Finally,

I will offer you some of my personal advice, guidance, and ideas for running a successful business.

I hope to inspire you to follow your dreams and maybe even help discover and bring to market yet another miracle drug that can save lives. Then you, too, can experience the deep emotional fulfillment of helping to bring back the magic of normal to the millions of people who have lost it.

How can you start a successful business or help a failing business survive?

Business is the process of overcoming challenges on the pathway toward progress, and that is what makes business exciting, interesting, and rewarding. Starting a new company or trying to turn around a failed company is a big challenge. As with any start-up, there is something metaphysical about taking a concept, turning it into reality, and creating a great new enterprise.

The huge challenge you will face is selling a new capability, gaining credibility, and building a substantial user/customer base. You must have the willingness to run a marathon. You need to always remember to focus on whether or not your company can stay in the race because you will likely have only one chance to create a world-class business.

Globalization is always a challenge. You are dealing with different languages and different cultures, as well as different laws in every country. As the company becomes more global, more people of diverse nationalities will join the company. This means you have to become more flexible. You have to understand the diversity of lifestyles each employee is experiencing. You have to understand the differences in language, culture, traditions, and mentality.

In order to succeed, you have to have the ability to manage all these complexities within the organization. The key to success is to try to understand all these differences and give every employee the opportunity to integrate their own culture into the company's culture.

I have learned that the skills it takes to start a company are not the same skills it takes to keep a company going. In the beginning, we needed to inspire a small team of people to meet deadlines and deliver results. We needed to provide a lot of guidance, focus, and direction. It may have seemed to others that we were trying to retain too much control. I was constantly telling people to stop just talking about it and instead take action (i.e., start doing). My philosophy was to lead, follow, or get out of my way. I will tell you that with this as my philosophy, I may not have been everyone's best friend. However, I realized we could not move fast if we planned slow.

We needed people who were flexible, people with the ability to make a decision on the fly. We needed people who could adjust to a constantly changing situation. But I found that flexibility was not easy to teach. We could not train people to be flexible. In certain companies, it's better to have fewer people, but people with multi-functional abilities.

To build a company, you have to find great people who operate at the top of their profession and who share the same passion for building that new company. And never forget people like to have fun, so make your workplace a fun place to work. Operate with a flat organizational structure so you can build a harmonious team.

You also have to find great investors who are going to help and support you in building the company. You should look for people who are networked and will generate good ideas. Do not build a business with the aim of selling it. Build a company, and the exit will follow. Also, make certain you never run out of cash. That means you have to plan ahead and raise more capital than you need. This will help build security and the ability to stay in the game during difficult times.

You have to get in front of the customer or the end user and reply quickly to realistic business ideas. Do not ignore market shifts. The advantage of a small business lies in its ability to adapt to the needs of users ahead of its rivals. And the last and most important rule for all new business success stories is, *be transparent with all stakeholders.*

After visiting Pharmacyclics in April 2004, Bob and I invested in Pharmacyclics—the start of a new chapter in my life. From 2004 to 2008, I followed the company everywhere. I went to all the scientific and investor meetings. I went to ASCO and American Society of Hematology (ASH) conventions. These are key conferences held every year, where scientists and companies from around the world come together to present the latest research and clinical trials of potential oncology therapies. Wherever Pharmacyclics presented, I was there. I met the principal investigator of Pharmacyclics's clinical trials, Dr. Minesh Mehta, who later became a board member at Pharmacyclics. Dr. Mehta is a radio-oncologist and an incredible person. He is also a very calm and peaceful man.

In June 2004, at the ASCO meeting, Pharmacyclics gave some presentations and announced some phase 3 trial results. The results were not as positive as expected. After the presentation, the stock price dropped to nine dollars a share. And from that time until 2008, Pharmacyclics stock went into a failing mode. So, in April 2006, Pharmacyclics decided to increase its portfolio of potential drug candidates and acquired multiple small molecules—a histone deacetylase (HDAC) inhibitor, a factor VIIa inhibitor, and a Bruton's tyrosine kinase (BTK) inhibitor—for the treatment of cancer and other diseases from Celera Genomics.

At that time, HDAC inhibitors were a very popular new class of drugs in the field of oncology. Everybody was talking about the potential of HDAC inhibitors, but no one seemed to know about

BTK inhibitors. If you were to look at the contract between Celera Genomics and Pharmacyclics, you would have seen that the focus of the agreement was on HDAC inhibitors and not BTK inhibitors. I give the previous management of Pharmacyclics credit for purchasing these potential drug candidates from Celera Genomics.

During the three years from 2004 to 2007, following the presentation at ASCO, the stock price of Pharmacyclics continued to drop, but Bob Duggan kept increasing his ownership during that time. He even joined the board of Pharmacyclics in September 2007.

In April 2007, Richard Miller, the CEO of Pharmacyclics at the time, initiated a series of four opinion editorials in the *Wall Street Journal*, addressing his disagreement with current FDA policies and procedures.

Shortly thereafter, in December 2007, the FDA sent a non-approvable letter for MGd for the treatment of NSCLC with brain metastases, as the phase 3 results from the clinical trials came back negative.

During this period, from mid-2005 to July 2008, I did not see Bob at all. He had moved to Florida with his family. But we kept in communication because of our Pharmacyclics investment. Unfortunately, we were losing money on this investment. It was devastating to think I was losing all my life's investments. Also, I was not too happy to be the one who got Bob involved in this whole thing.

I continued to keep my eye on Pharmacyclics, and from 2007 to early 2008, I spent a lot of my time learning more about BTK and HDAC inhibitors. The more knowledge I gained, the more potential I was able to see in these inhibitors. Around this time, I went back to Pharmacyclics to meet the scientists from Celera Genomics who joined Pharmacyclics in 2006. These three molecules were the only chance the company had to survive after the failure of the main molecule, MGd. After a lot of discussion with Bob and doing a lot of research to better understand the value of these potential drug candidates, around May 2008, Bob participated in a tender offer and purchased up to $4 million shares of Pharmacyclics stock at $1.05.

Finally, after three years, in August 2008, Bob and I met again in person. I felt it was time for me to take some responsibility for this investment. Bob and I went to Sunnyvale and met with Richard. I wanted to help the company succeed, so I asked for any position in the company, no matter the title, salary, or options. Richard offered me the position of vice president of business development, starting the last week of August 2008.

I was now an employee of Pharmacyclics, which is located in Silicon Valley. Silicon Valley is located south of San Francisco. This famous location is between San Francisco Bay and the hills. There are four thousand high-tech companies and approximately three hundred biotech companies in Silicon Valley. The valley was previously a farm area known as the Valley of Heart's Delight. Silicon Valley culture is the most conducive to entrepreneurialism, if you define that as the creation of new products for new markets in a risk-taking but ultimately rewarding way.

The Bay Area has always been a home for pioneers. Stanford University has played a large role in forming the entrepreneurial and scientific culture of Silicon Valley. The university was founded by Leland Stanford, who came out west after the gold rush and made his fortune building railroads. He bought an eight-thousand-acre farm, now known as Palo Alto or Tall Stick, named after a tall tree alongside the railroad tracks just across the street from the Stanford Shopping Center. Later, when the university faced some financial problems, a Stanford electrical engineering professor came up with the idea of leasing some of the property.

And that was exactly how things had worked with many high-tech companies for ninety-nine years. These companies were formed and settled in Silicon Valley, and an entire culture was born. Students began starting their own companies locally rather than returning east. And so the world experienced a series of inventions and innovations all coming from Silicon Valley. These included the semiconductor in 1947, the integrated circuit at Fairchild in 1958, and the first microprocessor in 1971.

The computer revolution was underway. Silicon Valley became a magnet for optimistic young entrepreneurs with innovative ideas. It became the home of today's billion- and trillion-dollar US companies, like Google, Apple, Facebook, and eBay.

Yet I was still living in Los Angeles. I began going back and forth between Sunnyvale and Santa Monica. As the head of business development, I participated in many meetings that Pharmacyclics arranged with some of the big pharmaceutical companies. Pharmacyclics was trying to negotiate several research agreements for BTK in autoimmune diseases. But at that time, none of these companies were interested. Pharmacyclics's BTK inhibitor was a covalent drug, and Big Pharma was not interested in covalent inhibitors[15] at that time.

So I spoke with Bob, who was a board member. And after several discussions about Pharmacyclics, we decided to help the company

15 Covalent inhibitors are small-molecule ligands designed to covalently modify and inhibit the function of specific protein targets. They can be reversible or irreversible, but many are irreversible, so the effect (inhibition) is permanent until the modified protein degrades in the cells. The advantage of a covalent inhibitor is once it finds its target and modifies its target, the effect is sustained, and therefore long exposure (PK) of these inhibitors is not necessary, significantly cutting down the need for continued exposure and having nonspecific effects on other normal tissues or targets. Before ibrutinib's success in B-cell lymphoma patients, most companies were not interested in developing covalent irreversible inhibitors from fear of toxicity of nonspecific covalent modified proteins. (However, most targeted covalent inhibitors use weakly reactive warheads that do not generate strong immunogenic responses.) Today, close to sixty covalent drugs are approved, mainly in cancer and anti-infectives.

in any way, shape, or form we could. In my opinion, Pharmacyclics could benefit from a fresh infusion of life and energy.

It was time to contact some colleagues and see if they would be willing to help us. Time was of the essence.

I met Dr. Cynthia Bamdad, CEO of Minerva Biotechnology, for the first time in June 2008, before starting at Pharmacyclics. She presented her company to me to see whether Duggan & Associates would be interested in investing. At that time, however, we were not interested. Through Dr. Bamdad, I met Dr. Glenn Rice, who was working as an adviser in her company. Dr. Bamdad and Dr. Rice were people who came into our lives at just the right time. Both were science-driven people with a good understanding of the biotech world. In addition to Dr. Bamdad and Dr. Rice, we also spoke with Dr. Mehta and Dr. David Smith. All these people were interested in working with us and willing to help us out at Pharmacyclics if we needed it.

About a month after I started working at the company, around September 10, 2008, Bob got a call from Richard saying that he and three other Pharmacyclics board members had resigned. Richard had voluntarily resigned as CEO and chairman of the board, and Liev Levy had resigned as chief financial officer (CFO). The remaining board members were Bob and James Knighton.

So the next day, on September 11, 2008, Bob flew in from Florida, I flew in from Los Angeles, and Ramses Erdtmann, an associate of Bob at the Duggan Investment Company, joined us from Berkeley. That was definitely a day I will never forget. I was actually very sick that day. I had a very bad case of the flu that had turned into pneumonia and ethmoiditis. I had received an injection of antibiotics, and normally, I would not have had the authorization to fly. I was told to stay home and rest. But that day, I got up in the morning and took the first flight to Sunnyvale. Looking back, the meeting that took place that morning marked the beginning of a life-changing adventure.

From that day on, we had just one mission: to make it go right. There was no time to waste. It was now or never. Failure was not an option. The clock was ticking, and we only had so much time to secure the jobs and people we needed for the company to survive.

On that day, Bob told all the employees at the company meeting, "We are here today as scientists, medical practitioners, innovators, early adopters, and entrepreneurs to play out our destiny of creating change. Change for the betterment of mankind." He set the tone of who we were and what we wanted to achieve.

By the end of September, I decided I was going to live in Sunnyvale temporarily. Bob, who was now the interim CEO, came to Sunnyvale from Florida, as he had also decided it made sense to live there temporarily.

On top of all the changes that were going on at Pharmacyclics, the market was crashing, and people were being laid off left and right. With unemployment soaring toward twenty-five-year highs, housing prices plummeting, and the nation's biggest banks facing insolvency, it was difficult not to wonder: Could any business facing cash issues survive? It was a no man's land. No money was being invested in companies. There were no IPOs, nothing.

A few months after we took over the company, the stock had dropped to $0.67 a share. That showed the lack of confidence the market had in us when we took over the company. There we were, two people with a background in the medical device field. Neither of us had ever run a biotech/oncology company. In December 2008, the company had a valuation of approximately $20 million. Bob had lent the company $6 million so we could end the year with $12.9

million in cash. He told us he never wanted to see the company with less than $10 million in cash.

The initial task was to assess the risks, assets, liabilities, challenges, and opportunities facing the company while a financial crisis of global proportions was occurring. There was so much uncertainty around any business at that time.

The employees of Pharmacyclics consisted mostly of a research team and a manufacturing group. Dr. Greg Hemmi was a veteran of the company. He had started with the company in 1992, spending years at Pharmacyclics before any of us even started working there. He was the head of the manufacturing department. Greg became a true partner and friend who welcomed us from the first day we stepped in. I will never be able to thank him enough for all those years of support.

Once we got to the company, we decided to look at each molecule in detail and see what we could do with each one of them based on the information we had on hand at that time.

The first compound we started to assess was our lead compound, MGd. This compound was reviewed by several different people in the company, and after months of looking at the data, we concluded that we had to stop the development of MGd. The mechanism of action was not clear, and the patient data was very confusing. We finally announced that we would stop all development activities of MGd. It was a very important announcement. Bob and I invested in this company because of MGd in 2004, and in 2008, we chose to announce the discontinuation of this drug. After that, we decided to evaluate our Factor VIIa inhibitor.

In October 2008, we were considering developing this drug for pancreatic cancer. Pancreatic cancer is a graveyard for all drugs. It is hard to find a cure or even a drug that can help these patients survive. We spent weeks evaluating and talking to key opinion leaders, specifically Dr. Daniel Von Hoff, a well-known oncologist and professor of medicine in Arizona who specializes in the field of pancreatic cancer. Based on discussions, evaluations, and the mechanism of action of this drug, we decided to move forward and start a phase 1 trial for pancreatic cancer.

But the biggest challenge for this specific drug was the eighteen steps it took to manufacture it. It would cost us $800,000 to make the drug for just a phase 1 clinical study. We asked our chief scientific officer to start the discussion with our manufacturing department and work with our chief medical officer for the phase 1 clinical program.

For some reason, which is hard to understand, the team did not follow the instructions they were given. The delay in the trial hurt us later on when the standard of care changed and the new drug was approved. We would need to start our clinical trial over and compare it to the new standard of care. Restarting all development again based on a new standard of care would have cost us a lot of money and time. Consequently, we decided to stop the development of Factor VII inhibitors for pancreatic cancer at that time.

The HDAC inhibitor was the only drug that had some advanced data, and we decided to go back to a French pharmaceutical company called Les Laboratoires Servier, which had shown some interest in the molecule a few months before we took over the management of the company. I went to Paris to see whether we could work with them and license the drug to them. The financial markets were down, no one was really investing, and the market had no confidence in our ability to lead a pharmaceutical company. On top of that, Pharmacyclics needed more money. It was important to do a deal, gain credibility in the industry, and do it quickly. And this compound was our best chance to do this.

From October until December 2008, I spent a lot of time going back and forth between San Francisco and Paris. Most of this time was spent negotiating with Servier. Finally, we signed a licensing agreement for $40 million, including $15 million up front and a research milestone. It was actually a very low-dollar-value transaction, but at that time, it was a good transaction for Pharmacyclics. We licensed only the ex-US rights, and we kept all the rights to the compound in the US. On top of that, the deal allowed us to gain a lot of credibility and provided $15 million in cash.

In 2008, no one was really able to raise money in biotech or form any partnerships with pharma companies. Looking back, I give a lot of credit to Dr. Borfiga, head of the Servier business development team, who was open-minded enough to get us rolling and helped us close the deal on April 17, 2009.

Parallel to working on our partnership for our HDAC inhibitor, we were treating eight dogs that had lymphoma with our BTK inhibitor (PC1-32765). We announced the data from this study at the ASH meeting in December 2008. The data showed that these dogs had an immediate response to ibrutinib (PCI-32765). This proved to be very important for us. The challenge with this drug, however, was that it was a covalent drug, and at that time, there was no confidence in the scientific and medical communities that a covalent compound could be a safe and effective drug.

At ASH 2008, we held an advisory meeting, and we invited a few key opinion leaders in the field of hemato-oncology to participate. One of the renowned physicians and researchers of the National Cancer Institute and a key opinion leader in the field of hemato-oncology, especially B-cell lymphoma, was there.

After looking at our preclinical data, he stated, "Even milk can dissolve this tumor, so I don't believe you have something all that special at this time based on this small dataset."

To be honest, it was very discouraging, and I remember Bob and I looking at each other. We both had the same thought: "What if he was right?" We decided to continue with our clinical trial anyway with the hope that our drug would still be able to help our patients.

The dog data gave us the confidence to start our phase 1 trials in humans. At this point in time, we needed to know whether this drug could work not just on animals but on humans as well. There are many drugs that work on animal models but fail in humans. The cost to bring a drug through clinical trials is quite expensive and can be hundreds of millions of dollars.

We asked the team to come up with a plan that would show safety and efficacy data in a phase trial. But in standard drug development, we never talk about efficacy in phase 1. I will never forget that day we were all at an executive meeting. We requested the development of a phase 1 clinical trial with safety and efficacy data. Everybody who was in our executive session and had been in this industry a long time thought that we were just the craziest people imaginable, who understood nothing about the pharma industry. Phase 1 is all about safety. Interestingly, all the blockbuster drugs to date have demonstrated some efficacy in phase 1.

Everybody looked at us as if we were from another planet. Who knows? At that moment in time, maybe they were right. But about six months later, they changed their minds. Bob put in a condition that if we did not see any signs of efficacy, we would discontinue the study of this compound. Phase 1 was a basket study (meaning we looked at multiple types of cancers at the same time) of four different blood cancer types (follicular lymphoma [FL], diffuse large B-cell lymphoma

[DLBCL], Waldenström's macroglobulinemia [WM], and CLL). We started the study by looking at different doses (low to high) to determine what would be a safe dose for patients. The study included only a total of forty patients during the dose-escalation phase.

By the end of February 2009, less than six months after I started with the company, we made some changes at the board and management levels. Bob became the permanent CEO, and I became chief of staff and chief business officer. Dr. Mehta, Dr. Bamdad, and Dr. Smith, as well as Dr. Rice, joined the board of directors. We also suspended the clinical development program of MGd, did a private placement for $1.4 million from Pacific Biopharma Group Ltd., and initiated our first phase 1, human clinical trial with PCI-32765. We enrolled our first patient on February 12, 2009.

During that period, we decided to change our logo, our website, and the overall look of our company. I give Bob credit for selecting the logo. He always liked the round shape of the logo with an arrow. He defined the meaning behind it as "energy with impact."

I started to work with one of our previous colleagues from Computer Motion on our new website. It was the first time I was involved in website development, and I was not willing to spend too much money on it at that time. But the website came out really well. It showed an animation of our molecule and a picture of our drug capsule, along with a well-written description of Pharmacyclics and the activities that were going on in the company.

In late April 2009, we decided to raise money through a rights offering, which gave shareholders the right to purchase additional stock shares in proportion to their current stock holdings in the company. The price to participate was $1.28 per share of common stock. Three hundred and seventy-five shareholders, roughly 80 percent of our known holders, participated in the transaction. The offering was oversubscribed, and at the end of the day, we raised $28.8 million without banker participation.

Bob's friend, Jonathan Fassberg from Trout Capital, assisted us in this transaction. Bob and I were the only ones from the company who participated in the rights offering. I personally borrowed money from a bank in France, with an interest rate of 7 percent, and bought whatever number of shares I could to support the company and show my confidence in Pharmacyclics and our team. Bob also continued to invest. He never accepted a salary or options from the company and always invested his own money so that the company could stay on track.

I give Bob credit for originating, strategizing, and executing this rights offering. At that time, not only were we enrolling patients in our phase 1 study, raising money, and signing a deal with Servier, but we were also building the company infrastructure. We were trying to hire the right people to take the company forward and make sure every team member was necessary for our future success. At the same time, we were also working on updating our facilities. It was clearly 24/7 work, nonstop.

On December 7, 2009, we presented the interim results from our phase 1 clinical trial of PCI-32765 at ASH. The presenter was Dr. Ranjana Advani from Stanford. The results turned out to be spectacular. All the categories of blood cancer patients in our study had responded with either a partial response or stable disease. The data was eye-opening, and it was right then that Big Pharma began to notice Pharmacyclics.

I will never forget when we found out that Dr. Windham Wilson had treated his patient with ibrutinib and saw the results just a few months later. He called Bob and told him, "You will not believe it. This drug is amazing. It melted the tumor after a few months … The tumor was like a rock and was melted after only a few months of treatment." Later on, Dr. Wilson became a big advocate of ibrutinib/ Imbruvica and actually helped the team develop this drug.

By the end of December 2009, the company valuation had increased to $37 million ($3.14 per share). We had $30 million in cash and forty-seven employees in the company. Additionally, Wedbush Pac Growth Lifesciences had initiated the research coverage of Pharmacyclics. The analyst Greg Wade predicted that the year-end price would be $5.50 when the actual price was just $2.79 per share.

We continued to get more data from our clinical programs and presented the results at several scientific conferences. The clinical data of ibrutinib seemed too good to be true. At that point, all the Big Pharma companies started looking at our data. They were interested and began contacting us to talk about how we could collaborate with them.

Suddenly, everything was different. The tide had changed in our favor. We were no longer running after Big Pharma. They were running after us. Now, they were the ones knocking on our door. Everybody kept telling us that our product was similar to Gleevec and Rituximab, the biggest blockbuster drugs in the field of blood cancer. This was such a rewarding stage for our company. We had not even started our phase 3 trials yet, but ibrutinib (PCI-32765) was already being compared to two of the biggest blockbuster drugs out there.

At ASCO in June 2010, we made our first oral presentation on ibrutinib (PCI-32765), followed by three oral presentations at ASH in December of the same year. Over the years, the data just kept getting better and better.

In December, we reported the combined data from the phase 1A and phase 1B clinical studies in CLL and small lymphocytic lymphoma (SLL) patients. We had approximately eight months of follow-up data on the patients from the phase 1A study. One patient achieved a complete response (meaning they had no signs of cancer), and eight out of thirteen patients who were assessed had a partial response (a decrease in the extent of cancer but the cancer did not go away). Two patients had a nodal response (decrease of cancer in the nodes), and two patients had stable disease (meaning the cancer or tumor was no longer growing but also not decreasing).

In the phase 1B study with two months of follow-up, eight out of thirty-two had a partial response, and seventeen out of thirty-two had a nodal response. Six other patients had stable disease. Thus, out of the total of forty-five patients, 2 percent had a complete response, 36 percent had a partial response, and an additional 42 percent had a reduction in lymph node disease (resulting in a total reduction in nodal disease alone of 87 percent). This was a phenomenal signal of efficacy in a phase 1 study.

In June 2010, Pharmacyclics raised another $40 million. By the end of 2010, we had $62 million in cash. But to continue with the clinical trials in the next stages, we needed even more money. So after presenting the data at ASH 2010, we decided to have a discussion with some of the pharma companies. During that period, I looked at more than three hundred deal transactions. I remember that some people were skeptical and did not believe we would be able to do the job, so they tried to introduce us to an expert. To be honest, it was a joke when we saw how it was going to work. We were expected to give one of those experts a 15 percent commission from the up-front payment. That was way too much money at that moment in time, so we decided to do the work ourselves.

The most important thing that needed to be done was to write a plan describing what we wanted from the collaboration, what we would achieve as part of the deal, and how the product would be developed during the term of the partnership. The one thing that was important to us was to not dilute our company anymore. This product deserved a full clinical development program and a worldwide launch and approval. All this was quite costly.

During the December 2010 time period, a lot of companies contacted us. But to be honest, it was too late. Where were they when we really needed them? They had rejected us. They did not believe that a covalent drug could have this kind of efficacy and safety. We finally decided to begin discussions with Celgene, Novartis, GlaxoSmithKline, and Millennium Pharmaceuticals. Celgene was very successful in oncology because of its main drug, Revlimid. Novartis was the number one pharmaceutical company in the field of oncology, and GlaxoSmithKline was an interesting company that was doing a lot of licensing and M&A during that period.

We began to prepare for a transaction by putting together our slides and setting up a due diligence room. The team put together an amazing presentation of the product, pipeline, clinical data results, manufacturing, regulatory pathway, commercial pathway, and revenue potential.

The first company that we presented our product to was Celgene. We were very excited that they had shown an interest in Pharmacyclics. Their product, Revlimid, was an oral therapy drug for MM and had shown a lot of success in this field. It was important for us to work with a company that already had oral therapy for cancer patients. But shortly after our meeting with Celgene, I found out they had met with one of our competitor companies, Calistoga Pharmaceuticals.

Honestly, I did not appreciate that. And for some reason, at that moment, I found myself acting more like a child than a businesswoman. We were all disappointed that they were talking to both companies, and on top of that, the clinical plan that they presented to us was a clinical development of ibrutinib combined with their own drug, Revlimid. We felt that our product would never be a priority in their pipeline, so we finally decided to discontinue our conversations with Celgene.

Later on, by the end of February, Gilead Sciences, Inc. announced that they bought Calistoga for $375 million, with an additional $225 million if certain milestones were achieved. By that time, we had moved on and decided to begin discussions with AstraZeneca as a third company to consider as a partner. In the meantime, Johnson & Johnson also called us, but at that time, we had three other parties to talk with already, so we were not really interested in speaking with them. At that time, they were also not considered very strong in oncology, and we needed a partner with diverse expertise in oncology. Their main oncology drug, Velcade, was primarily for MM patients.

We continued our communications with GlaxoSmithKline, Novartis, and AstraZeneca. But after multiple discussions with AstraZeneca, it was clear that they felt that the field of CLL was crowded. Also, their development plan did not really match our vision and philosophy. For those reasons, we decided to discontinue our discussions with them as well. But we still wanted to keep three companies in discussion with us so that we had options, especially if one or more dropped out during the process, which had already happened twice.

I remember it was late February when I got a call from Robert Wills at Johnson & Johnson. Rob is an amazing individual and a lot of fun. He was the vice president of alliance management at Johnson & Johnson. I decided to take his call and arranged a meeting between Johnson & Johnson and Pharmacyclics (see the letter from Rob in chapter 21).

Unfortunately, the day they came to meet with us was the same day I left for France because of my son's hospitalization for GBS. I ended up being in France with Shaun until mid-April. And believe me, trying to manage everything from France was not easy for me, but it was critical for the company.

During the first three months of our discussions with these companies, we met a lot of people. They included R&D teams, discovery teams, commercial teams, and top executive management teams. Our product was in phase 2 clinical trials, but everything looked very promising, which attracted a lot of attention. I believe that was why we began to see a lot of the top executives of all these companies showing up at our meetings at that time.

We had a specific process that we went through with all the different companies; while unconventional, it proved to be very valuable. The first thing I requested was that the development team of the other company present their plan and vision for our product. It was always interesting to watch and see so many ideas, concepts, and visions for our product.

The second thing I requested was their vision for commercialization, their pricing, their revenue model, and finally their forecast. That was the best thing we did. Once I got all the development and commercial plans of ibrutinib from each company and our own team, we mapped out our final Pharmacyclics development and commercialization plan. This included phase 1, phase 2, and phase 3 studies; approval times; and a revenue model.

The last thing was the term sheet. This was the bullet-point document outlining the material terms and conditions of the agreement. We met with the CEO of GlaxoSmithKline USA, as well as the CEO of Novartis USA, and the entire top executive team of Johnson & Johnson. Later on, we went to the East Coast for meetings with them. During that time, in April 2011, Dr. Stoffels, Dr. Bill Hait, and Mr. Joaquin Duato, the top executive team of Johnson & Johnson, came to Pharmacyclics to better understand who we were and why we seemed to be so picky about everything. I remember that meeting being quite a lot of fun. I remember feeling like we had built a very nice relationship with all the top executives of Johnson & Johnson that day.

After two months of discussions with these three companies, I asked for a term sheet. They could not believe that we would ask for a term sheet after such a short period of time. The only thing we told them was that we wanted a minimum payment of $100 million up front and a total of $750 million for the licensing agreement. Do not forget that we were just a phase 2 company at that moment in time. They found all this unreal, especially since our company's total valuation at that point was less than $750 million.

Anyway, we set a deadline and asked them to send us their term sheets. Once we received the term sheets, we realized we were an ocean apart from what we wanted versus what they proposed. We called them and told them that their terms were not acceptable, and they needed to come back with a different term sheet.

In the meantime, we continued to work on our plan. It took us a month to finalize our development plan and commercial forecast. I continued to review a lot of different deals. One agreement that caught my eye was an Abbott Laboratories and Reata Pharmaceuticals agreement from September 2010. Under the terms of the agreement, Reata granted Abbott exclusive rights to develop and commercialize bardoxolone outside the US, excluding some Asian markets. They received $450 million up front and a near-term cash payment. I found that quite interesting. It was $450 million up front. How could they get that amount as an up-front payment?

We needed to plan for $150 million up front and another $200 million if we wanted to hit our clinical objectives. Also, it was very important to us that we did not dilute our company. By October 2011, we had narrowed the parties down to two. One of them was Johnson & Johnson. They had clearly shown us that they wanted to help us build Pharmacyclics while developing the drug. Their vision for the drug completely matched our vision. Another thing that was so important was we shared similar cultures. They also shared our sense of urgency to launch this product because of the efficacy and safety data, as well as the need to put this drug in the hands of patients as soon as possible. It meant so much to us that they believed in the same philosophy: "patient first."

From that moment on, we worked together to build a final clinical development plan that both companies could agree on before signing the contract, as well as the expenses attached to this clinical development plan.

To support the international expansion that we were expecting as a result of this deal, we decided to establish two international subsidiaries: one in the Cayman Islands in October 2011 and another in Switzerland in November 2011.

We were so close to signing the collaboration, but every detail counted. One day, we were in a meeting room at the Wilson Sonsini law firm. For this transaction, we worked with Ken Clark, a top lawyer at Wilson Sonsini, who was very experienced in the field of licensing and M&A. I do not know exactly how many people were in that room. I just knew there were a lot of lawyers from Johnson & Johnson and Pharmacyclics in the room, as well as some other members of both teams. Dr. Stoffels was there, as well as me and Bob.

The lawyers were going back and forth, trying to get the best deal for each respective company. The disagreement was around the cost-sharing of clinical development expenses. At that time, I remember Dr. Stoffels asking whether Bob and I could meet him outside the board room. After just a few minutes of discussion, Bob and Dr. Stoffels agreed to split the expenses. I will never forget coming back into the room and Dr. Stoffels announcing the final decision to both teams. He explained that there was no need to continue going back and forth for hours on this subject. I think you can understand why we really enjoyed working with Dr. Stoffels. He always saw the big picture.

After that meeting, Bob and I met Bill Weldon, CEO of Johnson & Johnson, and Sheryl McCoy, vice chairman, for a private dinner in San Francisco. We told Bill and Sheryl that Pharmacyclics would control the commercialization, pricing, and regulatory decisions in the US.

I will never forget that after a few moments of silence, Bill looked at us and said, "You know, Johnson & Johnson has 120,000 employees, and you have less than 100 employees. So you're telling me that you want all this control and decision-making with the limited resources that you have?"

Then Bob, with full confidence and without hesitation, said, "Yes." He continued, "We did it in robotics, and we tried to convince Johnson & Johnson to work with Computer Motion at that time. But Johnson & Johnson didn't believe in robotics then, but look at where we are today with robots in the operating room. Now we are ready to do it again."

The truth was, we were ready to face all the challenges in front of us, and we were convinced that we could make everything happen just the way it should. And to Bill's credit, he concurred that we could do it.

The funniest part was, one hour before signing the deal, we were still negotiating to add the total amount of clinical development expenses to our contract, as well as the revenue forecast. We wanted the commitment of Johnson & Johnson on clinical development expenses, and that was not insignificant. I remember I told Rob, then head of Johnson & Johnson alliances, that we were not going to sign the deal if they did not add the revenue model and the amount of expenses to our contract.

Everybody was tired. After so many months of working on this deal, all of us were more than ready to finish it. But what I told Rob triggered such a huge upset at that point that Dr. Stoffels ended up calling Bob. Bob was in the parking lot at Wilson Sonsini. I explained to Bob what I did. I was convinced that we should have all these numbers in our contract to avoid any future disagreements. Then after just a few minutes of discussion between Dr. Stoffels and Bob, Dr. Stoffels accepted our proposal, and that was the end of a few intensive months of working on this partnership.

On December 8, 2011, we entered into an agreement and signed a contract with Janssen Biotech, Inc., a subsidiary of Johnson & Johnson, to codevelop and co-commercialize ibrutinib (the generic name for Imbruvica) for oncology. Pharmacyclics would receive $975 million, inclusive of a $150-million up-front payment. In addition, the agreement provided for fifty-fifty worldwide profit sharing of all sales.

In the US, Pharmacyclics would book the sales and take the lead role in the development of the US commercial strategy. Both Janssen and Pharmacyclics would share in commercialization activities in the US. Outside the US, Janssen would book the sales and lead and perform the commercialization activities. Up front, both companies agreed to a significant amount of money to be spent on clinical development. The details were set out in the contract between both companies for the development cost.

At the ASH meeting in December 2011, we presented our interim phase 1/2 single-agent trial of ibrutinib for mantle cell lymphoma (MCL), CLL, and SLL patients. The results were again impressive.

There was a 69 percent overall response rate in previously treated MCL patients, 86 percent progression-free survival (length of time during and after the treatment of a disease that a patient lives with the disease but it does not get worse) in advanced CLL/SLL patients after twelve months, and a 67 percent overall response rate, including partial and complete response, in CLL/SLL patients.

Pharmacyclics ended 2011 with 108 employees, $240 million in cash, and six ongoing clinical trials. The valuation of the company jumped to a $709 million market cap. Our stock price went up to around fourteen dollars, but as soon as we announced the partnership, we took a hit on our stock price. Investors were very skeptical about this partnership.

Some investors called us saying they were very disappointed. They said that going into a partnership at such an early stage would not be in our favor. They believed that Big Pharma would control us and never let us grow. To be honest, they were not fully aware of all our communications and agreements with our partner.

Our agreement was to build Pharmacyclics with the help of the Johnson & Johnson team. In reality, it turned out to be the best decision we ever made. The Johnson & Johnson team was an amazing partner all along the way, and it was a pleasure working on this project with them.

On top of this partnership, we also announced in 2011 that we signed a five-year cooperative R&D agreement (CRADA) with the National Cancer Institute.

Immediately after we signed the agreement with Johnson & Johnson, the teams began working together. We arranged for multiple meetings at ASH, and we built the governance and working groups for the parties on the development activities. We worked side by side to build the team and get Johnson & Johnson integrated into our activities without slowing down our own productivity. I will never forget that in December 2011, over the Christmas holidays, our regulatory team, clinical team, and manufacturing team were all furiously working to meet our deadlines.

I remember one day Rob called me and told me we needed to take time to get the right people together and figure out how we could work together. I told him, "We do not have the luxury of time. We, the Pharmacyclics team, will keep going, and Johnson & Johnson will just have to catch up." But the one thing I was aware of at that time was that we had formed an unbelievable collaboration.

In January 2012, I became the COO of Pharmacyclics. We initiated even more clinical trials, including our first phase 3 study of ibrutinib for CLL. For reaching this milestone, we received another $50 million from Johnson & Johnson. We were on time in the execution of our clinical development and had started multiple phase 3 trials, which gave us an additional $200 million in milestones less than fifteen months after signing the deal.

During that year, we presented a total of eleven oral presentations at ASCO and ASH. We conducted twenty-seven clinical trials, and we initiated five phase 3 studies. We had 224 employees, $317 million in cash, and a market cap of $4.1 billion. Multiple financial analysts began covering us in their research that year, including Piper, Jeffrey, Stiffel, and Berstein. This all increased the year's target stock price to between fifty-one dollars and eighty-three dollars per share. We ended the year with a stock price of $57.78 per share.

Analysts predicted that our drug could eventually grow into a blockbuster product and recommended a buy rating. One analyst cited, "Ibrutinib shows consistent robust clinical activity in several different hematologic malignancies,"[16] while others cited its "unprecedented efficacy."

---

16 Natalia Timofeeva and Varsha Gandhi, "Ibrutinib Combinations in CLL Therapy: Scientific Rationale and Clinical Results," *Blood Cancer Journal* 11, no. 4 (April 29, 2021), https://doi.org/10.1038/s41408-021-00467-7.

During that time, we also entered into a licensing deal with Novo Nordisk, where we licensed the rights to our Factor VIIa inhibitor, PCI 27483, for a restricted disease outside the area of oncology. Suddenly, the company was raised to a completely different level. And the data continued to look very promising. Everybody was talking about ibrutinib as a blockbuster drug. In our executive meeting in October 2012, I decided to set a goal for the company of one NDA submission per year. I can tell you it was the best goal ever because it resulted in us accelerating our enrollment, filing our FDA submissions, and getting our approvals over the years.

What really had an effect on me then was that the patients were so happy. They now had an oral therapy, a once-daily capsule, and were getting efficacy results with minimum side effects. As one patient told us, "This is too good to be true." Now, they could travel. They just needed to get one glass of water with their pills every morning. There was no longer the need to go to the hospital or infusion center. They could live their lives without having to deal with all the side effects of chemo or other drugs.

That year, at the ASH meeting, we had our first booth in the exposition area, and our presentation and data were honored as the best of ASH. We were even included in the ASH press program. We also received the award for Best Partnership Agreement from BayBio. That year, Bob wrote a wonderful letter to all the Pharmacyclics employees that spoke of the many things we did together and everything we accomplished as a team.

To all involved:

One is usually hesitant to over-celebrate a milestone success. But, I wish to express my admiration for the persistence and focused attention each of you has contributed to this team milestone and company-wide corporate goal.

While it is true there are a limited number of elements (in chemistry), 118 I believe, it is also true there exists an almost unlimited potential to combine them. The challenge and trick is to find a combination that creates the desired effect and only causes the desired effect. It is a truly adventurous journey, not for the faint of heart, not for the impatient ones, not for the uneducated, or those with limited resources of time, energy, creativity, money, and willingness to sacrifice.

So, the question is who does this kind of work and what are they made of? The who's are tough to name. However, the characteristics common to those hard-to-name who's are easy to define.

Among those characteristics are surely curiosity and caring about life and its forward progress. Extraordinary intellectual and creative power would be present to a great degree. Long and hard work goes without saying (although I just did). It takes courage to do things others consider impossible to have tried and failed. Perception, observation, knowledge, a sense of certainty and the quiet confidence that the work one is accomplishing is worthwhile, in the broadest sense will be found present. Certainly, a resident tendency to expect the best possible outcome fuels the energy always required to make a meaningful difference for the betterment of existing conditions. Emerson said, "Nothing great was ever achieved without enthusiasm." Boy, was he right. And Edison said, "I will not say I failed 1,000 times. I will say that I discovered a thousand ways that can cause failure." So, a willingness to take chances is part of a parcel of innovation.

The two P's of perception and perfection are worth validating. One must perceive if one's idea is or is not workable. Perceiving requires looking without prejudice and seeing what you see. Not necessarily what you desire to see or what someone else insists you see. But really see, perceive, what is truly there. This does require an intolerance of mediocrity, particularly in oneself. So a sense of perfection and consistently striving to do better in the direction of a known goal are characteristics of successful teams, organizations, cultures and individuals.

A sense of humor can act like the feathers on a duck's back and which allows the waters and emotions of failure to roll right off one's back. It does not stop one from accomplishing a vital target. As one moves up the ladder of accomplishment so does one's confidence and trust in one's self and one's team to develop. This can spark a willingness to adapt to changing circumstances, not always doing things the same old way. Instead, one is willing to consider new options. By striving to achieve great things not just for yourself, but for the betterment of mankind some will accuse you of being idealistic. Surely, there are worse things to be accused of. The cherishing or pursuit of high or noble principles, purpose and goals can lead to levels of creation that spark unparalleled joy.

With the application of the above characteristics, joy and happiness are not so elusive after all. This I am sure you know because your accomplishments speak volumes. Do continue as there is no limit to innovation, joy, happiness and wealth. Again, thanks to all who pitched in on this. We, working together, are making a significant difference for the betterment of mankind.

Another letter Bob shared with our Pharmacyclics team was a letter to his son Demian from Sam Walton of Walmart. In 1986, Demian received an answer to a letter he wrote to Sam as part of a school project. The letter said so much simply. Not only was it kind of Sam, the chairman and CEO of one of the fastest-growing companies in the world, to promptly answer the questions a young schoolboy had about running a successful business, but it also told you a lot about the values this famous entrepreneur lived by. In his reply to Demian, Sam expressed the importance of serving others at Walmart. I always found that interesting, as that was exactly the heart of our mission at Pharmacyclics.

I have included the original letter, which is a bit faded, and a clear version so that it can be easily read below:

WAL-MART *WAL-MART STORES, INC.*
CORPORATE OFFICES
BENTONVILLE, ARKANSAS 72716

Sam M. Walton
Chairman and Chief Executive Officer
(501) 273-4210
April 21, 1986

Mr. Demian Duggan

Dear Mr. Duggan:

Thank you for your letter and your interest in our Wal-Mart Company. I appreciate the honor you have given me and our company with your questions pertaining to the research you are doing.

My friend, you have asked some very thought-provoking questions and I am not sure I can respond adequately. (1) There were several persons who had an indirect influence on my business philosophy: my parents, teachers, friends, and associates. (2) The training and experience I received and the self-confidence I gained probably were the motivating factors that prompted me to enter the retail business. (3) My advice to anyone wishing to succeed in business is to first count the cost of time, energy and investment that will be necessary, then become dedicated to hard work, sacrifice, reinvestment into the business, obtaining all the knowledge that is possible, setting attainable goals, sharing profits with employees, practicing hospitality and aggressiveness, and having a willingness to serve others.

Thanks for taking the time to write and best wishes for success and happiness in whatever you pursue.

Very truly yours,

Sam Walton

SW/wpt/421/9

WAL-MART

WAL-MART STORES, INC.
CORPORATE OFFICES
BENTONVILLE, ARKANSAS 72716

Sam M. Walton
Chairman and Chief Executive Officer
(501) 273-4210

April 21, 1986

Mr. Demian Duggan

Dear Mr. Duggan:

Thank you for your letter and your interest in our Wal-Mart Company. I appreciate the honor you have given me and our company with your questions pertaining to the research you are doing.

My friend, you have asked some very thought-provoking questions and I am not sure I can respond adequately. (1) There were several persons who had an indirect influence on my business philosophy: my parents, teachers, friends, and associates. (2) The training and experience I received and the self-confidence I gained probably were the motivating factors that prompted me to enter the retail business. (3) My advice to anyone wishing to succeed in business is to first count the cost of time, energy, and investment that will be necessary, then become dedicated to hard work, sacrifice, reinvestment into the business, obtaining all the knowledge that is possible, setting attainable goals, sharing profits with employees, practicing hospitality and aggressiveness, and having a willingness to serve others.

Thanks for taking the time to write and best wishes for success and happiness in whatever you pursue.

Very truly yours,

Sam Walton

The year 2013 was the greatest year yet for ibrutinib. We finally launched the product. November 13, 2013, was quite a day. It was the day we got approval from the FDA for the treatment of patients with MCL who had received at least one prior therapy. We now called ibrutinib "Imbruvica."

It was the year JP Morgan initiated research coverage of Pharmacyclics, as well as Morgan Stanley, Goldman Sachs, Brean Murray, William Blair, and Deutsche Bank. The analyst coverage was nothing short of amazing.

It was the year we got three breakthrough therapy (BT) designations. The BT designation is a program designed to expedite drug review by the FDA. It came into existence in July 2012 through the Food and Drug Administration Safety and Innovation Act.

Pharmacyclics was the first company to get three BT designations from the FDA. They were for MCL, WM, and CLL/SLL with deletion 17p (a genetic mutation). The FDA team worked side by side with our team. They worked as advisers and collaborated with us to help put our drug in the hands of patients. The team from the FDA worked when the government was shut down, they worked Friday nights to give us their feedback, and they pushed our team to make sure the reporting and submission of data were all done with excellence and perfection. The speed of their review was remarkable.

I want to take this opportunity to thank Dr. Richard Pazdur, the director of the FDA's Oncology Center of Excellence, and his remarkable team for all their advice and collaboration with Pharmacyclics and our partners.

Our scientific data was published in the *New England Journal of Medicine*, which is a prestigious journal in the medical world. We presented a total of forty clinical and preclinical presentations at ASH, five of which were oral presentations, and one was awarded the Best of

ASH. That was the year that our drug and company were all over the media. We were featured in *Time*, *Bloomberg*, *The Wall Street Journal*, *The New York Times*, and on CNN with Sanjay Gupta. We were even featured on *MAD Money* with Jim Cramer. The truth of the matter was, we were all over the place.

Time wrote, "A pair of recent studies hint that for some leukemias the answer [to whether the end of chemotherapy is near], may soon be 'yes.' Patients who had failed to respond to existing treatments tallied a survival rate up to 83 percent after two years on a drug called ibrutinib that blocked the activity of signaling molecules responsible for the cancer."[17]

It was the year we started to hire everyone in our sales and marketing team. We ended the year with 484 employees, which was double the team from the previous year. We also had forty-one ongoing clinical trials, including ten phase 3 studies. Our cash position was strong. We had $636 million in cash and an $8.15-billion market cap.

That was the year I was honored by Fierce Biotech as one of the Top Women in Biotech and by Ernst & Young as a finalist candidate for the Ernst & Young Entrepreneur of the Year 2013 award.

The year 2014 was the year when our attention was focused on our sales, the continuation of our other clinical trials, NDA submissions, and approvals. We received our second approval for CLL patients with at least one prior therapy. We got approval in Europe as well on phase 2 data. It was unheard of that Europe would approve a drug with only phase 2 data. By the end of the year, we had approval for relapsed/refractory MCL, CLL with one prior therapy, and CLL/SLL with deletion 17p.

17 Alice Park, "The End of Chemo?" *Time*, July 29, 2013, https://time.com/archive/6643836/the-end-of-chemo/.

Early in 2014, Bob invited a friend of his, Cheryl Berman, to come talk to us about our branding. Cheryl is the former chairman and chief creative officer of Leo Burnett, one of the largest advertising agencies in the world. She is what you might call a female advertising icon. She was named Ad Woman of the Year, as well as one of Ad Age's Most Influential Women and Adweek's Most Inspiring Women. She also received a journalism medal of honor from the University of Missouri. After leaving Leo Burnett, Cheryl started unbundled, her own successful branding and creative company. Both Bob and I were impressed by the work she did for brands like McDonald's, Disney, Altoids, and Morgan Stanley.

So we started our branding project with Cheryl. It began in a hotel with a branding session she ran with about ten of us from Pharmacyclics and a small group of her people. The session started with some inspirational films about Apple, Altoids, and Disney. I especially remember watching the beautiful "Think Different" video for Apple. I had seen it before, and I knew Steve Jobs himself played a role in writing it and getting it produced. His thoughts and advice always influenced my viewpoints and decisions in business and life. "The Crazy Ones" was a beautiful video about people like John Lennon, Amelia Earhart, Jim Henson, and Picasso. These were the ones who pushed the human race forward. The ones who were crazy enough to change the world. I always wanted to be one of the people in that ad. Looking back, I remember that this video really spoke to me and our team. We had definitely become the ones who saw things differently and, in the end, changed the world for cancer patients everywhere.

After watching the inspirational videos, we began the process of defining the Pharmacyclics brand. We each had to come up with an elevator pitch describing our brand to someone about to get off the elevator on the next floor. Then we had to come up with words and phrases we thought best described our brand. The next step was actually creating collages using words and pictures from a variety of magazines that expressed the look, feel, and essence of the Pharmacyclics brand. This was an unusual process for those of us in the biotech industry, but Cheryl assured us we were much more creative than we thought.

At the very end of the session, we did what Cheryl called "power dotting" to help identify not only the words and phrases that best described our brand but also the multisensory traits of the brand. This also took into account defining our color palette. We did an exercise that involved what the brand looked like, felt like, smelled like, tasted like, and sounded like. Cheryl called this a multisensory experience. We spent a good hour immersing ourselves in all the senses, including the sense of responsibility, which really resonated with what Pharmacyclics and our mission were all about.

Part of our session also involved coming up with brand attributes. Brand attributes are vital in keeping a brand relevant, authentic, and differentiated. These are the words that can be used throughout a company to evaluate everything, from product design to marketing. The following is a sentence from our brand book, featuring the brand attributes we landed on:

> *Pharmacyclics could be referred to as a Courageous Game Changer and Ally that operates with Integrity and Transparency.*

I was very proud of how our team aligned with the ideas, data, and answers that day. They really put their hearts into it, although it was quite a new experience for them. I also appreciated the passion and knowledge Cheryl and her team provided throughout the session. I knew Pharmacyclics was very different from the brands Cheryl was used to working with. We were not trying to improve sales of hamburgers or curiously strong mints. And our magic was quite different from the Disney magic Cheryl helped bring to life for fifteen years during her career at Leo Burnett. But most of the people in our team knew that what we had created at Pharmacyclics was a kind of magic that would actually change the lives of many people.

The most important part of the session was coming up with words and phrases that led to our "Big Idea." The Big Idea is what makes a brand unique and differentiates it from its competitors. This is the idea or positioning that creates a well-defined brand in everyone's mind.

We expanded the concept that Bob introduced years ago at Computer Motion. Bob's idea was to be patient-friendly and establish a therapy that consists of being a patient's true ally in support of their struggle to overcome their cancer. The goal of the patient and everyone involved is to have the person return to normal with the least amount of trauma or pain, as well as remain cancer-free for the long term.

The Big Idea is the same one you will still find today on the AbbVie/Pharmacyclics website. "Bringing back the Magic of Normal" was our Big Idea. It spoke not only to the results of Imbruvica, our lifesaving drug, but also to how this drug would change the lives of the patients taking it.

The magic of normal was our goal so many years ago when Bob and I stepped into our leadership roles at Pharmacyclics. We always believed and lived by "patient first." And one of the things we learned from all our trials was that more than anything, patients wanted their normal lives back. This concept actually showed up time and time again in studies and interviews with patients, doctors, and caregivers. Taking a pill with a glass of water was much more normal than having to undergo chemotherapy.

Patients were so happy that they would not lose their hair or suffer from diarrhea or vomiting. They could travel during this treatment and basically live their lives with very few or no side effects. They could actually get back to the magic of normal.

Cheryl was blown away by the results of our trials and the detailed comments we received from our patients, doctors, and caregivers, which were perfectly aligned with Pharmacyclics's mission statement.

She and her graphic designer created a very beautiful and useful brand book, *The Brand Manifesto. The Brand Manifesto* is a declaration of who we are, why we are here, and how we are making the world a better place.

Here is our Pharmacyclics Brand Manifesto:

Who Are We?

We are visionaries, innovators, the ones who believe anything is possible. We are optimists, scientists, doctors and friends. We are resilient and courageous. The ones who fight for you, encourage you, respect you and stand by you. The ones who made a decision that no one ever stands alone. We are the allies that step in with knowledge, confidence, integrity and a willingness to be of service.

We are the game changers who look at things differently. The ones who see stars where others see only darkness. We come with a goal and passionate intensity to restore lives, bringing back happiness and the freedom to dream again.

We are not waiting. No challenge is too big. We will never stop striving to transform hope into reality. We will never stop trying to make a difference.

We are determined to change the world for the betterment of mankind, by finding ways to give back the true "magic of normal" to those who have lost it.

Who are we? We are Pharmacyclics.

One of the highlights of 2014 for me was our launch party on April 11. It was such a magical night. We were finally able to make our drug available to all those patients in need. It was a dream come true after so much hard work by so many people. We did not have much time to organize this party, but I wanted it to be fun, elegant, and magical. It was a formal black-tie event, and we invited the entire company, as well as the C-level executives of Janssen. We worked hard to organize that party right when I was in the middle of an unbelievable amount of work. One night before the event, Shaun and I were watching *America's Got Talent*, and there was a young, upcoming, and very talented performer named Collins Key, who did a magic show and became one of the finalists.

The next day, I called Naomi Cretcher, our event planner, and asked her if she could find Collins and hire him for our launch party. And she made it happen. Naomi did an outstanding job coordinating this event. "The Magic of Normal" was one of our marketing campaigns, so Collins and his magic show fit perfectly in the event. We found the perfect magician, and he totally wowed the audience with his magic. Ramses and I were the hosts for the event that evening.

Ramses is very tall. I believe he is six feet four. I am only five feet four, so the week before the show, I decided that I had to buy some new high heels. I really didn't want Ramses towering over me all night. I finally found the right shoes that were over ten inches high. At the end of the night, after the party, after standing in these shoes for over eight hours, I couldn't feel my feet anymore. But I was right up there with Ramses the whole night. We were almost the same height. It was fun but painful. In any case, it was a truly magical evening at the Palace Hotel in San Francisco, one of those very special times I will never forget.

That year in December, we received the Pantheon DiNA Award for Outstanding Company from BayBio for the rapid development and commercialization of Imbruvica, and the Society for Medicines Research award for Drug Discovery for ibrutinib. We ended the year with 607 employees, fifty-five ongoing clinical trials—including thirteen phase 3 studies—and a market cap of $9.15 billion.

While we accomplished some amazing things in 2014, it was also the year that everything turned around. The stock price dropped suddenly because of some old news that was not clear to the market, as well as competition with ABT199 (a drug from AbbVie) and a PI3 kinase drug (from Gilead Sciences). Additionally, some investors started to doubt the ability of our management and leadership because of the turnover rate of the top executives of the company.

Between April and October 2014, two of the executives at Pharmacyclics were let go, and one resigned, so the market became very nervous. But to be honest, everything was under control. We were on time with our trials and approvals and on target with our revenues and collaboration with Johnson & Johnson.

I had been working nonstop for the past six years. A lot was going on. Instead of hiring outsiders for some key positions, we decided to promote internally with existing team members and build a horizontal organization chart so everyone could work closely together.

We entered into multiple collaboration agreements, which included Bristol Myers Squibb, AstraZeneca, and Roche, to evaluate ibrutinib in combination with other therapies. We decided to move into solid tumors and pancreatic cancer and began our collaboration with the Celgene team. This was also the year we terminated our contract with Servier and took back all the rights of our HDAC inhibitor. It was a year filled with activities left and right as we continued to expand and hire more people.

We were disappointed that our autoimmune drug did not perform the way we expected. But we were confident that Imbruvica would work for graft-versus-host disease (or GVHD, a condition that occurs when donated stem cells or bone marrow [the graft] see the healthy tissues in the patient's body [the host] as foreign and attack the tissue). In early 2014, early data observed by Dr. Miklos at Stanford in two to three CLL patients showed some biological activity indicating that ibrutinib might work for GVHD.[18]

The question was whether this drug would work for GVHD. No treatment had been approved, so there was really no standard assessment for efficacy by any regulatory authority. The Pharmacyclics team, with Bob's and my support, decided to conduct the development of ibrutinib for this indication. We did this because we believed it would benefit the patients, although it was not a big commercial prospect at that time.

Our team had a series of meetings with each of six key thought leaders to obtain their input on disease assessment, efficacy endpoint assessment, and their interpretation of the preliminary data from the phase 2 trial of the GVHD study. We also wanted to get their assessment of approvability by the FDA based on the results at that point. Interestingly, all the key thought leaders believed that the benefit of ibrutinib was there, and the biological rationale made sense, but they were skeptical about the approvability of our data based on their experience.

18 David Miklos, et al., "Ibrutinib for Chronic Graft-versus-Host Disease after Failure of Prior Therapy," *Blood* 130, no. 21 (2017): 2243-2250, doi: 10.1182/blood-2017-07-793786.

For GVHD, all phase 3 trials in the last ten to twenty years had been negative. There were no accepted endpoints. The National Institutes of Health (NIH) had some groups working on methods/guidelines to assess the disease and response. But we did not give up. Since no drug had obtained a label for this disease, people were skeptical, and that was understandable. But that did not mean we could not make it happen. God knows patients were desperately in need of our help.

Although there were a lot of skeptics, we also had a number of supporters. A few key leaders in the NIH's GVHD division had the enthusiasm to support our effort. Through our contact with them, we were invited to attend the NIH working group consensus meetings on the disease classification/definition set and efficacy assessment criteria. The team based their work on our knowledge and understanding of defining the endpoints.

We also made every effort to collect data and clean the data so that we could derive those endpoints with reasonable data quality and clarity of the measurements that could satisfy an FDA review. In August 2017, the FDA approved the use of Imbruvica for GVHD. And that was really an amazing achievement for all of us at Pharmacyclics, but mostly for the patients.

Summer 2014 was a very busy summer. I was doing all I could to work as closely as possible with the team. There was a huge amount of work to do, and there never seemed to be enough time to get everything done. We were performing at the speed of light, and everyone felt stretched.

During the entire summer and through November, the team worked nonstop, enrollment after enrollment, submission after submission. There were several research activities underway. We had around one hundred investigator-sponsored clinical trials ongoing, along with our own trials—all working in parallel.

Our collaboration with Johnson & Johnson was just spectacular. It portrayed the speed of execution beyond imagination. The Johnson & Johnson team could not have been more supportive. Together, we had one mission: to bring this product to market. And we could not have chosen a more incredible team: Rob Wills, vice president of alliances management; Patrik Ringblom, global strategy commercial leader; Peter Lebowitz, senior vice president of global oncology therapeutics; Craig Tendler, vice president of oncology clinical development and global medical affairs; Scott White, group chairman for North America pharmaceuticals; and many other incredible people at Johnson & Johnson. Patrick and Rob were always there to help us speed up our work with Johnson & Johnson. I cannot thank them enough for everything that they did to make our collaboration so successful.

By the first week of December, Bob and I decided to talk with some bankers about possibly selling the company. On December 4, 2014, we spoke with Marc Robinson, a partner at Centerview Partners. We met at the Four Seasons restaurant in San Francisco. Centerview suggested we explore the possibilities, and perhaps in nine months, we could envision a sale. But that was not our target. Our target was a sale within a maximum of four months.

That same week, Gilead Services announced a collaboration with one of our competitors in the BTK space. They decided to buy the company. On that day, I sent a message to Mike Gaito, the global head of healthcare investment banking at JP Morgan, at three o'clock in the morning and asked whether he could meet with Bob and me at our famous restaurant, Mayfield Bakery in Palo Alto. Bob and I had known Mike for many years. At the meeting, we told Mike that we wanted JP Morgan to collaborate with Centerview on the sale of Pharmacyclics.

From that moment on, everything moved very fast. Nobody in the company was aware of this decision, except Bob and me. On December 18, 2014, Bob went to Costa Rica for Christmas vacation. We had many discussions before he left and decided to tell Manmeet Soni, our CFO, what was going on. Manmeet and I both stayed in the office over the holidays. There was still so much work that had to be done. Manmeet is definitely one of the best CFOs you'll ever find in our industry. He is young, full of energy, and super smart in the field of finance and business. On top of that, Manmeet is a true friend. And he is one of the most hardworking individuals I have ever met.

Manmeet started to work on the revenue model and forecast for our Pharmacyclics products. I worked with the research team to prepare a five-year plan for the research activities. This included our board member Dr. Robert Booth, our consultant Dr. Jim Palmer, and our research team, as well as our preclinical team. We had a very tight deadline. Our plan was to finish everything by the end of the holidays. We put together a very good research plan. I could not tell everyone why we needed this plan. I just told them I needed to talk to our partners Johnson & Johnson at the JP Morgan investor meeting in January.

The JP Morgan meetings started around January 10, 2015. I remember we met with the JP Morgan and Centerview teams at JP Morgan's office in San Francisco to discuss the plan. We were firm. We wanted a maximum of three months of work, no online due diligence, and all the team members of the potential acquiring companies that were selected—just three of them—would come to our offices to look at our data.

I told them we would be ready by the end of January or the beginning of February to show our due diligence room. I believe that was the biggest challenge I ever put in front of our team. We had to have everything ready in three to four weeks. We had to prepare all the departments in the company and come up with a complete five-year development plan not just for Imbruvica but also for other potential pipeline products. We had to prepare a regulatory plan, as well as a sales and marketing plan. On top of all that, we had to prepare the due diligence rooms for three Big Pharma companies.

To assess that amount of data in such a short time would require between fifty and sixty people from those companies to look at and dissect all our data. Preparing the team to present the data while running the day-to-day activities of the company without telling anybody what we were doing was quite a difficult position to be in. Talk about pressure!

We initially chose fifteen employees to be on the due diligence team, and then expanded it to twenty-five. Besides Manmeet, the first team included Will Black, executive director of information technology (IT), and Ramses, head of corporate affairs. We needed high-speed internet, big data storage, and God knows how many computers with loaded datasets up in three different locations. We spoke with Betty Chang, PhD, head of research; Barbara Stewart, PhD, head of nonclinical safety; Juthamas Sukbuntherng, PhD, head of clinical pharmacology and drug metabolism and pharmacokinetics; and Wei Chen, PhD, senior director of medicinal chemistry, so they could work on the five-year research plan, as well as present all the research data. We also had to load all this data into the due diligence room for all the R&D programs.

We spoke with Dr. Darrin Beaupre, Dr. Thorsten Graf, Dr. Danelle James, Dr. Alvina Chu, and our clinical/medical team leaders; as well as Fong Clow, head of biostatistics, statistical programming, and clinical data management; and Urte Gayko, PhD, global head of regulatory affairs. They prepared a presentation of all of our clinical data, clinical development, and regulatory plans.

We spoke with Heow Tan, chief of quality and technical operations; Greg Hemmi, PhD, vice president of chemical operations; and Mark Smyth, PhD, executive director of chemical development and manufacturing, in order to present our quality and manufacturing plan.

We spoke with Matt Outten, head of market access and commercial liaison, to present our marketing and market access data, and Elaine Stracker, JD, PhD, general counsel, to present all intellectual property (IP) and legal data.

Naomi, senior director of events and media production, coordinated and set up all the due diligence events. Some other people who joined us were Anthony Souza, IT manager; Rick Love, PhD, legal; and Christophe Suchet, head of IT.

We camped at Wilson Sonsini's office. We worked day and night, twenty-four hours a day, seven days a week. I did not keep track of time. We were just working. I was looking through page by page, correcting all the presentations and preparing a five-year plan for the company. The team practiced, prepared the presentations, reviewed approximately seven thousand contracts of the company, and prepared all the job descriptions and résumés for over 750 employees. I made the decision that all this would be done in four weeks!

We were ready as planned and on time. And so we invited the first group. Over the next three weeks, people came and went. We had one group at the Four Seasons, one group at Wilson Sonsini's offices, and one group at our company, looking at the data.

The organization operated way beyond anything I could have imagined. We became experts at presenting and answering questions. By the end of February, we were ready for all negotiations. I will never forget that in just one day, we met the CEOs, COOs, CFOs, chief business officers, and group chairpersons of all three Big Pharma companies in Palo Alto. Bob, Manmeet, and I went from one meeting to another.

Our board members were the following: Kenneth Clark, Richard Van Den Broek, Dr. Mehta, Dr. Booth, Dr. Smith, and Eric Halvorson. Our corporate lawyers, Adam Fineman from Olshan, and our M&A lawyer from Wilson Sonsini were all on call so we could communicate with them at any moment. This would allow us to get their agreement to proceed and execute as quickly as possible.

We asked for the companies' proposals by the end of February. Bob made a decision to make a two-round process. It was not an auction. There would be two rounds of offers, and the best offer would win at the conclusion of the second round. In the first round, the offers from the three companies were within 12 percent of each other. In the second round, on March 4, two companies matched the leading offer from the first round, and the third company, which was AbbVie, offered us $261.50 per share.

One thing we did that perhaps nobody has ever done in the history of due diligence was, we decided to show the nonpublic IP data only to the company that won the offer. After we accepted their offer, they would only have a few hours to look at the IP. If they decided after a review that they did not want to proceed, the company with the next highest offer would have the right to see the IP. I will never forget when the bankers told us that this was not the usual process, and we could be putting multibillions of dollars at risk.

Nobody would ever offer to pay that kind of money without seeing the IP. To be honest, at that time, nothing we were doing was usual, but we stuck to our principles. And I will tell you it was an unbelievably stressful process. I give a lot of credit to Dr. Stracker, our patent lawyer and general counsel at Pharmacyclics, who diligently protected our IP over the years. She is very experienced and extremely knowledgeable. And I will always admire her integrity and loyalty. I learned a lot about her loyalty to our company when I found out she spent two hours driving to Pharmacyclics and then another two hours driving home every day.

One hour before the offers came in, I could not find Bob. I looked everywhere for him. I called Naomi and asked if she could go to the Palo Alto Town & Country Village shopping mall to see whether she could find Bob at the newspaper shop or Peet's Coffee. Sometimes, Bob can become really cool and do something totally unexpected. I have always admired his calmness. This was one of those times. Bob finally showed up at 11:45 a.m., fifteen minutes before the deadline for all the offers!

By noon, we had received all the proposals. Bob called Rick Gonzales of AbbVie and announced that he had gotten the deal, and we gave the green light to our lawyer, Dr. Stracker, John Desmarais from Desmarais LLP (a law firm in New York), and the AbbVie lawyers to look at the IP. The other legal and patent lawyers from all the other companies were waiting in their due diligence rooms.

No one apart from AbbVie knew yet that they had the highest offer. It took four hours to go over everything. Finally, it was done, and AbbVie acquired us. Directly following the acquisition, Bob called each of the CEOs of the other two companies, thanked them for their participation, and informed them of their status.

After my experience with the Computer Motion and Intuitive Surgical merger (my first experience of M&A), I knew that going through M&A is not always easy for the employees of the acquired company. So the one thing I am very proud of and the biggest thing I think we did for our employees was the severance package.

Generally, senior executives get two years of salaries as severance. But I requested in our merger agreement that all employees—including juniors, who made up most of the staff, and seniors, who were most of the executives—receive one year's salary and health insurance as severance if they were let go without cause within two years of completion of the merger. AbbVie agreed.

So we ended up merging the company with AbbVie for $21 billion.

Anyway, Pharmacyclics was an amazing story: record time to clean up the company, prepare the company, and put together a five-year plan for the company! The sale of Pharmacyclics became one of the best sales of all time in the biotech industry. Imbruvica became one of the ten top blockbuster drugs in history. And most importantly, many patients have been treated, and many have survived because of Imbruvica. And for those of us who put our hearts and souls into this, we ended the story the same way we began it: operating at the speed of light.

On May 26, 2015, AbbVie announced the completion of the acquisition of Pharmacyclics.

Following the announcement, we received quite a few very nice emails from a lot of people, including this one from Steve Biggar of Baker Brothers Investments:

Bob, Maky, Ramses and team,

Honestly, I am not sure how best to capture my heartfelt congratulations. When I reflect on the past 5 years and the progress you have made, it is stunning to see what can be accomplished with a blend of conviction and talent and serendipity. Your vision in what could be achieved with ibrutinib and Pharmacyclics has driven successes that we are proud to have been a small part of. You have achieved so much for so many people—you should be infinitely proud of all of it.

Patients are living longer and better lives because ibrutinib is available, and they will continue to do so all over the world. You have found a home for the company where your employees will continue to have amazing jobs and possibly more products to work on with AbbVie's portfolio. And obviously, you've generated a tremendous amount of value for your investors. Our only regret is that we would have enjoyed continuing to build the company around you and ibrutinib.

We are so grateful for your efforts, energy, honesty, and conviction. We tremendously value our relationships with you all, and the conversations we had over the years. We are awed by your accomplishments, and we learned a lot by supporting them.

Steve

PS When I say "we," I am at the front of the line to offer my thanks and congratulations, but I know everyone here at Baker Brothers Investments shares my thoughts. It has always been a team effort.

My last day at Pharmacyclics was in September 2015. I will never forget that day. The Pharmacyclics team arranged a beautiful farewell for me and Bob. To be honest, it was hard to let everything go. I was supposed to give a speech right after a beautiful speech Bob gave. I stood up and realized I was not prepared to give any kind of speech at all. My heart was too heavy in my thoracic cage. I remember that in a fraction of a second, just like in a movie, all those years at Pharmacyclics flashed in front of my eyes. There they were: all the pressure, all the challenges, and all the wonderful memories.

It was the first time in my life that I could not feel my own feet after leaving Pharmacyclics in September 2015. That was my last day! My last look at the company and thirteen years of hard work. It was the first time I thought, "Now that all the plans are set, the team is in place, and the company is in the best shape ever, why not run it?" Sometimes, it is hard to let go, but I knew that the decision to let AbbVie and Johnson & Johnson continue to put this drug into the hands of patients was the right thing to do.

It was an incredible and beautiful adventure—full of emotion, hard work, happiness, and joy. And I can never thank every single member of our team at Pharmacyclics enough, as well as so many amazing people at Johnson & Johnson and AbbVie. I also have to thank our investors, our clinical team, and every patient who committed to this journey and helped us achieve the unbelievable success we experienced.

CHAPTER 21
Teamwork

> **None of us is as good as all of us.**
>
> —Ray Kroc, founder of McDonald's

There is no way we could have ever achieved the success we experienced at Pharmacyclics without the incredible talent, brilliance, and passion of the people working there. As in every company, there were those who came and went, but the team we built over the years was made up of individuals who put all their blood, sweat, and tears into everything they did to help us reach the very ambitious goals we set forth to achieve at Pharmacyclics.

I would like to take this opportunity to share the experiences of some of our team members who took the time to tell the stories of their personal contributions to Pharmacyclics, as well as their experiences of working at Pharmacyclics. Their memories of this incredible adventure we went on together will never be forgotten.

Michael Wang, MD, professor at the Department of Lymphoma and Myeloma at MD Anderson

The history of mankind has evolved into an era of rapid progress in science and technology. Our human generation has more science and technology than any other generation in history. This is especially true in biomedical science where we are enjoying rapid translation of science and technology into clinical outcomes. Pharmacyclics is a classic example of modern biomedical success. I always believed that the investors in this area have to be visionaries who could see opportunities arising far from the horizon before others could see them. Not only they can see before others, but also, they possess the unique ability to change it into a success.

Dr. Maky Zanganeh and Bob Duggan are these visionaries. For reasons still mysterious to me, they began to invest in Pharmacyclics. Before the development of ibrutinib therapy for B-cell lymphoma, a group of diseases affecting 0.5 to 0.7 million Americans, has mainly relied on chemotherapy, which is toxic and only transiently effective. Chemotherapy could not cure B-cell lymphoma.

In 2010, I began working on an international multicenter clinical trial with ibrutinib in relapsed and/or refractory mantle cell lymphoma, one subtype of B-cell lymphoma. Ibrutinib as a single oral agent induced an overall response rate of 68 percent in relapsed mantle cell lymphoma patients. Everybody in the field was surprised that a single oral pill was equally, if not more, effective than the combination with chemotherapy, which requires a central intravenous catheter with low blood counts, nausea, vomiting, and many other side effects.

Ibrutinib was approved by the US FDA to treat relapsed mantle cell lymphoma in November 2013 as its first indication. Subsequently, it was approved in more than five other indications in B-cell lymphoma. This drug brought a revolution in the therapy of B-cell lymphoma.

In November 2011 in San Diego at the American Hematology Society annual meeting, I presented the preliminary results of ibrutinib in relapsed mantle cell lymphoma patients. During my fifteen-minute presentation before an international audience of hematologists and oncologists, there were three standing ovations—many felt that was the first and last ever in the history of the American Hematology Society annual meeting. The audience was so excited that I had to ask them to calm down so that I could finish my presentation. Ibrutinib is now being used in daily practice and has saved the lives of thousands.

My other rewarding experience was that I worked with many outstanding colleagues and leaders in industry. Dr. Maky Zanganeh, the chief operating officer of Pharmacyclics, certainly stood out among her colleagues. Maky had the unique combination of charisma and effectiveness. She thinks fast and acts even faster.

I worked in academics for many years and was used to waiting for a while before anything got approved. Ibrutinib could drive the lymphoma cells from their home environment into the peripheral blood circulation. These lymphoma cells left their home and therefore were vulnerable to a second attack we call synthetic lethality. In order to improve the efficacy of ibrutinib further, I proposed to use a monoclonal antibody by the name of rituximab as a second attack after ibrutinib in relapsed mantle cell lymphoma patients.

Maky got my proposal approved the same week of my proposal. The efficacy was improved from an overall response rate of 68 percent to a historical record of 88 percent. The ibrutinib-rituximab combination is used in routine practice these days and served as the basis of chemo-free therapy used in other trials such as window 1 and window 2 trials. I often want to express my gratitude to industry leaders such as Maky for this lifesaving therapy.

Robert Wills, Vice President, Alliance Management at Johnson & Johnson

I first met Maky in 2008 at BioEurope, a business forum where companies who have the technology to partner meet with companies who have the money to buy. I was the lead partnering head for Johnson & Johnson. Maky requested a meeting, which I accepted. The format was a thirty-minute allocation for Maky to present her pitch to me. It was a new oncology compound at an early stage from her company Pharmacyclics. The opportunity was too early for Johnson & Johnson at the time. I subsequently met with Maky two more times in both '09 and '10 at the same meeting. Maky was persuasive and passionate, but there still wasn't enough data to capture the interest of Johnson & Johnson.

It [was then] February 2011. I received an internal email that was sent by a director of Oncology Business Development asking if anyone in our group knew any of the board members or anyone on the executive team at Pharmacyclics. The oncology R&D group was extremely interested in the lead opportunity, ibrutinib, their BTK inhibitor. I clearly knew Maky, so I was asked to reach out to her because our business development lead could not get Pharmacyclics to agree to a capability presentation from Johnson & Johnson. It was somewhat ironic that the roles had flipped, Johnson & Johnson was now on the pitch side, and Pharmacyclics was on the decision side.

I called Maky, and as usual, she was her energetic self. We caught up on life, and then I told her that Johnson & Johnson would love to come to Pharmacyclics and present our capabilities as a partner for ibrutinib. Maky was quick to say, "Rob, Rob, we are far along with other companies, and we didn't view Johnson & Johnson as a strong oncology company. In fact, you ranked seventeenth [never was told out of how many but clearly not competitive], and we didn't engage beyond the first five." I then said, "Maky, you always told me I was the only Big Pharma company that took meetings with you in the early days. So I am asking that you give me ninety minutes, which is equivalent to the three thirty minutes meetings I gave you." She laughed and said she would get back to me.

A day or two later, Maky called me. She again reminded me that they were far along with two other companies. Maky then asked me who would likely come as part of the Johnson & Johnson contingent. I told her we were very serious and that we would bring decision-makers along with experts. This would include our worldwide head of R&D, our head of oncology, our head of business development along with experts in drug development and commercialization. I then told her I would attend as well and we are prepared to come as soon as Pharmacyclics would have us. Maky paused and then said yes.

We scheduled a visit within days after the call. Internally, we discussed our approach, and given how important we viewed this opportunity, we actually would now have the top executive of JNJ to join. I called Maky to let her know that Dr. Paul Stoffels, Mr. Joaquin Duato, and Dr. Bill Hait would be present. We arranged a meeting for her and Bob to meet the CEO of Johnson & Johnson, Bill Weldon, a few weeks after. She was stunned. I told her that we knew we were in a competitive situation with a huge time gap to close, so we felt we only had one shot at convincing her we would be the best partner.

After the presentation, Maky told us they were impressed. In particular, they felt we truly conveyed that we weren't about control but about partnering where control was shared. They agreed to continue discussions. Over the next several weeks, it became clear to us that we were not only in the hunt but likely the preferred partner. We were not told that until near the signing, but we knew based on the time we were spending negotiating and working on a contract that Pharmacyclics could not have the time or resources to do this with anyone else. We were right, and a definitive agreement was signed on December 8, 2011.

Post the signing, I was part of the steering committee set up with equal members of the partnership. Maky and I were the key interfaces for our respective companies. Over the years of the partnership until the acquisition of Pharmacyclics by AbbVie in March 2015, I got to know Maky extremely well.

As with all partnerships, there were times where the relationship was stressed and we had our normal share. Maky was always level-headed and rational. This made my interactions with her and the state of the partnership productive. We always could solve any issue and we did.

One part of Maky's persona or style especially impressed me. Maky pressure tested each situation and operational plan. She would not accept "no" or "it can't be done." Maky pushed timelines and results to levels I honestly didn't think were possible. This came from someone who trained as a dentist and did not have any biotech experience until she joined Pharmacyclics. Quite remarkable.

The partnership was extremely successful, which led to a tremendous new medicine, Imbruvica, that has been a breakthrough for hematologic cancers and a godsend for those patients who are being treated. Maky made her mark in a big way, and I am sure she is most proud of what she contributed to the betterment of those patients suffering from these cancers. We keep in touch occasionally and catch up on our lives post the partnership. I am a better person from knowing and working with her. It was my pleasure.

Ken Clark, Partner at Wilson Sonsini Goodrich & Rosati and Board Member of Pharmacyclics

Pharmacyclics was transformative, not only for the people involved but to some degree for the entire biopharma industry. It went from complete failure of its core business to near bankruptcy and a takeover by an activist shareholder, to identifying a potential drug that by conventional wisdom could not be developed, obtaining regulatory approval and achieving $1 billion/year revenue run rate of a now industry-leading oncology drug—all in less than six years and led by two executives who had no prior experience in the pharmaceutical business.

Along the way, Pharmacyclics established covalent binders not only as a viable but in many cases a preferred modality for small molecule drugs, established a groundbreaking partnership with Johnson & Johnson, became the first company to receive marketing approval in the US for a breakthrough therapy, and was the target of a $21 billion acquisition by AbbVie. That culminated in a more than 2,900 percent return to early investors and saved untold lives of leukemia patients with relatively inconsequential side effects.

It also proved that a small relatively inexperienced biotechnology company with limited resources can consistently outperform the largest of pharmaceutical companies in nearly every aspect of the business from patient recruitment to manufacturing challenges, to innovative clinical development strategies, and commercial execution. At the same time, it showed how both small innovative biotech companies and large pharmaceutical companies can mutually benefit from the resulting synergies, albeit in ways that pharma company leaders who were not involved still seem unable to comprehend.

In the beginning, it was a matter of survival. In response, Pharmacyclics got a small amount of funding from Pacific Biopharma, executed a pharma partnership with Servier on a noncore, HDAC inhibitor program in a matter of days, and pursued a rarely used "rights offering" to raise additional capital.

With that capital in hand, it then focused on the work of developing ibrutinib, which in and of itself was remarkable. Until then, the pharmaceutical industry held the view that covalent binders could not be developed because of potential toxicities. But based on the data alone, Pharmacyclics defied industry dogma and quickly proved that ibrutinib was not only highly effective but unusually safe as well. Having done so, it opened an entirely new path to develop drugs for difficult-to-drug targets, which has and will lead to a number of other highly effective therapies. It also established BTK inhibitors as a major drug class.

In 2011, Pharmacyclics's partnership with Johnson & Johnson both broke new ground and defined a new paradigm for biopharma partnerships. Not only did it achieve a governance structure of equal control, which had been done before but only rarely, but it also retained the right to book sales and effectively control commercialization in the United States, which had never been done before in an arrangement of this type. The fact that it had never been done before barely registered for management, and by force of their vision booking US sales became the centerpiece of the alliance. They also engineered a financial structure under which the partnership was completely self-funding.

After its signing, Pharmacyclics would never have to raise additional capital (although it chose to do so opportunistically some [eighteen] months later). Today, ten years later, it is unsurpassed as a model for building value while partnering with a larger company, certainly in the biopharmaceutical industry and possibly in other industries as well.

Three and a half years later, Pharmacyclics broke new ground again in its $21.5 billion acquisition by AbbVie. In typical fashion, it bent the curve again on the time to complete such a transaction—some ten weeks from the first conversation to competitive offers from three suitors to signing. Despite the compressed timeline, the company nonetheless achieved a level of preparation that far exceeded any similar effort I have ever seen.

Heading into the first substantive discussions, the entire management team recused themselves for three full weeks at an off-site location to prepare a presentation on ibrutinib's potential. That and the clarity with which the company pursued the transaction resulted in three competitive bids in two rounds of bidding that were remarkably close in value (a testament to management's preparation and presentation of the opportunity), and the most efficient sale process I have ever witnessed.

Part of Pharmacyclics's success was its demanding culture. Anyone who did not share a passion for speed, who rested on their past achievements, who was bound by convention, or who distracted others through political maneuvering, did not survive. Those who did survive were relentlessly hardworking, humble, and capable. The result was a team that could accomplish the unexpected on timelines that were nearly unthinkable. In that regard, it stands as a reminder that people can accomplish anything if they refuse to accept that they can't.

Manmeet Soni, Chief Financial Officer of Pharmacyclics

My first interaction with Maky was while interviewing for a job at Pharmacyclics. Through our initial conversations, it was evident that Maky is bright, quick-witted, and passionate. As a successful and flourishing business leader, she is confident, proactive, optimistic, enthusiastic, and committed to her work yet humble, kind, empathetic, and full of compassion. Her loud laugh would always capture the room, and her smart, innovative, ingenious ideas will shock anyone with her depth and breadth of knowledge.

Most of my recollections of Maky were when she needed a project or analysis done. She ensured diligence and that the tasks were executed efficiently and as scheduled. I appreciated these qualities in her and was elated to satiate her meticulous approach and assiduous research.

Maky is a woman with a strong voice and cares what she believes in. Once you've known her for a while, you will appreciate that as a manager her priority is work, but her soft corner is very visible. She always wanted to ensure that all her company staff were well-rewarded and taken care of. For instance, not so many people are aware that when we were in the M&A process for PCYC [Pharmacyclics], she ensured that everyone in the company from the receptionist to an executive was well taken care of in case they were let go from the company.

Generally, you would note that senior execs get two years of salaries as severance. But she ensured in our merger agreement that all employees including junior-most staff to the senior-most executives receive a one-year salary as severance if they would have been let go within two years of completion of the merger. I am not aware of these generous terms in these agreements. Only a compassionate and bold leader can support and bring those terms to the discussion.

Maky is a symbol of patience and strength. Normally you would find people confident and strong when they are at the peaks of their professional career, but Maky is an exception to this norm. Even though 2019 started with cancer diagnosed for her father and then eventually her, I have seen Maky, even stronger and more determined through this difficult time in her life in 2020. She is one brave girl I know.

I am proud to say that as expected of Maky, she came, even more, stronger than ever. If you meet Maky today, you can never imagine that she is a cancer survivor. Her persistence and resilience were visible all along her journey of deep pain while going through chemo and its side effects.

I am extremely lucky to call Maky a great mentor, friend, and support. Her attention to detail and memory of an elephant never ceases to amaze Bob Duggan and me. I am grateful for the opportunity to be working with you Maky and to get to know you very well. Maky, you are the best and always stay as you are.

I am writing this page on the morning of February 7, 2021, Super Bowl Sunday, which reminds me that winners are always winners. All the best to one of the finest quarterbacks Tom Brady who challenged all established rules of the football game and came again to the Super Bowl for the tenth time. Maky has been successful, accomplished, and I wish that she will be the winner in her future endeavors.

Betty Chang, Vice President of Research and Biology at Pharmacyclics

As I recall, I had many memorable times at PCYC, the type of things that do not happen often in our lifetimes, but when it does, we grab onto it as a huge blessing. I was at Pharmacyclics from 2009 to 2018. When I joined the company in 2009, the entire company was less than fifty people, and I was hired to lead the immunology programs at PCYC.

I had studied PCI-32765 in various autoimmune indications as the scientific understanding of the time was that BTK was a better target for autoimmune disease indications than cancer (not to mention the sizable market of autoimmune indications versus B-cell malignancies—blood cancer). However, Syk inhibitors (another

B-cell kinase inhibitor) have been tested clinically in B-cell malignancies with good outcomes.

Since I had worked on Syk with Rigel company for five years before I joined Pharmacyclics, I had a head start in understanding BTK of both cancer and autoimmune diseases. I headed the immunology programs, but I was also in charge of the clinical biomarker labs. PCI-32765 was starting to give good results in 2010, and I started to work almost exclusively in cancer by 2011. After PCYC initiated collaboration with Janssen in December 2011, our objectives became very clear and aligned to push forward for ibrutinib to be the first BTK inhibitor approved for MCL/CLL.

Our bandwagon started to move like a train, and the train moved faster and faster toward the goal. With the new resources coming in, we were able to purchase the needed capital equipment and hire new scientists to work on our expanded BTK programs, and by early 2013, I was promoted to executive director of research. Then the unexpected happened: both my supervisor and my colleague decided to leave Pharmacyclics in the middle of 2013.

I was promoted to vice president of research biology of Pharmacyclics and overlapped with Joe Buggy, my supervisor, for a month, and then I was fully in charge. I was very excited to have the opportunity to be the head of our small department and felt very confident about my scientific abilities to lead the strategy and operations of our team. I worked aggressively to fulfill my responsibilities, and I put in more than seventy hours weekly until I left PCYC in 2018. I was almost always the last person to leave building 995 each and every day and one of the few to come in on weekends.

The company kept on growing exponentially, and I envisioned we needed around fifty people in research to continue to explore the BTK franchise from a preclinical setting and new diseases including the support of in-house preclinical biomarker efforts for the ever-growing list of clinical trials that expanded from CLL, MCL, FL, DLBCL, AML, MM, and GVHD (where we had planned forward and reverse translation); drug discovery efforts of next-generation BTK inhibitors (which included various platforms), combination therapy with ibrutinib, resistance mechanisms and solutions to break resistance.

In early 2015, we were about forty-five people, the majority of them with doctoral degrees. With the success of ibrutinib in the clinic, more new studies were planned, initiated internally and externally, my responsibilities kept on growing each day, and even with seventy-hour weeks, I could not keep up with all the happenings in research.

For the first time in my life, I felt behind. I could not attend all the meetings I needed to, and I was behind in reviewing MTAs [medical technology assessments], CTEPs [cancer therapy evaluation programs], patent applications, collaboration proposals, manuscripts, posters, CSRs, IBs, and other regulatory documents. I could not hire people fast enough to replace key functions. Our labs were too small and could not accommodate more people in the lab—having more people in the lab did not mean increased productivity because the lab was too packed with people and instruments.

It was very disheartening to go into the lab to see how little space our scientists had to work in, and we worked on reorganizing the lab to create more space again and again. It was a tremendous time of exponential growth but also a challenging time albeit an exciting one.

As the clinical success of ibrutinib became more evident and its strong activity was demonstrated, the news was released at major international meetings and published in first-tier scientific journals, such as the *New England Journal of Medicine* among others. The success of Pharmacyclics became a focal point of prestigious media starting from 2013. Following the interviews with our company executives, the media and photographers came to the labs to capture our staff in action.

After the photographers from the *New York Times*, the *Wall Street Journal*, and other media took photos, we would see photos of our lab and staff featured in the *NYT* and *WSJ*. We had a very humble biology research lab at PCYC, which was about 2,800 feet squared (and it stayed that size until it was renovated in 2017 by AbbVie). I would collect those photos of our lab and staff and hang them on the bulletin board outside the lab. In a matter of months, the bulletin board was completely filled with our published articles on ibrutinib and coverage by the national media. It was an incredible time of productivity and success for our department, even more so for the company.

I headed the strategy and operations of our internal and external research at PCYC. External research included the more than one hundred academic collaborations of US/ex-US major universities with an interest in BTK research. Internally, I built out the research team from a team of five to forty-five capable of internal drug discovery, pharmacology, translational medicine, core flow cytometry and sorting facility, and bioinformatics.

We retrofitted our labs to be CGCLP compliant and ran the majority of our clinical biomarker and pharmacodynamic assays in-house with a two-week turnaround running all the assays twice. This is lightning speed; actually, our biomarker lab had processed sixty thousand samples from 2010 to 2015. Being able to read out receptor occupancies from our trials internally was a big benefit since it meant we would be able to determine the dose needed for the next study in weeks rather than months.

My main achievement was to define the mechanism of action of ibrutinib in CLL and MCL. Ibrutinib's mechanism of action was unconventional. It was not a cell-killing molecule; rather, it penetrated deep tissues and mobilized malignant B cells from tissue, lymph nodes, or bone marrow into the blood circulation where it gradually died without its tumor microenvironment. This made our drug safe and effective in B-cell malignancies. In addition, I also demonstrated ibrutinib was effective in models of autoimmune diseases, such as rheumatoid arthritis and lupus nephritis models by inhibiting both BCR [B-cell receptor] signaling and FcR [Fc receptor] signaling, making BTK an attractive target for autoimmune diseases.

We were first to identify BTK mutations that led to ibrutinib resistance but also demonstrated BTK-mutated cells can be inhibited with reversible BTK inhibitors, and that resistance can be broken when combined with other drugs. And last but not least, we were the first to identify BCL2 inhibitors as the best combination partner for ibrutinib with or without resistance.

But my main achievement was to give PCI-32765 the name ibrutinib and work on the drug to shed light on the way it works. The name will stay on even after I stop working on the drug, helping many patients all over the world. Many of our contributions will be forgotten over time, but ibrutinib will continue to benefit patients, and it is now used as a gold standard as a control in basic and translational research.

The story is that in 2010 or 2011, we had a drug naming contest within the company for PCI-32765, our first-in-class BTK inhibitor in the clinic that was working well in phase 1 studies. Business development held a contest with a one-hundred-dollar gift card as a reward for the winner. It came down to either abrutinib or ibrutinib. Many people had named the molecule abrutinib while only I used ibrutinib for "I am a BTK inhibitor" (it was also the time when Apple came up with all *ix* products such as iPhone, iTunes, etc.).

One of the key elements for the drug name was not to have another foul meaning in other languages. Apparently, someone had brought up abrutinib sounded like stupid (*abruti*) in French and we certainly did not want a "stupid BTK inhibitor," so ibrutinib won, and I received the one-hundred-dollar American Express gift card.

At PCYC, we always had the opportunity to become our best. Women and minorities were given equal opportunities; in fact, I recall we had more women than men as leaders of the company. In addition, we had quite a diverse background of people. Despite all the above, we were quite aligned on major decisions. We had intelligent people who were top of their field but were also nice to work with. No one came in with arrogance or attitude. We all rolled up our sleeves to do the work when it was needed.

During regulatory filings, I would see the parking lot full of cars on the weekends and evenings. The team was extremely diligent and hardworking, and management gave recognition to their contributions, which boosted morale in the organization.

I had several wonderful supervisors, but Maky was the one who believed in my abilities and gave me tremendous growth opportunities and always offered strong support when I needed it. She believed in promoting people from within who were doing the hard work.

Joe Buggy and David Loury hired me in 2009 to lead the BTK immunology program; both David and Joe retired in 2012–2013. In 2013, Maky (and Bob) promoted me to vice president of Research. There were other options, but Maky took a chance with me, and I am forever grateful for that opportunity. Without this opportunity, I would have never had the chance to experience drug development at a higher level and take on responsibilities of operations management in a very high-paced yet rewarding environment.

Having been born in Japan and growing up in Taiwan, I grew up in a culture where being a junior high school teacher or a nurse was recognized as an ideal career path for women. Although I was shy and reserved, I was also confident in my abilities, ambitious, and ready to lead if I was given the opportunity. I had studied tyrosine kinase signaling for fifteen years and B-cell kinases for five years before joining PCYC, and I had solid training in not only drug discovery but also cancer pharmacology and PK/PD [pharmacokinetic/pharmacodynamic] studies using flow cytometry methods. I had dreamed of being the research head since I was in high school and wrote essays about it when I was fifteen. My break came in June 2013.

Although I reported to Maky, we did not have a regular weekly one-on-one, but we would talk when needed and only when we had issues that needed to be resolved. Maky was extremely busy, but she gave me her trust. Maky was running the company while Bob, the face of the company, gave inspirational speeches.

Maky was very intelligent and intuitive. I did not have to explain to her in detail, and she did not ask more than once about any issue or incident; she would quickly understand the cause and consequence of the various events. She was 100 percent supportive of my decisions and explanations, and we did not have to talk much because she trusted me. That was the most important that I cherished—to have the trust of my boss, Maky. Maky also gave me opportunities to represent the company to accept the Best New Drug award from SMC in London 2014 and the Prix Galien Award (which we did not win in 2014 but won in 2015).

That was the most important and beautiful thing we had at PCYC; we wanted the best for the company. We always had the company's best interest in mind for all our decisions. We all had to play the bad gal from time to time for the sake of our company, and it wasn't pleasant, but it needed to be done.

I liked the fact that all the executives in the company were very passionate when we had meetings. We all wanted the best for the company, and we would spend long discussions to sort out our differences before we informed Bob and Maky for the final decision-making.

I was fond of the Pharmacyclics leadership of Bob and Maky because they were a great team together. For the tough and large decisions, Bob and Maky were always there together. Bob obviously was very seasoned, experienced, and understood how to deal with all sorts of people whether they were head of the FDA or a custodian. He spoke sincerely, was inspirational and intuitive, and had a way to interact with people from all walks of life in a remarkably positive way and resolve conflicts. Maky was very perceptive, highly intelligent, and her ability to analyze the situation, decide, and execute the strategy was quick and spot on. Together, they made great decisions and the right ones when we faced big challenges.

On multiple occasions, I had the opportunity to experience instances where the company went through various findings that might be seen as negative at least for the temporary. Bob would always be transparent and would inform the investors. Bob built out his trust in business by being transparent with his team of investors so he had a sizable team of investors that would follow his lead.

In addition, I liked everyone on our research and translational team. We were one big tightly knit family, and we all cared for each other, stepping in when others needed help in the lab, especially during big in vivo studies. As we added more people to the team, we were all careful to hire people that were not only highly skilled, experienced, and industrious but also great team players.

The team got along very well, and we had lots of fun together in team-building activities, such as playing Bio-Jeopardy, having white elephant Christmas parties, sailing in the Bay, etc. I had many fond memories of us having fun as a team. As the department head, I always had it in my mind to hire someone that I could help nurture and grow in their career should they accept our offer to work in research.

I remember the first several Christmas parties I attended; they were small and intimate. Bob would often tell us how it was important to have a purpose in life and how we should focus, have courage, and commit to this purpose as long as it could benefit mankind and society. He often said he would invest in companies with clear purposes that resonated with him. He came to PCYC because PCYC was developing a drug for brain cancer—the cancer that took the life of his son—but soon after he invested in the company, the brain cancer drug had failed in two Ph3 pivotal trials.

Rather than give up on the company, he invested his personal funds to keep the company alive, and it was the only reason why PCYC still existed (after that, the rest is history). Even when the most painful things happen in our lives and darkness falls, it is important to move on with even greater momentum and energy in fulfilling that purpose in our lives. I really admire and respect that and often think about his leadership. Bob was truly a leader in understanding people and life. He inspired us to live a life in a meaningful way that scientists could relate to.

As Pharmacyclics had not received FDA approval in the last two decades, the Imbruvica launch was meaningful to us in many ways. It was on this day that the toil and exhaustion from years of seventy-hour workweeks all of a sudden melted away. It was a time when PCYC and Janssen truly rejoiced as one as we reached our common goal.

The Imbruvica launch party was in April 2014. We had all looked forward to the launch party for a long time ever since we submitted our NDA for ibrutinib. It was such an important milestone for our hard work and teamwork after so many years. The attendees of the party were from PCYC and Janssen. The party was absolutely perfect. I remember Ramses and Maky were the masters of ceremonies for the launch party. Maky arranged most of our meetings and parties. They were always carefully choreographed without missing a tempo. Ramses is a tall man, and Maky was as tall as Ramses at the party.

The launch party was an affirmation of our belief that although we were a small biotech company that never had a drug approved, we were capable of getting ibrutinib approved as a first-in-class BTK inhibitor among all the competition from large pharma. *We* had a great drug, but we needed to get to the finish line first to be successful. We are small, but it can be done if we all focus on this goal. It was such a wonderful time to celebrate this achievement that so many have contributed to and a testament to PCYC's hard work and commitment.

Fong Clow, Head of Biostatistics, Statistical Programming, and Clinical Data Management at Pharmacyclics

The crucial part of achieving excellence is having a good team with good leaders. Bob Duggan and Maky Zanganeh are some of the best leaders you could ever have. Without their excellent leadership in Pharmacyclics, many of my accomplishments would not have been possible. Identifying and working with excellent leaders is essential to success. That's one lesson I have learned over the years.

Leaders like Bob and Maky have a huge impact on people's lives. Because of their efforts, people who have CLL, a kind of lymphoma, can live without the need for chemotherapy. Our drug, Imbruvica, was a very big commercial success story. It is the oncology drug with the second or third highest sales globally. Although the hematology field is much smaller than the solid tumor market, it's still one of the top-selling drugs in the world.

Under their leadership, Pharmacyclics grew from a small fifty-people company when I joined to become one of the big houses in oncology. At Pharmacyclics, we obtained our first FDA approval less than five years after the first patient was treated. We have had at least one to two approvals every year since then. We have obtained four breakthrough designations and a total of eleven sNDA [supplemental new drug application] approvals. Three of those indications that we obtained are the first and, at this time, the only approved drug for the disease.

I had the chance to be a key part of a team under the leadership of Bob and Maky that created $21 billion in value in four years before the sale to AbbVie.

When we got our first approval for the drug, one of the colleagues at Johnson & Johnson, our codevelopment partner, told me this project might be the first one in the Johnson & Johnson history of over one hundred years where the codevelopment project was more than a year ahead of schedule.

Lots of factors came together to make it a success, but it all came down to one thing: the pursuit of excellence, with an excellent team and superior leaders, like Bob and Maky.

For me, the criterion of a good leader is that they consistently want to achieve and do not accept the mediocre, they have their own opinions and stand for what they believe in, and they have the goal of wanting to make the world better. They are there to achieve great gains for the world. People can talk about this and say it, but it is what you are able to do that distinguishes for me what a true leader is.

As Bob wrote while we were at Pharmacyclics, "The two *P*s of perception and perfection are worth validating. One must perceive if one's idea is or is not workable. Perceiving requires looking without prejudice and seeing what you see. Not necessarily what you desire to see or what someone else insists you see. But really see, perceive, what is truly there. This does require an intolerance of mediocrity, particularly in oneself. So a sense of perfection and consistently striving to do better in the direction of a known goal are characteristics of successful teams, organizations, cultures, and individuals."

During my time at Pharmacyclics, I always felt confident that Bob and Maky would see and support the excellence of my work. My efforts and abilities were perceived and never wasted. I decided to join the company because I believed in their leadership. I believed that they had passion about success, the desire to change society, and the capability, perception, and will to enact their vision.

Thinking back over my experience of the last thirty years, I have come to see that the lesson is that if you want to achieve excellence, you need to be willing to deal with adversity. You might be one of few individuals, or the only one, to have an idea. You sometimes have to be willing and prepared to take on some strong disagreements, misunderstandings, and even accusations in pursuing this idea. You might have some powerful people against you. Nevertheless, if you are sure that you have good science and that the outcome of your struggle is good for society, then the personal sacrifices are worth it. In the end, a majority of people will join you and you will make a big difference for the betterment of life.

Let me tell you some of my recollections at Pharmacyclics, our achievement, and how we overcame obstacles:

Understanding of lymphocytosis and bleeding to assess whether ibrutinib could be a good drug

When I joined Pharmacyclics in May 2011, a key task for me was to work with the statistician and programmers to perform analyses for publication and presentation in ASCO and ASH. Two key observations that became the center of concern for evaluation of ibrutinib as a potential good drug were bleeding and lymphocytosis in CLL. We needed to determine how to evaluate the impact of bleeding on the value of ibrutinib. Would bleeding dramatically reduce the therapeutic index and become a big liability for the drug? At that time, a few people thought so. We were also nervous about lymphocytosis, whether lymphocytosis is indicating PD [Parkinson's disease]. If not, how can we apply the existing CLL efficacy assessment criteria? Can we predict who will have lymphocytosis? Were there any prognostic factors for lymphocytosis? How does lymphocytosis impact the efficacy of ibrutinib?

To evaluate safety, we needed to know what the impact on patients was. It is not a simple total event rate. Based on my many years of previous experience analyzing and discussing the evaluation of bleeding with the FDA, we could categorize bleeding as minor (manageable) and major, such as an Adverse Event. The analyses showed that the major bleeding rate is relatively low for ibrutinib. Therefore, we did not think that bleeding would lead us to change our assessment of the value and the development path of ibrutinib.

How to assess efficacy was also somewhat problematic due to the lymphocytosis phenomenon that we observed for some of the CLL patients. During the first few months of ibrutinib treatment, some patients reached a high ALC [absolute lymphocyte count] level, which would be one of the measurements indicating disease progression by narrowly applying the existing efficacy assessment criteria.

However, it was observed that almost all patients' ALC eventually came down; some reached the normal level along with other assessments of the disease when patients continued ibrutinib treatment. Lymphocytosis might not be the indication of the disease's progress but rather a measurement that might reflect the mechanism of action of the drug. Clinically, many treating physicians, especially some key thought leaders, observed that in patients with lymphocytosis, their clinical symptoms of CLL continued to improve to minimum disease. Patients feel normal and return to their normal life.

This led us to believe that ibrutinib was effective for treating CLL regardless of lymphocytosis. Instead of thinking ibrutinib did not work, we needed to have modified or clarified efficacy assessment criteria that the FDA understood and accepted. This work ultimately took us until early 2013 to complete. The clinical scientists, especially Danelle James, were the major drivers to achieve this. We collaborated with some thought leaders and published a few papers on this topic as well as one with more statistical modeling to describe lymphocytosis.

This allowed us to find a way to accurately measure the success of the drug, changing the criteria away from the ALC level.

At ASH in 2011, the big question was how to present efficacy data. Ibrutinib had achieved an unprecedented overall response rate in CLL. The question was how to demonstrate the durability of the response. Ibrutinib-treated patients could stay responsive for a long time, and they did not get disease progression. The traditional measurement of duration of response did not fully present this.

Another measurement is the PFS (progression-free survival) curve. Most PFS curves are a decay curve, but the ibrutinib PFS curve was a straight line with a couple of steps, which was not a common shape. I compared our straight line with some curves in the literature, and it appeared to me that the length of follow-up in our study was reasonable, not too short, compared with other reported data. The interpretation of the straight line was the drug is highly effective.

I decided to produce a quality graph on PFS, and even include the confidence interval, and had it presented to ASH. My proposal got a few critics and a few strong opinions against presenting it within the company. I was nervous about this decision. To my pleasant surprise, the presentation got an incredibly positive reaction from the audience and investors. That straight line PFS curve put ibrutinib on the map.

For me, it indicated that our understanding of the drug was right. Our interpretation and presentation had been accepted by the medical community and wide audiences. Most of all, patients would greatly benefit from our work on ibrutinib.

Using phase 2 data to obtain approvals for MCL in US

After 2011 ASH, with one phase 1 and two phase 2 (one in CLL and one in MCL) ongoing, a few questions came to my mind. How could we deliver this drug to patients as fast as possible? How could we deliver this drug to as many patients (types of diseases) as fast as we could? To design the most efficient phase 3 trial with a high probability of success is one way, which we would have to do no matter what. But could we use existing data to support the approval? I thought we could. Here were my assessments to support this:

1. Does the drug show clinical benefit? Yes, based on review of many published papers (including CLL-related treatment, diagnostic, and prognostic effects [i.e., Del 17p, Del 11q, Zap20, beta-macroglobulin, etc.]), the observed treatment effect in the phase 2 trial demonstrated the drug was efficacious and reasonably safe.

2. Was the data quality obtained in the phase 2 trial good enough to support labeling? My previous successful experience using non-standard industry clinical trials as label-enabling studies helped me to say yes to this question.

During 2012, I worked hard to pursue and work with my clinical and regulatory colleagues to continue moving toward the decision to use phase 2 data to file the MCL indication. By October, we reached the decision to use phase 2 data to file an NDA for the MCL indication. Just after we had made the decision, Bob told us that he heard that the FDA had a new initiative, "breakthrough therapy designation," which supported innovative drug development.

The team felt this was a great opportunity for us to apply for this designation. We applied and obtained a breakthrough therapy designation for ibrutinib in MCL.

We also continued working with some key thought leaders to understand the data and interpretation of the result. It was exciting working with Dr. Wang on his presentation in 2012 ASH on MCL for an updated analysis. We observed that ibrutinib continues to improve its treatment effect with longer treatment. This was a new finding and a new understanding of how ibrutinib works. The presentation of Dr. Wang at ASH was a very memorable one.

Submitting phase 2 CLL data for labeling of CLL together with the phase 2 MCL NDA submission

In considering the data package that we would use for MCL NDA, the phase 2 trial in CLL was included as the part of the safety database since, at that time, we had only three trials:

1. One phase 1, first in human trial with dose escalation and various histology of B-cell malignancy,

2. One phase 2 in 3 different populations of CLL, and
3. Phase 2 MCL.

Based on the assessment of efficacy and safety data, it seemed to me that the phase 2 CLL showed ibrutinib is efficacious and safe for the CLL population. I wanted to use the phase 2 study to obtain the label approval for CLL. Of course, there were many more hurdles for CLL than MCL, such as

1. the data that can be used as pivotal support for labeling was limited (i.e., N = 48 or 51); while for MCL, we had data from more than one hundred patients;
2. the criteria of efficacy assessment needed to be clarified in order to obtain a reasonable and proper estimate of response and duration of response (the key efficacy endpoints); and
3. the indication population was more complicated with a smaller sample size for population definition.

I understood all those hurdles; however, based on the reactions that I observed in the conferences, discussions with key thought leaders, interaction with regulatory authorities, and hearing the feedback of patients from medical affairs and clinical colleagues, I strongly felt that it was our responsibility to try to bring this efficacious drug to patients as soon as possible. We needed to do our best to make it happen.

During the late part of 2012, I brought this topic up from time to time. CLL phase 2 data were proposed as supportive safety data for the MCL NDA package. For me, if that had happened, the door for using CLL phase 2 as the pivotal study to support a CLL label would have been closed. On the flight back from the pre-NDA meeting with the FDA for MCL, I could not eat or drink, wondering if there was anything we could do about this. Urte Gayko, our head of regulatory, saw me and asked me what I was thinking, and I brought this topic up with her. She agreed with me and was supportive of this proposal. Without her support, history would be different. With Bob and Maky's support and good teamwork, we overcame all the hurdles.

There were so many details that I could not include them. One important one is that the CLL approval ultimately needed a published clarification of international CLL efficacy assessment criteria, which had to be done within a few months. This could not have happened without our clinical colleagues, especially Danelle James, who was amazing in making it possible. At the beginning of 2014, FDA granted the CLL label with a forty-eight patient phase 2 as the pivotal study.

Overall survival on label based on phase 3 CLL study

Demonstration of overall survival (OS) benefit is the gold standard outcome to show the benefit of a drug. How we could demonstrate the overall survival benefit of ibrutinib was a question in my mind when we designed and monitored the progress of the randomized phase 3 trial, RESONATE. I wanted to show that ibrutinib could prolong patients' lives if ibrutinib was capable of doing so. It was our responsibility to show this, which would lead to the proper information being provided to patients and health care professionals. I read many key papers published on CLL and went to conferences to understand the facts that could influence the analysis of OS and what analyses might be applicable in this setting.

Based on that, I believed the results we had did show that the drug was efficacious to this degree. But to demonstrate an OS benefit is a high bar. Only one regimen had shown OS benefit previously in CLL. One reason is that CLL is an indolent disease, and patients could live a reasonably long time with the disease. It might take a long treatment time and/or follow-up to observe the OS benefit, and the benefit must be of a large magnitude in order to overcome the noise in the data.

During the middle and late part of 2013, while RESONATE was in progress, it was more widely recognized that ibrutinib was a benefit to CLL patients. A question came up of whether we should make a protocol amendment to allow patients that receive the standard therapy/control treatment to cross over to ibrutinib treatment after their disease progressed. We all knew that the crossover would have a negative impact on demonstrating OS benefit.

Should we allow crossover? How and when? How would we minimize any negative impact on demonstrating OS benefit? As with most complicated issues, there is no simple answer. After many debates, I was satisfied that the PCYC leadership team came to the best solution: allowing crossover while tightly managing operation of the crossover process to minimize the negative impact on the crossover in demonstrating OS benefit.

Meanwhile, the statisticians performed many simulations to evaluate the analysis methods for the final analysis that might minimize the bias of crossover, which might be acceptable to the FDA. In addition, we also developed a statistical test scheme to maximize the probability of demonstrating OS benefit at the interim analysis and submitted it to the FDA to obtain an agreement. The testing scheme was somewhat unconventional or, to use another word, risky. There were many discussions and debates among the team and with Bob and Maky. In the end, the team made the decision to proceed with this.

There was an issue about when to perform the interim analysis. Many people wanted to perform the interim analysis earlier than the protocol prespecified to satisfy the FDA request. In the end, Bob and Maky made a decision to wait until the protocol specified events of interim analysis were observed.

To implement the statistical test scheme, we also had certain procedures that the independent DMC needed to follow. It took a couple of hours of discussion with the IDMC [independent data monitoring committee] to finalize the procedure before the interim review. By the way, we had world-class IDMC members. They had made many first-class decisions in their monitoring of the trial. Even today, I am still grateful with deep respect for their correct decisions, which resulted in benefit to patients.

A little story: we started our pre-meeting in the late evening when some of the members flew in. After we finished our discussion of the procedure, it was midnight. IDMC members decided to continue their closed session meeting to review the data. Several of us with Bob and Maky stayed in a small conference room waiting for the outcome. About 3:00 a.m., the chair of the IDMC called us in to inform us of their decision. The trial had achieved statistical significance in its primary endpoint, PFS, and the secondary endpoint, OS. It was a big day for PCYC.

Waldenström approval

Dr. Treon had performed an investigator-sponsored study that showed that Imbruvica had efficacy for Waldenström's macroglobulinemia (WM) a rare disease with only about 1,500 cases per year in the US and no FDA-approved treatment before Imbruvica (and no other treatment since). Pharmacyclics was willing to do an in-house study, but that would delay approval for a few years. After seeing his presentation and the study results as well as his scientific and biological rationale for WM, I thought the data he generated could get us through the FDA review and allow us to obtain a label.

As you know, the requirements for a study that supports a label are many and rigorous, from database structure to data quality, from design to data monitoring. It is rare that an investigator-sponsored study can be used to support a label. But because the science of Dr. Treon's study was strong and the result was good, I proposed that we use his study data. We would work through the issues related to trial conduct, database, and endpoint assessment.

Based on my assessment and my early experience working at Dana Farber Cancer Institute, I thought we could help Dr. Treon and his team to clean the data to be submittable. In the end, both Dr. Treon's and PCYC's team worked together to successfully submit the NDA and go through the FDA review and audit; ultimately, we obtained the first label for Waldenström.

Building a biometrics organization for ibrutinib

It is important to have the right strategy in drug development, but it is also important to have a strong world-class biometrics team that is agile, creative, willing to take risks, seeking to make the impossible become possible, dedicated to science, and devoted to patients, to produce excellent submissions.

When I joined PCYC, we had three full-time employees in the biometrics department, and the statistical analysis produced by statisticians and programmers needed to be approved by the operations group using an Excel spreadsheet.

With Bob and Maky's support, we were able to build an in-house organization with up to ninety full-time employees. We hired all employees without help from professional recruiting firms because the reputation of the department was so strong in the industry. We produced analyses supporting three breakthrough packages, orphan designation packages, pre-NDA packages, and NDA submissions, leading to eleven label approvals within six years.

Deepali Suri, Executive Director of Clinical Operations at Pharmacyclics

I worked at Pharmacyclics from 2012 to 2017 when Maky was the chief operating officer. It was one of the best and most enriching experiences of my life, which gave a brilliant exposure to my professional life, driving me to innovate and strive to excel every day; at the same time, grow by leaps and bounds as a person and a team player; and have a sense of making the difference for the better. It was truly Maky's brilliant leadership, larger-than-life persona, aiming for the stars for herself and her team, and top-notch operative execution that led to every day being a fulfilling day at work.

The drug being researched at Pharmacyclics, Imbruvica, was an unheard therapy in the world of hematologic malignancies when Maky ventured into the area of a huge unmet need. When I joined in 2012, there were some critical global clinical trials starting, comparing Imbruvica to the treatment of choice/approved therapies in chronic lymphocytic leukemia and other hematologic malignancies. It was hard to convince the hematologists, investigators, investors, and community at large that the BTK inhibitor drug Imbruvica could even be researched against some well-established treatment of choice, let alone be approved at some point.

Maky's team was clearly embarking on an unknown, extremely tough-to-achieve path, and reaching the finish line was nothing short of a far-fetched dream. I always saw a sense of solid belief and conviction in Maky's leadership and persona that led me to follow that conviction. I started creating various out-of-the-box scenarios with her support, building the Imbruvica story day by day, brick by brick, with that brilliant guidance, rock-solid support, and care she provided to me and all the team members. The result was Imbruvica creating history by getting approved by regulatory authorities in multiple regions and multiple disease areas across the globe. The drug today is one of the biggest blockbuster drugs in the history of hematologic malignancies.

The daily work environment was extremely positive, where each team member challenged each other in a competitive but a positive way to achieve fast-track goals with utmost quality and speed. During Maky's tenure as the leader at Pharmacyclics, the team saw exponential growth in the number of employees, from around one hundred to around eightfold in less than five years. While the growth was fast and goals were tough, the backbone of the organization always remained patient first, striving to create the difference for the better, and a quest to recreate the magic of normal in the lives of patients. There were some fantastic patient support programs built while the drug went on toward commercial success. I was fortunate to be a part of the stellar group and organization that created history under Maky's leadership.

Heow Tan, Chief of Quality and Technical Operations at Pharmacyclics

In early 2012, Pharmacyclics hired a very capable senior director of global supply chain and logistics. This senior director was a good friend of mine who had worked with me and for me for many years. She knew I was looking for an opportunity to return to the San Francisco Bay Area to work for a company developing oncology products. She said, "Hi, there is an opportunity here that fits you. We can work together again. It is a great opportunity." She suggested I send my résumé to the company.

To make the long story short, I sent my résumé to Pharmacyclics, and the human resources team soon reached out to me to schedule an interview here in Sunnyvale, California. I knew of Pharmacyclics and knew a few acquaintances who had worked for this company before. What I knew of this company was it had continued to struggle to get a footing in the oncology development space and in the early 2000s was close to going under.

As I was preparing for my interview, I was surprised to learn of this molecule called ibrutinib. Johnson & Johnson had just signed on as the corporate partner to co-develop and co-market this molecule worldwide.

I realized I needed to get this job. I could not screw this up. This is a once-in-a-lifetime career opportunity!

I came in early April 2012 and interviewed with all the chiefs and the technical operations team. I enjoyed my interview and discussion with everyone, especially the CEO, Bob Duggan, and the COO, Dr. Maky Zanganeh. They were very open and clear about the position I was interviewing for. They were also very clear about the timeline. They said, "We have two years to get CMC [chemistry, manufacturing, and controls] ready to file an NDA." Two years, OK, I was not sure how many holes or how big the holes were in this function. I just nodded, pretending I understood.

As I was interviewing with the technical operations team, which I later came on to manage, the team later told me that they knew I would be hired. This was the beginning of the lightning strike.

I came on board a few weeks later. Like any new employee, the first week onboarding process consisted of learning who was who and what was their job. I also needed to learn the CMC development status of the molecule. The most surprising thing was that many very senior executives from Johnson & Johnson were reaching out to me, wanting to discuss the manufacturing process of this molecule with me, especially the manufacturing of the capsules.

Being a new kid on the block, I tried my best to schedule to talk to them as soon as possible so I could create a good impression and build a good relationship. They asked me about my thoughts on this capsule manufacturing process and shared their concerns that this process could not flow well and thus was not scalable. Well, maybe I was naive. I told them this was only a phase 2 process, and together, Pharmacyclics and Johnson & Johnson would find ways to make this process work. For some strange reason, they seemed to feel more comfortable and asked me to lead the development of this process. Well, now the challenge was on.

Here came the lightning. In July 2012, the US Congress passed the PUDFA [Prescription Drug User Fee Amendments] IV Act, which included the award of breakthrough therapy designation (BTD) for molecules the FDA deemed to have exceptional efficacy and safety in the early phase studies.

Pharmacyclics reached out to our partner Johnson & Johnson to understand how to utilize this new act to accelerate the development of ibrutinib. FDA had not issued any guidance yet for this BTD. So the pharmaceutical industry didn't know how to utilize this designation. They wanted to understand more before proceeding. Sounded perfectly reasonable.

But Pharmacyclics was gung ho and fearless. We wanted to take advantage of this BTD to accelerate the development of ibrutinib in the US. We believed in this game changer act. So we proceeded, and within a few months, Pharmacyclics received three BTDs for ibrutinib. We were proud to receive these three BTDs. Ibrutinib was the only molecule at this time to receive multiple BTDs. Little did we know that from the two years to filing, the NDA was now reduced to months.

It was now racing to the finish line, to get the NDA filed as soon as possible. But I told Bob and Maky, "Wait, I do not have enough stability data to file the NDA." FDA needed six months of accelerated condition and twelve months of long-term storage condition data to file. We only began our stability studies for both conditions. I tried to educate Bob and Maky that they could not accelerate time. There was no time machine to do this. I argued that there was no precedent to file less than this amount of stability data, or we would receive an RTF (refusal to file) letter with the NDA. Bob, in his great wisdom, said, "Talk to the FDA." I relented and reached out to the FDA.

At this time, I had been in the Pharmaceutical industry for more than twenty-six years. As far as I remember, it was always the industry that tried to convince the FDA that they had sufficient data in all aspects of CMC, including stability data to file the NDA. It was then the FDA that pointed out all the holes that needed to be completed before the NDA could be filed.

When my team and I reached out to the FDA, we reversed our roles. We pointed out to the FDA the holes we had in the CMC development of ibrutinib. We did not have enough pivotal stability data, and many of the impurities were in the process of being qualified.

When I finished presenting these holes to the FDA in our meeting, the FDA CMC lead said, "Do you have twelve months of long-term stability data from your supporting lots? Did these stability data trend similarly to your current pivotal stability data?"

One attribute of ibrutinib that helped us a lot was the molecule's stability. I said yes to both of these questions.

Then she said, "Why don't you substitute the supporting data for your pivotal data as they trend similarly?"

I was dumbfounded for a few seconds. When I quickly recovered, I said, "Will do. Thank you."

When Pharmacyclics planned our CMC NDA timeline with our partner, Johnson & Johnson, collectively, we determined that we could complete and file the NDA at the end of 2013. Only two weeks later, with all the excitement of the BTD and good news from the clinical fronts, Bob and Maky asked me to come and meet with them on the timing of the NDA filing. They told me the CMC modules were on the critical path for the NDA filing and asked me when these CMC NDA modules could be finished and filed. I told them the end of 2013.

They said they heard me, and again, they asked the question, "The CMC module is on the critical path. When can you finish and file?"

Only then did I realize they wanted the NDA to be filed earlier than the end of 2013, and they asked me to come back in a few days to let them know the timing.

Well, the Pharmacyclics and the Johnson & Johnson CMC team just determined that we could file the NDA at the end of 2013. Now my two bosses were not satisfied with this timing from the team. Should they push back at Bob and Maky, or go back to the CMC teams to work out a new timeline? They decided they would work on this timeline and give it to Bob and Maky. As I had an ibrutinib joint project meeting with Johnson & Johnson on the East Coast the following day, I decided to take a couple of pencils and erasers to work on this new timeline on my red-eye flight.

Prior to landing, I put this new timeline on a PowerPoint for presentation for the joint project team meeting. There I announced that the new timeline for the NDA filing was midyear 2013, a reduction of six months. I knew what I did was bad management, micromanaging, and overriding a joint team decision. The Pharmacyclics and the Johnson & Johnson CMC teams were shocked and thought I was out of my mind.

As Pharmacyclics conducted our manufacturing activities with contract manufacturers overseas, we visited them quarterly to ensure they executed their activities at a very fast pace. We were also there to brainstorm and discuss challenges they encountered and offered "out of the box" solutions. When I first visited these manufacturers, we told them they had two years before we filed the NDA. A few months later, when we came back after developing the joint Pharmacyclics and Johnson & Johnson CMC teams timeline, we told them they had twelve months before we filed the NDA. After Pharmacyclics received the three BTDs, I told them the NDA would be filed midyear 2013. They responded by saying, "Please don't come back."

Even with my unilateral setting of the timeline to midyear 2013, the joint Pharmacyclics and Johnson & Johnson CMC teams proceeded to author each subsection of the NDA in an expeditious manner. It did not matter whether it was after 5:00 p.m. on a weekday or weekend, the toils continued for both Pharmacyclics and the Johnson & Johnson teams. Our overseas chemical and domestic capsule manufacturing plants continued their work 24/7. The collaboration between both teams was exemplary. As Pharmacyclics was a small company and Johnson & Johnson was a multinational conglomerate, Johnson & Johnson supported Pharmacyclics with their best scientists and engineers so that Pharmacyclics could manage these development and manufacturing activities overseas and domestically around the clock.

Bob introduced the corporate culture for Pharmacyclics. He put together his thoughts on the twenty-four characteristics of a genius. These were simple and practical characteristics that helped each person to be a better person and a more thoughtful and efficient coworker by invoking these characteristics inherent in every human being. Seminars for these characteristics were presented to all employees of the company.

At Pharmacyclics, we had a solid cohesive team. The teamwork among the various functions was commendable. Each team took risks to achieve traditional pharmaceutical practices and think outside the box for ideas and yet still comply with all FDA and international pharmaceutical regulations and guidance. When a team was at risk of not achieving its objectives, other teams stepped in to help. While the work at Pharmacyclics was challenging as we wanted to get ibrutinib to the patients as soon as possible, the leadership and culture created allowed its employees to have a very satisfying feeling of achievements and contributions.

It is particularly true for the technical operations CMC team. The CMC development activities were on the critical path for the NDA filing, but the team in collaboration with our corporate partner, Johnson & Johnson, came through to complete the NDA in midyear 2013 with only a day left. The team ensured ibrutinib was manufactured at the highest quality, and any patients who wanted the drug could get it through its proper channels on a timely basis. While ibrutinib, whose commercial name was now Imbruvica, was not the first BTD molecule to be approved, the Pharmacyclics supply chain launched the product out of our warehouse on the same day as its NDA was approved to the wholesalers and allowed our patients access to this wonderful molecule.

The team was incredibly focused. Their teamwork and support for each other was second to none. Not only were we teammates, but we also became friends and family.

As they say, we need to give credit where credit is due. We must thank our corporate partner for their support to Pharmacyclics and the development and registration of Imbruvica. Johnson & Johnson is a giant pharmaceutical company with vast resources and experience. They have great facilities and people that came to be very helpful to Pharmacyclics. All the problems Pharmacyclics encountered in the development, manufacturing, and registration of Imbruvica had been encountered before by the Johnson & Johnson team.

For example, in manufacturing in our commercial manufacturing sites, we needed to use reagents that were flammable and explosive. We reached out to Johnson & Johnson to ask them to send their safety engineers to ensure the equipment used was adequately designed, the safety procedures were in place, and that the production operators and supervisors were all thoroughly trained. As mentioned earlier, in the early days of scaled-up activities, as Pharmacyclics did not have enough staff to cover 24/7 operations at our manufacturing sites, Johnson & Johnson provided their scientists and engineers that allowed Pharmacyclics to develop a 24/7 person-in-plant coverage. When we needed highly specialized equipment to analyze samples, Johnson & Johnson was there to provide the instruments with their technicians.

At Pharmacyclics, we did all our GMP [good manufacturing practices] manufacturing at our contract manufacturer's site. We also leveraged Johnson & Johnson's purchasing power to help us obtain the manufacturing schedules and services we needed.

Johnson & Johnson took care of Pharmacyclics like a big brother takes care of a young brother. Besides providing technical experience, facilities, and staff, they provided many invaluable pieces of advice. They utilized their vast corporate international affiliates infrastructure to check and explain how they responded to many of the local regulatory agencies' filing questions and inspections.

The Pharmacyclics technical operations team would not have been able to achieve the CMC development and manufacturing at this lightning speed without the Johnson & Johnson CMC technical team's support. While we were experienced professionals and very motivated, sometimes, in our haste, we did not see the speed bumps or the walls. When we ran into the speed bumps and walls, the Johnson & Johnson team was there to support us. For this, I am very thankful to our corporate partners and friends at Johnson & Johnson.

When I came for my interview, Pharmacyclics's chief medical officer showed me some preliminary phase 2 clinical data. Though it was very impressive, and I was truly impressed, deep down I was skeptical. I have been shown impressive phase 2 data before when I went for interviews with other companies. Then after I joined the company, I would find that the eventual phase 3 data had failed.

But the clinical trials here at Pharmacyclics were different. As the follow-up of the patients continued, more patients responded and responded more completely. Like wine, the longer the wine is stored, the better the taste. Ibrutinib was like wine—the longer it went, the better the results.

I have never worked for a company where there was good news after good news. First, the US Congress passed PUDFA IV with the BTD designation. Then each of the completed clinical trials for the various leukemia indications continued to be successful. There appeared to be some magic here.

Truly, I must credit these incredible successes to the leadership of the CEO, Bob Duggan, and the COO, Maky Zanganeh. They had "for the betterment of the patients" corporate vision. They hired a very professional executive team and many other employees. Bob and Maky empowered and trusted the decisions of their executive team. Most important, they were always available to lend their leadership whenever any executives or employees reached out to them.

Wall Street and the Financial World rewarded the company richly. Since I joined, the stock price had only one direction to go (i.e., up). In every quarterly earnings call, I only heard praises from very appreciative analysts.

What can I say, it was a once-in-a-lifetime career opportunity. Not only did I have the opportunity to work on this spectacular molecule called ibrutinib, but I also had the opportunity to work for two of the best corporate leaders, Bob and Maky; without them, ibrutinib would probably not have become Imbruvica in such a short time.

For me, it was such a very rewarding and satisfying career to be part of Bob and Maky's winning team. The satisfaction I experienced was beyond words. I will always be thankful and grateful to Bob and Maky for this opportunity.

Matt Outten, Head of Market Access and Commercial Liaison at Pharmacyclics

I almost never came to Pharmacyclics (PCYC). I went to interview with a few individuals in the fall of 2012 and really liked the opportunity but afterward was told that I needed to fly to New Jersey and Pennsylvania to interview with the copromote partner. I said that I was only interested in working for the lead in a copromote situation and was uneasy if the partner was making the hiring decisions. So I pulled my name out.

A few months later, I received a callback and was told that if I were still interested, I would not have to interview with the copromote partner, but I would have to come back to California to interview with the COO and CEO, Maky and Bob. The interview was supposed to be thirty minutes, and an hour later with the discussion ongoing, I said, "I'm not sure if I should say this, but I am having a lot of fun."

The interview became a strategic working session, and I could tell what it would be like to work at Pharmacyclics and I wanted to be a part of it. I began commuting weekly from Boston for several months before moving with my family to California.

My most memorable moment at Pharmacyclics was being a part of the successful launch and copromotion of Imbruvica, a drug that benefits the lives of oncology patients around the world. While I chose to work here for this purpose, what also remains indelible of my time at Pharmacyclics was the unique and non-conforming leadership style versus what you see in the Big Pharma arena. One was able to push boundaries, be heard, and think outside the box in a way I believe set Pharmacyclics apart and far above its competitors and other companies I had worked for previously.

I was initially hired as the VP of market access, later promoted to an interim chief commercial officer position. On my second day on the job, Maky came into my office, asking if I was settling in OK. Barely finishing my response of "everything is great," she asked me to put together a full strategy with tactics to present to JBI, our copromotion partner in the following days. I literally laughed, thinking she was joking. She laughed because she found humor in my believing she was joking. Turns out she was not joking, so I proceeded with the plan. I was excited for the chance to implement my knowledge and excited to be part of this biotech company.

One of my proudest achievements at PCYC was creating and later implementing a novel distribution model. This limited distribution model not only made accessing lifesaving oncology medications easier but also simultaneously saved the company millions of dollars in unnecessary fees. I was able to do this by leveraging my specialty pharmacy relationships in conjunction with my negotiation skills and working with an amazing group of market access professionals.

This distribution model has been successfully adopted by several biotech companies and is still being used today by many companies. There were many aspects of working at Pharmacyclics I enjoyed, but what stood out to me was the generosity of the leadership team. While Bob and Maky had high expectations and goals to be met, they also appreciated and in turn rewarded success and achievement. At one point, Bob Duggan gave away ten Teslas in a company lottery from his own personal finances. When twelve names were accidentally drawn, he honored all twelve without hesitation.

Deepa Venkataraman, Senior Director of Drug Safety and Pharmacovigilance Operations at Pharmacyclics

An Unforgettable and Magical Journey.

I feel deeply grateful and fortunate to have been part of the magical journey of Imbruvica, aka Pharmacyclics, aka a journey with Bob and Maky.

At Pharmacyclics, I was brought in to build the clinical drug safety ops team in preparation for the first NDA filing and launch. It was not an easy road ahead. When I first started, I had a team of two with minimal infrastructure in place, three months for filing, and six months for launch. I went on to build a robust operating model and oversaw more than one hundred members in onshore and offshore teams through all eleven approvals and integration with AbbVie during my more than eight years' tenure. I was responsible for the safety of our patients throughout the product life cycle and compliance with regulatory requirements worldwide.

None of this would have happened if it were not for Maky and Bob. They believed in me more than I did in myself. I am forever grateful for them. I am a better person and a better leader today because of them and my journey at Pharmacyclics.

It all started when a colleague of mine at Johnson & Johnson, UK, had put me in touch with my hiring manager at Pharmacyclics when I was moving to San Francisco to start the next phase in my life. I gathered from her that the team at Pharmacyclics was very committed and that both companies could mutually benefit from having me there to further strengthen the relationship of the Pharmacovigilance (PV) teams.

Working in oncology has always held a special place in my heart since my grandmother passed away from leukemia at a young age. I was excited to work for a company whose goal was to find a cure for cancers that have personally affected my family and that focused so much on the patient journey.

I still vividly recall my first interaction with Maky in the fall of 2012 when I was interviewing for a manager role in patient safety/PV. I could see the passion and confidence in her eyes toward the company, the people, and the product; it was so contagious. Suddenly Bob surprised me by dropping by from the room next door during my interview. I was in awe seeing such an inspiring and committed leader yet very humble in every way. After meeting with the two, I knew at once that this was the company that I wanted to invest myself in and I could not wait to start my journey with these exceptionally passionate and committed folks.

The words of Bob and Maky to me resonated throughout my time at Pharmacyclics. "We are here to make a significant difference to the betterment of patients. Let us channel all our energy to make it happen. We can and we will. We are all in this together."

The path to success was not an easy one and was not meant for everyone. Only those who dared to dream big, take the hard path, challenge the norm, and believe in themselves and the mission could deliver.

The bond we formed among colleagues during the days at Pharmacyclics was nothing less than magical. It was so strong and special. We were never afraid to challenge one another, yet we always had one another's backs and support every step of the way. Many of them have become my lifelong friends. This special bond built a lot of trust among colleagues and was instrumental in our combined success as one team. Such was the unique culture created by Bob and Maky.

At Pharmacyclics, we were able to see the impact on the patients in a very tangible way. Bob and Maky made sure that we got to hear from the patients firsthand about how our product brought back the magic of normal to the patients and their families. I still remember the times when Maky and Bob had brought patients onsite. At the end of every patient's talk was a room filled with a teary-eyed audience. We knew every day that we were there to make a lasting impact. We just could not stop aiming higher and higher. Nothing could stop us.

Both Maky and Bob were a constant source of inspiration and guidance. Their leadership was instrumental in the success of the company.

Maky was the powerhouse, whose enthusiasm, confidence, and guidance fueled us to stay focused on execution with excellence even at lightning speed. Maky possessed a rare combination of a brilliant mind, perceptive leadership, and a very friendly personality. She brought out the best in everyone and challenged us in a healthy way to be a better version of ourselves every day. Maky trusted her team and empowered and enabled them to be independent thinkers and leaders. It is this secret sauce that kept us moving toward our goal without pausing.

I am grateful to have been part of this journey, an unforgettable and magical journey that would go down in history, something that I never thought even in my wildest dreams could happen when I first met with Bob and Maky.

I knew all along that I would do it all over again in a heartbeat should there be another opportunity to work for Bob and Maky. I did not expect it to come this soon. … I cannot wait to recreate the magic of normal.

Naomi Cretcher, Senior Director of Events and Media Production at Pharmacyclics

Working at Pharmacyclics was life-changing for me. Before starting at PCYC, I had recently reentered the workforce after raising four kids. In my prechildren life, I was a media producer, and the biotech world was very foreign to me. I had a lot of catch-up in learning about drug development and commercialization, and I had a lot of insecurities, but the truth and encouragement that Maky showed allowed me to find my way. She trusted me to organize high-profile events and help create the branding of the company.

There are so many great memories for me during my six years while working at PCYC. One of them was my first day; while I was working at my desk, I kept hearing a foghorn throughout the day, but it did not make sense because we were in Sunnyvale. There is no fog in Sunnyvale. Finally, I asked someone about the foghorn sound, and I was told it was in honor of patients as they enrolled in our trials. I knew I made the right decision accepting the job because patients were the priority at Pharmacyclics.

What I will never forget is interviewing patients and their families about their experience with Imbruvica and bringing their stories back home to the office to share with the employees who worked tirelessly to bring the drug to market and to see the fruits of their labor. One of the most memorable ones was about a gentleman who was given a few months to live, and understandably, he was devastated but especially because he was going to miss his daughter's wedding.

Once he started on Imbruvica, his symptoms started to dissipate right away. He was able to attend his daughter's wedding after all. The whole experience gave him a new perspective on life, and he started meditating and doing yoga regularly. This was so opposite of who he was before, and it was rewarding to see how our company played a small part in making a difference in his life.

The most memorable day was on November 13, 2013, the day we received accelerated approval for ibrutinib (Imbruvica capsules, Pharmacyclics, Inc.). I knew patients would be able to receive our drug for mantle cell lymphoma. When we received the news, everyone in the office started hugging, crying, and celebrating because we could make a difference in the lives of leukemia patients. Following that, Maky asked me to organize the launch celebration. She was very clear that it was going to be magical, elegant, and fun.

I walked out of that meeting, thinking, "Oh my God, what an opportunity" and "Oh my God, how am I going to do this within a few weeks?"

The invitations for this black-tie formal event went out, and we invited the entire company and C-level executives from Janssen. One night, Maky and her son, Shaun, were watching *America's Got Talent*, and there was this young and upcoming talent by the name of Collins Key who did a magic show and was one of the finalists. The next day, Maky asked me to find Collins and hire him for the launch party.

The "Magic of Normal" was one of our marketing campaigns, and the magic fit perfectly into the event. We found the magician, and again, he wowed the audience with his magic. It was truly a magical event at the Palace Hotel in San Francisco. Maky and Ramses Erdtmann were the emcees, and the event went well into the night and is remembered by everyone.

Maky gave me an opportunity that I will never forget and will forever be grateful for. She asked me to coordinate the due diligence events for the eventual acquisition of PCYC. This was a first for me, and I wasn't sure if I could pull it off. But with Maky's guidance and leadership, it was a huge success. We were working around the clock for weeks. We created pop-up offices within days. It was challenging but rewarding to pull it off. It was a highlight in my career. Being part of such an event can be a once-in-a-lifetime opportunity, and I consider myself very fortunate to be part of it.

Dawn Bir, Vice President of Sales at Pharmacyclics

What Bob and Maky created at Pharmacyclics is nothing short of remarkable. At the time, some people called it "lightning in a bottle" and a "once in a lifetime" event. The real-life lessons I learned in only four years are priceless. They come from understanding the how and why behind this success and center on empowering people more so than on the business itself. Below are just a few lessons I learned from my time at Pharmacyclics that I wish I had known and embraced earlier in my career:

The best decisions are made when you listen to your head, your heart, and your gut. Never just one.

Your head will evaluate the data available. Your heart will let you know it is the right thing to do. Your gut will make you dig beyond the surface because more information is needed. It will also let you know when something is wrong. Your gut will also feel an overwhelming sense of energy (some may call it butterflies in your stomach) when the decision is a big one. Get used to that and use it to your advantage. It's why some people lead and others don't. It's why some people take chances and others won't. Trust these instincts and listen to them. When was the last time they were really ever wrong? I will forever hear Maky say, "Trust your gut. Always."

Attention with intention.

Don't invest in a company and turn your back. Your investment may grow, but it will never reach its full potential. Follow your intentions and invest your money in something you believe in deeply and then invest all of you and your attention to ensure it will be a success. Don't walk away or turn your back when things get tough. Try again. Greatness doesn't just happen. It takes your full attention and personal commitment. Investing in people works exactly the same way.

You are capable of so much more than you know at this moment in time.

Maky Zanganeh believes in hidden potential, and by doing so, she brings out the best performance in others. She didn't believe in everyone but took chances on only those whom she trusted, who were consistent, those who had demonstrated selflessness and cared about doing the right things the right way. Maky empowered people she knew would make her proud and represented Pharmacyclics well with "clean hands."

And by believing in someone, even before they believed in themselves, Maky expanded their potential. She would often say, "I know you will do this," "You won't fail. I won't let you," and "Everything you need is inside you. You've got this."

She helped others be fearless and confident, and with both, you can achieve more than you ever thought possible. This is life changing. How lucky am I that I was one she believed in. The lesson learned: *Give people a safe place to do the job you hired them to do. Let them be themselves and trust in their experience and commitment. This is how you bring out the best in people.*

"Make a difference for the better" (Bob Duggan). These are words I will remember forever. Do good without causing harm. Leave your

legacy in the people you touch. Create a change in the world through every person you influence. Make a difference for the better.

The business of biotech and drug development is especially difficult, and even more so for a non-revenue-generating, early-stage company heavily reliant on investors. Companies lack the infrastructure, process, and resources of a large established company. External scrutiny and the risk level are high. Employees discover very quickly if they will love it and thrive in this environment or hate it and leave. It is not uncommon to see people depart quickly or be escorted out the door if they can't handle the pressure, exposure, and unique dynamics of a start-up company. Pharmacyclics was no different. A lot was asked of every employee because the success of the team was on the line. Not everyone made it.

It was a Thursday afternoon late in the day and only a few weeks after joining the organization. This was my first time with a development stage company, and Bob and Maky asked me to trust them. "Trust us and what we will do." Not scripted or packaged, their honesty, directness, and unfiltered conversation felt very different and so welcome. That afternoon, I knew I was where I needed to be. The chaos of our world became the perfect place to flourish, and I did. For that, I am forever thankful.

Will Black, Executive Director of Technology Operations at Pharmacyclics

Bob and Maky established clear objectives for the company; what was unusual was that these objectives did not change over time or with market pressures. They were simple yet, for an early-stage biotech, inspiring:

- Patient first/patient-friendly
- Quality, then speed, then cost

Throughout the years I spent at Pharmacyclics, this patient-friendly, quality-driven philosophy was clear and emphasized at every company meeting and literally painted on the walls. For me, it quickly became clear that this was not a normal job. The overwhelming belief in science and that we had the ability to address unmet medical needs was pervasive.

This did not come without a price—we absolutely lost some good people who just became overwhelmed by the pressure and pace we were working under. So although there was clear excitement and the clinical trial results were very positive, a company quality mindset striving for a patient cure came at a cost, and that cost did see some intelligent, motivated people who simply could not maintain their balance in a high pressure, results-driven organization. The mission was quite simply to save lives and return patients to a normal lifestyle. With a wife who has stage 4 lung cancer, the power of normal is very appealing.

I was fortunate to join Pharmacyclics when the total headcount was less than fifty people. There were really no politics. I really felt that we all shared the company mission and really strived toward that objective. Bob had great vision and leadership—Maky transformed that vision into the strategic imperatives that would enable a tiny company to receive three breakthrough designations from the FDA.

At one of the first company meetings, when we had probably grown to about eighty people, Bob's true colors were very evident. Bob passionately asked if everyone was participating in the ESPP [employee stock purchase plan]. He emphasized that he felt this was a great long-term investment and strongly encouraged everyone to invest in the company. There are very few CEOs who would go out on a limb like this to encourage people to participate actively in the ESPP. In our litigious society, either the CEO or the board would feel that this was an unjustified risk. This really struck me as being very typical of the Pharmacyclics leadership. They truly did what they thought was best for everyone and not just for themselves.

Bob took no stock options or salary; as CEO and chairman of the board, he would have been justified in awarding himself millions of stock options between 2008 and the AbbVie acquisition in 2015. Taking no salary and no stock options and instead personally investing in the stock truly showed integrity and desire to share this opportunity with others.

ClinOps [Clinical Operations] used to celebrate every new patient coming on trial—Tammy would sound an air horn that echoed through the building. Everyone knew where we were with trial enrollment. We had great people who wrote brilliant protocols and a great ClinOps group that strived to find patients to participate in the trials. In the early days, this was an uphill battle. It was not until we had ASCO and ASH presentations with our great PI's [principal investigators] presenting that allowed prescribing oncologists to see that though we were in clinical trials PCI-32765 (ibrutinib) was truly a special treatment.

The final highlight of the Pharmacyclics story was being part of the internal group that would prepare the due diligence data for the 2015 acquisition. I'd been part of the earlier DD when we had selected Johnson & Johnson as a partner to help develop ibrutinib and to market and sell internationally. The final due diligence (DD) was a whole new level of complexity though.

At the final point, we had three simultaneous due diligence meetings in three separate locations. As additional data was requested by one group, the data was produced, QC'd [quality controlled], and passed legal review. This new data was then made available to all three DD meetings simultaneously. All three groups were sequestered and using PCYC systems, they could view the data, but they were not allowed to copy the data. This meant that there were between thirty to forty people in each DD and everyone was working around the clock.

After Bob and Maky had made the strategic decision that a sale of the company was the correct decision, they expanded the core group who would operationally execute to fifteen. This group worked evenings, weekends, and holidays (and through the Super Bowl) to bring together and present all the relevant data.

Though this was the end of the journey for independent Pharmacyclics, it was just the beginning relative to the impact Imbruvica would have on patients' lives.

Elaine Stracker, General Counsel at Pharmacyclics

There were so many things that I really liked about the company. The camaraderie with my team though I think was the best. We complemented each other very well; we were a well-balanced team in terms of personality. Everyone worked hard, but we also had fun together (e.g., Segway riding, wine tasting, assembling "briefs" together, etc.). Even during the stressful times, we would laugh, and I knew I could count on them.

Many times, my team members would put in very long days and nights to accomplish things that needed to get done. There were no comments or issues that this was someone else's work. Everyone jumped in and participated when needed. I liked the fact that if you worked hard and contributed that you were recognized. PCYC was good about this and allowed one to grow professionally if you were willing to take on the challenge and be accountable.

I remember, in executive meetings, people presenting ideas and the leadership allowing the presenter to go forward to execute on their ideas even though they were risky if the person was willing to accept full responsibility. The other thing that was great was that the company had a very flat organization and that everyone was encouraged to express their opinion in executive meetings. People were allowed to disagree, but once a decision was made, everyone was aligned and moved forward as a single team to execute it.

Another thing that was refreshing and that I really appreciated was the speed at which decisions were made. There was none of this need to convince a large number of committees and waiting months before a decision was made. You did not have to slog through committee after committee to push an idea. You could present an idea/suggestion in a meeting, and you generally had the decision regarding your idea/suggestion before the meeting was over. However, you definitely had to come prepared to answer any questions that may be raised at the time you presented your idea.

My most memorable time was the couple of months spent preparing for and handling the due diligence for the sale of PCYC. First was the ominous non-disclosure agreement that we were asked to execute before being accepted as part of the small team that would participate in getting the company ready for the sale. Then after you signed, they would tell you that the company was up for sale. I remember having mixed feelings, as of course, it was exciting to be part of the team that would get to participate in the due diligence, but you also knew that the company would change with a sale. Also, it would be very difficult to keep this from your team members, who would have to support your requests for data and information without knowing what was going on.

As I headed up legal and IP, and the company had been in business for about twenty years, I knew that there would be many things that would need to be looked at and possibly need to be cleaned up, not the least of which was the over six thousand active contracts that the company had. Also, I would need to have a way to look at all the clauses to ensure that there was no issue with a contract that had been in place for years with regard to an acquisition. Moreover, there were many records that would be required that we did not have in-house, as they had in the past resided with outside counsel, that we would now need to get copies of and index in a very short period of time.

I started by telling my team that we wanted to have all outside counsel documents in-house not just electronically but also paper copies, as we were considering changing counsel. I also said that we were also preparing for a potential audit, so we needed everything organized as this was likely to occur in the next six weeks or so. Both of these were true statements as we were considering changing our counsel and certainly would likely do so after the merger, and we had a number of audits that could occur at any time: FDA, IRS [Internal Revenue Service], JNJ, etc.

The contracts were another matter. At first, we tried to look at them manually; however, when I explained the issue to one of our IT heads, Will Black, who also knew about the sale, he proposed that he and his team could OCR [optical character recognition] every contract for me so that I could select words or phrases and conduct a global search for all documents at the same time to look at key paragraphs or sections. This was a great time saver for me. He was such a great help then and throughout the process.

The decision had been made that there would be only three parties that would participate in the due diligence and that we were going to set up the due diligence at three different locations, so three different data rooms needed to be set up. Additionally, each of the parties was making different requests for different information. I was responsible to work with IT and Ramses Erdtmann (head of IR and facilities) and all the department heads that were privy to the sale to ensure that all the responsive documents were ready for each data room.

Additionally, as we were parsing out the nonpublic IP that was being provided (including trade secret information) from the rest of the data, I needed to review the information being provided to ensure nothing was disclosed too soon. It was an incredibly hectic time, and as my daily commute to and from the company was so long (over two hours each way), it was decided that I should take an apartment near the law firm handling the transaction for PCYC so that I could be available when needed.

The team worked late into the evenings every day to put together the presentations for the due diligence. I am certain that people at the company were wondering where we were all the time. We would all arrive and work out of the law office of the law firm handling the transaction as we prepped for the due diligence. It seemed like we ate and slept there for weeks.

Finally, the time for the due diligence arrived. Each company participating heard our presentations and was allowed to access the data for three days and to ask us questions. All the due diligence was to be viewed locally. It was decided that the participants could not use their computers or phones during the due diligence (they had to check their phones with someone outside the data rooms when they arrived). Each team brought about sixty people to assess the data. So our small team was running from site to site.

As PCYC had decided early on to tier disclosure of information depending on how serious the bidders were and not to disclose trade secret information or non-published IP until after the final offers from each participant came in, it was important for me to sit in with the various groups to ensure that in responding to questions, trade secret information was not inadvertently disclosed. Also, during the day and in the evenings when requests for additional documentation came up during the due diligence from the bidders, it had to be reviewed by me to ensure that we were tiering the information correctly (i.e., not disclosing trade secret information until it was appropriate).

During this process, I was also working with our outside legal team to review the sales agreement and ensure that the disclosure schedules for the transaction were accurate.

Finally, the time arrived for the parties to put in their final bid (it was their second offer each). Even while their bids came in, they were still looking at the data in the data rooms. I remember during this process, Maky called me while I was with one of the companies answering their questions. She insisted I come quickly to the office of the law firm.

I remember running to get there, and she called me twice while I was running there. I was told who had the winning bid, AbbVie, and was instructed to provide their group with access to all the highest-tiered information including the IP and trade secret information not previously disclosed. I met with their counsels and had discussions to answer questions and explain a number of items.

At this time, the other parties were not aware that the highest bidder had been selected or that they were viewing this additional information yet. As part of the process early on, the bidders were informed that they could back out of their offer if after disclosure of the high-tiered information they did not want to proceed. We were confident that this would not be an issue. AbbVie had the highest bid and was comfortable moving forward after completing their review. We informed all the other parties at that time that AbbVie was to acquire PCYC. Everyone was exhausted but exhilarated at the same time. One of the largest sales ever, at that time, in biotech history, with probably one of the best due diligence processes ever.

My main achievement was the handling of the due diligence. This was a very stressful and critical time for the company. As an example of what it was like, I will describe the last night and day before the offers were to come in and we were trying to finalize the disclosure schedules for the deal. For the past several days, I had basically not slept as there was so much to do. I was working on the disclosure schedules for the transaction. I was also answering questions from our attorneys on the last evening, clarifying disclosures, before the offers were to come in. It was about two o'clock in the morning. I was tired and trying to recall all major agreements that needed to be disclosed for the specific reps and warranties, etc.

All of a sudden, after working for hours, my computer screen went completely black. I was in a panic. I could not imagine starting all over again; as it was, I was going to be up all night. I called our IT person on the team, Will Black. He answered immediately, and even though I woke him up out of a dead sleep, he assured me he would have it fixed and not to worry. He did! When I finished, I went to the apartment I was staying at during the due diligence to take a shower and then to come right back as this was the critical day.

When I arrived at the law firm office that morning, the lawyers handed me the disclosure schedules to review one last time before the contract was to be signed. I was shocked these were not the disclosures that I had provided. There was a mix-up and they had put a much earlier version of the disclosures on the agreement. It was these types of things that kept one constantly in upheaval during the process.

Thus, getting through and handling all the unexpected surprises that arose during the due diligence was my main achievement at PCYC. However, I could not have done this without the fantastic support provided by my direct reports and the other due diligence team members.

Greg Hemmi, Vice President of Chemical Operations at Pharmacyclics

My journey at Pharmacyclics began in June 1992. I was a newly minted PhD chemist from Texas, hired as the third employee of a new start-up company. My first day started in a rented office in Palo Alto, California, with no computer, no laboratories, no spending accounts to buy equipment, and no idea what I was doing. Shortly after, William Dow was hired to manage the science operations and quickly got me focused on making radiolabeled texaphyrin at SRI International for biological research studies.

As the company needed drug material for preclinical research studies, my next task was to work at Seres Laboratories in Santa Rosa California to manufacture as much drug substance as we could. Jim Eldridge was also hired to head quality assurance and taught me how to document drug manufacture using good manufacturing practices (GMP—often referred to as generate more paper). So began my journey down the chemical development and manufacturing career path.

Over the next fifteen years, I learned much about chemical development from William Dow, chemical manufacturing and contract manufacturing management from Hugo Madden, and GMP documentation from Jim Eldridge. I learned the importance of high-quality analytical methods from Alice Lin and Johanna Lang and how to work with regulatory agencies from Diane Ngami. I learned much from many other people at Pharmacyclics and contract companies and learned it takes a team of dedicated professionals to move a drug forward.

Success in developing a marketable drug not only takes a team of dedicated professionals but also a drug worthy of development. After fifteen years of effort, motexafin gadolinium had failed to show statistically significant efficacy in a second phase 3 clinical trial. By this time, Pharmacyclics had nearly exhausted its financial resources, had a poor relationship with FDA, and had to downsize its workforce to save money.

The company had purchased three early-stage drug programs from Celera Genomics and was essentially starting over. For the remaining employees at Pharmacyclics, the mood was not optimistic. Then to make matters worse, upper management and the board of directors resigned. Robert Duggan took control of the company. Little did we know this was the start of a better future.

The next year was a very trying time at Pharmacyclics. There were old employees and new upper management and board of directors. There was an old failed drug and new early-stage potential products. There was old poor investor interest and a new vision of a better future for the company. Maky Zanganeh came on to manage business development and soon developed a corporate partnership for the HDAC program to bring much-needed funding back in. Robert Duggan convinced investors to stay on and put more money in to keep the faith alive.

A difficult decision was made to abandon the old texaphyrin drug platform and look to the new. The new management looked at the old employees and chose to give them another chance. The stage was set, but where to go? The least developed of the Celera early-stage drug programs turned out to be the diamond in the rough.

Celera did extensive medicinal chemistry to search for a suitable compound to inhibit Bruton's tyrosine kinase (BTK). A sizable compound library was generated, but no one compound was active enough to develop into a drug. The only compound sufficiently active was a tool compound (later designated PCI-32765) considered unsuitable because it covalently (that is, irreversibly) bound to BTK. The mantra in pharma at the time was covalently binding compounds could not be developed into drugs because of potential long-term toxic effects.

The tool compound was tested for toxic effects and found to be acceptable for further preclinical development. Not only did PCI-32765 pass all preclinical testing, but once it was administered to lymphoma cancer patients, it quickly demonstrated safety and an ability to reduce a patient's cancer at low dose in phase 1. Finally, a drug that worked and was worthy of development! Finally, the employees of Pharmacyclics could put all their training to work and management's ability to lead a viable program to success!

The next five years became a blur of activity. More drugs were never enough. FDA went from "don't bother us" to "tell us more." A corporate partner was found who brought on a team of experienced people to help move the product forward. In the end, the drug was shipped for marketing on the very day approval was granted by the FDA, a feat seldom accomplished even by the largest pharma companies (and masterfully orchestrated by Heow Tan).

In a short one and a half pages, it is impossible to name all the people who contributed to the successful development of PCI-32765 (Imbruvica as it is now marketed). The list would span not only Pharmacyclics but also Celera, our corporate partner, and all the contract organizations who worked their expertise on the project. I was but a small part of the effort but learned a great deal from all I had contact with.

I once commented to Bob Duggan that Pharmacyclics was like a plane jetting straight to the ground when he and his team arrived. Thankfully, Bob and his team had the courage to run to the cockpit and pull the plane back up before hitting the ground. The plane ride became a wild new adventure thereafter. Thanks for the ride, Bob.

Adam Finerman, Lawyer at Olshan Frome Wolosky LLP

I first learned of Pharmacyclics from Bob Duggan. He passionately explained to me that PCYC was a little company with some extraordinary intellectual property. When Bob and Maky first joined PCYC, the company did a financing of several million dollars so that at year-end, the company would be able to report cash in the bank of $10 million. Over the years, as the team switched PCYC's focus to the ibrutinib molecule and began seeing confirmed positive results and working through the required regulatory testing process, raising money became easier, and ultimately hundreds of millions of dollars were raised.

Maky was, and is, relentless in pushing herself, the company, and everyone else toward the finish line. She never accepts the status quo, nor does she let anyone else. In meeting after meeting, she would challenge people who confidently told the group something was true or impossible to accomplish or who otherwise accepted facts without support. She would innately grasp what the weak assumption was and press—asking why—and demand support.

Engaged and prepared coworkers would welcome her challenge to common assumptions and freely consider if there were possible alternatives, frequently leading to better solutions. Those less confident, or less prepared, would become defensive and would ultimately leave the company, not being willing, or capable, of pushing against the status quo and looking for more.

Through sheer force of her will, Maky worked to create a team that was capable of developing, testing, working to get approved, and marketing one of the world's breakthrough cancer treatment drugs, including partnering with a leading international drug company. Maky helped hire, manage, motivate, encourage, and weed out when necessary the extraordinary group of people who worked at

Pharmacyclics and were crucial to getting Imbruvica to market in an unprecedentedly short period. Of course, this created huge value for all involved. Pharmacyclics went from a company with a value of only several million dollars and practically insolvent to being sold to AbbVie for over ten billion dollars.

It was my privilege to work with Maky and the Pharmacyclics team on this tremendous and exhilarating journey.

ACKNOWLEDGMENTS

I would like to extend my deepest gratitude to my family for their boundless love and support. I also want to thank my friends, my medical staff, and my collaborators. Over time, all these wonderful people became intertwined: friends who cared for me and collaborators who became friends. Together, we formed a big family, united for life and eternity.

I also want to acknowledge the many people whose encouragement and contributions made my books possible. I would like to thank my sister Mahshad Zanganeh, whose unwavering love and support have been the heartbeat of this book, guiding me through every word with her wisdom, compassion, and belief in me. I would like to extend my heartfelt thanks to Cheryl Berman, Shelley Spray, Chelsea Lauwers and the entire Forbes team, especially Suzanna de Boer, Lauren Steffes, and Alison Morse, for their invaluable assistance in editing and reviewing this book.

Their keen eye for detail, insightful feedback, and unwavering support have been instrumental in shaping the final manuscripts of my first and second books. I am deeply grateful for their dedication and expertise, which significantly enriched this work.

Special thanks to my friends, who supported me through publishing the first edition of my book. I would also like to express my gratitude for their help and contributions to the second edition of this book.

There were countless colleagues, mentors, and coaches who taught and inspired me throughout my life. I am also grateful to the amazing team of individuals who dedicated their time to work with me, as we strived to turn hope into reality. I will always treasure every moment spent with each and every one of you.

I am forever grateful to those who believed we could bring *the magic of normal* back to those who had lost it.

ABOUT THE AUTHOR

DR. MAKY ZANGANEH

This is Dr. Maky Zanganeh's first book, where you will become immersed in her life story, which includes leading a major biotech company restructuring that ultimately became one of the largest M&A in the biotech space. *The Magic of Normal* is a firsthand account of one woman's journey from Iran to Silicon Valley. The book will speak to each of you in the way Maky speaks and writes. It is a high-energy story that offers wisdom anyone can relate to. Maky is a woman with exceptional drive and passion, who takes on business and life at full speed. As this is her first book, Maky has made a special effort to relate to and connect with her readers. She was determined to create a fascinating and refreshing experience, as if she and the reader were meeting for the first time.

Maky is a cancer survivor who has dedicated her life to reducing the suffering of others in similar positions. She will take you on the journey of someone in the cancer business who actually experienced cancer. It should be noted that she wrote this book during her cancer treatment and although you can feel her pain at times, there was never a lack of hope.

Maky earned the Fierce Biotech Top Women in Biotech 2013 award and was nominated as a finalist for the Ernst & Young Entrepreneur of the Year 2013 award. She has more than fifteen years of leadership, management, corporate, clinical, and business experience in the pharmaceutical and medical device industries. She has also held positions of global responsibility for such corporations as Pharmacyclics, Inc., and Computer Motion, Inc. She is the founder and CEO of Maky Zanganeh & Associates and is currently the CEO and president of Summit Therapeutics. In addition, she serves on several boards for private and public companies. Maky was awarded her DDS from Louis Pasteur University, France, and received an MBA from Schiller International University, France. Although she lives in California, Maky speaks four languages and thrives on the many personal connections she has made around the world.

To connect with Maky or learn more about her, please visit the QR code below:

www.ingramcontent.com/pod-product-compliance
Lightning Source LLC
Chambersburg PA
CBHW070820100426
42813CB00039B/3475/J
* 9 7 9 8 8 8 7 5 0 5 1 5 2 *